Texts and Monographs in Computer Science

F. L. Bauer
David Gries
editors

Adaptive Information Processing

An Introductory Survey

Jeffrey R. Sampson

Springer-Verlag

New York Heidelberg Berlin

1976

Jeffrey R. Sampson

Department of Computing Science
The University of Alberta
Edmonton, Alberta T6G 2E1
Canada

editors

F. L. Bauer

Mathematisches Institut der
   Technischen Hochschule
8000 München
Arcisstrasse 21
West Germany

David Gries

Cornell University
Department of Computer Science
Upson Hall
Ithaca, New York 14859
USA

AMS Subject Classification: 68-01, 68A25, 68A30, 68A35, 68A45, 68A55, 92A05
(C.R.) Computing Classifications: 3.12, 3.6, 5.22, 5.26, 5.6

Library of Congress Cataloging in Publication Data

Sampson, Jeffrey R.   1942–
   Adaptive information processing.

   (Texts and monographs in computer science)
   "Began as a series of lecture notes for a course . . . at the University of Alberta . . . first
taught in 1973."
   Includes bibliographies.
   1. Machine theory.   2. Information theory in biology.   3. Artificial intelligence.
I. Title.
QA267.S25   001.53   76-8470

Printed in the United States of America

ISBN 0-387-07739-1   Springer-Verlag   New York

ISBN 3-540-07739-1   Springer-Verlag   Berlin Heidelberg

Preface

This book began as a series of lecture notes for a course called Introduction to Adaptive Systems which I developed for undergraduate Computing Science majors at the University of Alberta and first taught in 1973. The objective of the course has been threefold: (1) to expose undergraduate computer scientists to a variety of subjects in the theory and application of computation, subjects which are too often postponed to the graduate level or never taught at all; (2) to provide undergraduates with a background sufficient to make them effective participants in graduate level courses in Automata Theory, Biological Information Processing, and Artificial Intelligence; and (3) to present a personal viewpoint which unifies the apparently diverse aspects of the subject matter covered.

All of these goals apply equally to this book, which is primarily designed for use in a one semester undergraduate computer science course. I assume the reader has a general knowledge of computers and programming, though not of particular machines or languages. His mathematical background should include basic concepts of number systems, set theory, elementary discrete probability, and logic.

As befits an introductory survey, on the other hand, I have kept the need for specialized knowledge both circumscribed and minimal. Probability is used only in Chapters 1 and 2, and logic only in Chapters 3 and 13, for example. Nowhere is the treatment so rigorous as to preclude use of the book by college students in other disciplines (mathematics, psychology, biology) or even by advanced high school students. The book could also serve as a useful adjunct to more specialized computer science courses, where it would introduce the student to material related to the study of, say, Artificial Intelligence.

With this last possibility in mind, I have kept each of the three major parts of the book as self contained as possible. Although each part begins with some prefatory remarks and a survey of the chapters to follow, I have also included an Introduction which provides a general and unifying overview of the book. A short list of references and annotated bibliographical items is appended to each chapter, as are a few suggested exercises.

Although fully responsible for the views expressed and the topics included in this book, I am deeply indebted to John Holland and others in the Department of Computer and Communication Sciences at the University of Michigan. My graduate training there remains the major source of ideas for how this book should be put together and what it should say.

Several of my colleagues at the University of Alberta, including I-Ngo Chen, Wayne Davis, and Kelly Wilson, have provided useful suggestions concerning the content and organization of the course out of which this book grew; Wilson also commented extensively on the manuscript. Ken Morgan of the Genetics Department read Part II and made many helpful suggestions, as did Dick Peddicord of the University of San Francisco. I am most deeply indebted to my Computing Science colleague Len Schubert, who tested the manuscript in the classroom and supplied numerous major improvements. Many sections of Part III rely heavily on Schubert's observations and unpublished notes.

Preparation of the manuscript was done using the *FMT system on the University of Alberta IBM 360/67 computer. The assistance of Glynis Dorey, Mireille Dubreuil, Anton Kritzinger, Robert Mercer, Fran Russell, Jennifer Semchuck, and Elaine Soetaert, and the support of the National Research Council of Canada, are gratefully acknowledged.

Reference

Sampson, J. R. An introductory adaptive systems course for undergraduate computer science majors. *ACM SIGSCE Fourth Technical Symposium on Computer Science Education, SIGSCE Bulletin*, February, 1974, 6(1): 148–151.

Contents

Introduction

Machinery has always fascinated man. In both the workings of his world and the devices of his creation he marvels at intricacy of design and cleverness of function. He is perhaps most often impressed by a machine, natural or artificial, which is designed to modify its function to suit changing circumstances. A prerequisite to such adaptive behavior is the ability to process information—to receive, store, retrieve, use, and transmit it. Modern computers represent the ultimate artificial information processing machines so far created. In the realm of natural information processing machinery nothing rivals the brain of the computer's creator.

This book is about information processing machines. It is especially but not exclusively about machines which process information in order to work better. Our domain of discussion will be wide ranging, traversing abstract models of computation, biological information processing systems, and efforts to program intelligent behavior in computers. It is in the nature of our exploratory survey that we shall not dwell at length on individual topics or detailed examples. Rather I will sketch information processing features in broad strokes, highlighting instances of adaptive behavior.

This book is not about computers. At least it is not about electronic stored program digital computers. I assume you already know something about these machines and how they are programmed. In another sense this book is entirely about computers, if the term may embrace machines built of abstract components, of biochemical molecules, or of complex algorithms. I hope this book will induce you to appreciate the fundamental similarities which underlie so diverse a collection of information processing machines.

Each of the three parts which follow can be read more or less independently of the others. And each has its own introduction which previews the chapters that follow. For the moment then, let me loosely weave together the material of all fifteen chapters.

We begin with information, that abstract elusive stuff which must somehow be processed. We discover that information can be mathematically defined and measured, allowing us to find efficient and reliable ways of coding messages to be transmitted. Our first information processing machines are the highly abstract ones known as automata. We study the formal descriptions which allow us to characterize the information processing, or behavior, of any finite automaton. Turning to a kind of infinite automata known as Turing machines, we discover a form of behavior that can compute anything which is computationally possible. Such an ultimate computer might signal a happy ending to our search for adaptive machines, were it not for insurmountable practical limitations on the use of Turing machines. Another approach to universal computation behavior arises in the last type of abstract machine we study, the cellular automaton. Made up of relatively simple component machines or cells, these automata derive their information processing power from the interconnection of large arrays of components.

From the abstract cells of an automaton we turn in Part II to the biological cells of an organism. Here we encounter an overwhelming richness of adaptive behavior. The nature and expression of the long mysterious genetic code can now be almost completely explained. And we learn something about the ways in which biological information is transmitted from an organism to its offspring. Yet even the awesome information processing ability of a single cell is dwarfed by that of large intercommunicating networks of specialized nerve cells. In the brains of higher animals and man we find the ultimate in nervous system function. After a quick look at how such brains are put together we study the ways in which information is transmitted throughout the nervous system. Yet all this computing power would be useless for adaptive purposes if the organism could not acquire information from and influence its environment. So we look at some of the input–output systems with which the living computer has been endowed. Perhaps not surprisingly, both neural and genetic information processing techniques will give us cause to recall and apply the fundamental notions of information and coding with which we began. Finally we look at some examples of how computers have proved useful in simulation studies of natural adaptive systems.

When computers became powerful enough to simulate natural adaptation people began to consider ways in which a computer might be programmed to behave intelligently. Part III is concerned with aspects of Artificial Intelligence. To see what has been done on the information input side we look at various efforts in pattern recognition. Then we discuss how and with what success computers have been programmed to play games, prove mathematical theorems, solve problems, and converse in human language. We will be tempted to compare the artificial accomplishments with those of the natural systems already considered. And the artificial intelligentsia will usually disappoint us. But we must realize that the natural adaptive systems are the product of millions of years of evolution (itself a natural adaptive process).

At the end of each chapter you will find, in a section called Bibliography, a short list of some of the works that have most influenced my thinking about the subject of that chapter, with a comment or two about each item. Following the Bibliography will be a short set of Exercises. These range from solution of specific problems to suggestions for thought or essay, as appropriate to the subject matter of the chapter. In many cases the answers involve integration of material from two or more chapters. The exercises are mainly intended to stimulate your thinking and should not be regarded as thoroughly testing your knowledge of the contents of the chapter. By the same token, your experience with all these subjects will probably be far less rewarding if you do not at least attempt most of the exercises.

Part I
Information and automata

The five chapters which follow contain the most abstract material in the book. Yet it is appropriate to begin here, rather than with biological systems or intelligent programs, so that we can approach these latter subjects equipped with suitable formal tools and useful ways of thinking about information processing machines. We will not encounter much adaptive behavior in the automata of these chapters. But we will lay the foundations for a later understanding of how such machines can be used to model or simulate the behavior of other adaptive systems.

The first two chapters outline a formal approach to information. Chapter 1 treats the mathematical theory of communication in terms of the components of an idealized communication system. We learn how to measure the information contained in a message or set of messages. We review some truly surprising results concerning how accurately a given amount of information can be transmitted over a communication channel with a given capacity.

Chapter 2 first describes ways in which we can encode messages in order to obtain the fastest possible communication. For cases where accuracy is more important than speed, we study a group of special codes that can detect, and in some cases correct, errors in a transmitted message.

In Chapter 3 we meet our first information processing machines, finite automata, in three different but equivalent forms. We build automata to perform simple tasks, using networks, functions, and formal language expressions as components. And we learn some ways of transforming some of these representations into others.

The Turing machines in Chapter 4 are in many ways a natural extension of finite automata. Yet the computational ability of these infinite automata turns out to be essentially unlimited. We will quickly forsake the original formulation of Turing machines for a programmable version which is more natural for those with computer programming experience. We sketch a programmable form of Turing machine which can do anything that can be done by any other Turing machine. Such universal Turing machines will lead us into questions of just what classes of problems can be solved and whether there are questions that can never be answered. Finally we explore the relation between automata and formal grammars.

Chapter 5 recounts selected developments in the relatively new field of cellular automata. Of particular interest to those who work with these large arrays of simple machines are questions of the limits on computational power. What sort of cellular machine is required, for example, to emulate the behavior of universal Turing machines? How can self-reproducing machines be realized in cellular spaces? We look at two rather different kinds of answers to these questions.

1
Communication theory

In the late 1940's two wartime research efforts were troubled by the problem of faithfully reproducing a signal in the presence of interfering noise. At MIT, Norbert Wiener, better known as the inventor of cybernetics, was seeking reliable prediction for automatic fire control. Claude Shannon, working at the Bell Telephone Laboratories, wanted to make optimal use of communication channels for transmission of coded messages. These two men laid the foundations of what is now known as statistical or mathematical communication theory (or, more popularly, information theory). In this chapter we explore aspects of Shannon's contributions, as set forth in his 1948 paper entitled "The Mathematical Theory of Communication."

It is important to clarify in what sense the terms communication and information are to be used in our discussion, since they have a great variety of nontechnical interpretations. In his excellent essay on Shannon's work, Warren Weaver distinguishes three levels of communication problems: (1) the technical level, concerned with accurate transmission of the symbols of a message; (2) the semantic level, concerned with precise conveyance of the intended meaning of the message; and (3) the effectiveness level, concerned with appropriate impact of the message on the recipient's behavior. Communication theory deals only with technical problems. The meaning, significance, veracity, and effect of a message are of no concern to us in what follows. Messages are treated strictly in terms of their probabilities of occurrence. The numerical measure of information may be equal for two messages, one meaningful and moving, the other unintelligible nonsense.

1.1 Communication systems

Shannon's contributions to communication theory can best be understood with reference to the general model of a communication system schematically diagramed in Figure 1.1. We now discuss the basic components of this system.

An information *source* generates *messages* which may be in virtually any form, such as alphabetic characters, radio waves, or visual images. These messages are selected from some finite set of possible messages, called a message *ensemble*. Since the messages we deal with will typically be composed of elementary discrete units called *symbols*, we must be careful to

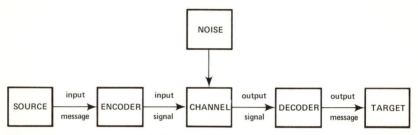

Figure 1.1.   Schematic model of a communication system.

distinguish between a message and a symbol. Thus we might choose to regard as a message ensemble the set of letters and punctuation marks transmitted in a Morse code system. Several symbols (dots, dashes, and pauses) would then be needed to represent each message. We call the set of all symbols an *alphabet*. Since most results for 2-symbol (binary) alphabets can readily be generalized to larger ones, we usually work with the alphabet $(0, 1)$.

Defined over the message ensemble is a probability distribution, so that we know the likelihood of occurrence of each message. In the Morse code example an "e" would be much more likely to occur than an "x." This probability distribution determines a measure of the rate at which the source produces information (called its *entropy*) which we will formally define later.

The input messages produced by the source enter the *encoder* (or transmitter in Shannon's original terminology) which applies some physical transformation to the messages so that they are suitable for transmission over the channel. The resulting (input) signals may be discrete (composed of distinct entities) or continuous (composed of waveforms). In the Morse code example, an encoder might simply transform each dot and dash to a voltage change of equal duration. More sophisticated encoding schemes can transform each message (or even groups of messages) into a representation in some different symbol alphabet. Again, we deal only with discrete signals, and can use a binary alphabet without loss of generality.

The *channel* is the physical medium of signal transmission and might be a pair of wires, a light beam, or the like. The channel accepts input signals and delivers output signals. Ideally, the input and output forms of a signal will be identical, but in reality there is always some *noise*, in the form of atmospheric disturbance, faulty equipment, or whatever, which may cause an error in the output signal. A transient transmission failure, for example, could cause the loss of a Morse code symbol, or make a dash into a dot. The maximum rate at which symbols can be transmitted through a channel is called its *capacity*. Channel capacity is usually limited by technological factors, in much the same way that hardware performance limits the speed of computers.

The *decoder* (or receiver in Shannon's original terminology) takes an output signal and produces an output message. It performs a transformation inverse to that of the encoder. The *target* (or destination) is just the person, place, or thing for which the message is intended.

The fundamental problems of communication theory relate to the design of encoders and decoders which will maximize the rate of information transmission through the system, particularly in the presence of noise. Shannon's major contributions or "fundamental theorems" relate the maximum rate or accuracy of information transmission to the source entropy and channel capacity of the communication system. For example, Shannon proves that for any discrete *noisy* channel which has capacity equal to or greater than the entropy of its associated source, there exists a coding scheme such that messages can be transmitted with arbitrarily small probability of error. This ability to achieve arbitrary levels of fidelity despite noise is truly an astounding result. Unfortunately Shannon's theorems do not always tell us how to *build* the encoders which guarantee optimal information transmission. The design of efficient and noise resistant codes is the subject of the next chapter.

In the remaining sections of this chapter we will make mathematically precise such notions as the information content of a message, the entropy of a message ensemble, and the capacity of a channel. These formalisms will give us a better appreciation of Shannon's remarkable results.

1.2 Information and entropy

We seek a numerical measure $I(x)$ of the amount of information contained in, or conveyed by receipt of, some particular message (or event) x. Since communication theory recognizes nothing about x other than its probability of occurrence p, it is clear that the information must be a function of the probability, that is $I(x) = f(p)$. It seems intuitively plausible that receipt of a less likely message conveys more information. For example, compare the information contained in the following messages: "the sun rose this morning" ($p = 1$); "the coin fell heads" ($p = 0.5$); "he lived to age 200" (p nearly 0).

Therefore f should be a decreasing function of p over the range $0 < p \leq 1$, with $f(1) = 0$. Another intuitively desirable property of the information measure is that if x and y are two independent events with probabilities p and q respectively, then the information conveyed by receipt of x and y should equal the sum of their individual information measures, that is $I(x$ and $y) = I(x) + I(y)$ and hence $f(pq) = f(p) + f(q)$. The only continuous function which satisfies both this and the decreasing property can be shown to be $f(p) = \log(1/p) = -\log p$. Thus the negative logarithm of a message's probability has been chosen as the measure of its information content.

The base of the logarithm determines the unit of the information measure. For a base of 10 the information unit has been dubbed the Hartley, after an early investigator of theories of communication. But by far the most common choice is a base of 2. From now on when we write "log" we will mean the base 2 version (i.e., if $\log x = y$, then $2^y = x$). Use of the base 2 logarithm causes the receipt of either of two equiprobable messages to convey one unit of information, a situation most people find intuitively satisfying. The name of this unit is identical to the familiar computerese contraction of "binary digit"; we refer to *bits* of information.

For our purposes then, the information content of a message x with probability p is *defined* as

$$I(x) = -\log p \text{ bits.} \tag{1.1}$$

Incidentally, some authors call $I(x)$ the *self*-information content of x, to distinguish it from the definition of the mutual information $I(x;y)$ provided by the occurrence of event x about event y. The concept of mutual information permits a more rigorous derivation of Equation (1.1) but is not particularly useful in our discussion.

From Equation (1.1) it is easy to derive the average information content of a message ensemble. Let X be a set of messages x_i with probabilities p_i, $i = 1, \ldots, n$. Then the average information content of X is just the sum of the individual message information contents weighted by their probabilities of occurrence:

$$H(X) = -\sum_{i=1}^{n} p_i \log p_i \text{ bits.} \tag{1.2}$$

$H(X)$ is called the (communication) *entropy* of the ensemble X. If X is the set of messages produced by some source, we may refer to the entropy of that source.

The term entropy is derived from a related measure used in classical thermodynamics, where entropy roughly refers to the amount of disorder in a system. Communication entropy resembles thermodynamic entropy in that it measures the uncertainty associated with an ensemble or source before a message is received. Thus when all but one of the p_i are zero, only one message can occur and $H(X) = 0$. At the other extreme, we are most uncertain about the source when all messages are equally likely ($p_i = 1/n$). So we can compute the maximum entropy of a set of n messages as $H_{max}(X) = -n(1/n)\log(1/n) = \log n$. Figure 1.2 shows the entropy of a set

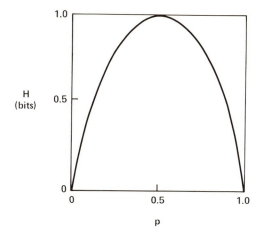

Figure 1.2. Entropy of a binary source.

two messages with probabilities p and $1 - p$. Note the maximum value of 1 bit when $p = 1 - p = 0.5$.

The *relative entropy* H_r of a message ensemble is defined as the ratio of its actual entropy to the maximum entropy for an ensemble of that size. The value $1 - H_r$ is often referred to as the *redundancy* of the ensemble. Thus when $H = H_{max}$ each message carries a maximum amount of information and there is zero redundancy. To illustrate these concepts, let us consider English text as the output of a source which contains 27 messages (26 letters and a space). The maximum entropy of a set of 27 messages is $\log 27 = 4.75$ bits. Various estimates of the actual entropy of English text, where the letters are far from equiprobable and independent, suggest that it is about 2 bits. This gives a redundancy for English text of about $1 - 2/4.75 = 0.58$, which suggests that it could be recoded for far more efficient communication. On the other hand, as we shall see in Chapter 2, redundancy can be a useful property in a noisy communication environment.

As a final example let us calculate the entropy and redundancy of the following message ensemble:

Message	Probability
x_1	0.50
x_2	0.25
x_3	0.125
x_4	0.125

$$H(X) = -0.5 \log 0.5 - 0.25 \log 0.25 - 2(0.125 \log 0.125)$$

$$= 0.5 + 0.5 + 2(0.375) = 1.75 \text{ bits}$$

$$H_{max} = \log 4 = 2.00 \text{ bits}$$

$$H_r(X) = 1.75/2.00 = 0.875$$

Redundancy $= 1 - 0.875 = 0.125$

The above results show that receipt of a message in the ensemble conveys an average of 1.75 bits of information, 0.25 bits less than if all the messages were equally likely. On the average 12.5 % of the information in a long string of such messages is "unnecessary." In the next chapter, we will discover how the messages could be encoded in a binary alphabet so as to maximize transmission of information.

1.3 Channel capacity

As already noted, Shannon's fundamental theorems derive the maximum rate or accuracy of information transmission in terms of source entropy and channel capacity. In this section we discuss some simple types of discrete channels and their capacities, concluding with a statement of Shannon's theorems in their original forms.

The *capacity* C of a channel is the maximum rate at which information can be transmitted over the channel. C is often expressed in bits per second. But if all symbols sent over the channel take equal time to transmit, we can just as well measure capacity in bits per symbol (and multiply this figure by the rate in symbols per second when actual transmission time is of concern).

For noiseless channels transmitting a set of N symbols with identical transmission times, the channel capacity is simply $C = \log N$ bits/symbol, since each of a set of N symbols can carry at most $\log N$ bits of information. Of course the channel will not always transmit at this rate. Whether the actual rate attains the capacity depends on the source of the information. In the case where the symbols have different transmission times, Shannon has shown the channel capacity to be $C = \lim_{T \to \infty} [\log N(T)/T]$ where $N(T)$ is the number of sequences of duration T.

Capacity determination for noisy channels is far more complicated. We begin by characterizing a noisy channel as a matrix which contains the probabilities of any input symbol being transformed into any of the possible output symbols. In the matrix shown in Figure 1.3, for example, input symbol

		Output Symbol				
		a	b	c	d	e
	a	.8	.05	0	.1	.05
	b	0	.9	.02	.08	0
Input Symbol	c	.1	.1	.7	0	.1
	d	0	0	0	1.0	0

Figure 1.3.   A noisy channel.

a is transmitted correctly with probability 0.8. It is transformed into the other input symbols *b*, *c*, and *d* with probabilities 0.05, 0, and 0.1, respectively, while with probability 0.05 it will be output as a spurious symbol *e*. Only the input symbol *d* enjoys error free transmission in this example.

For channels disturbed by particularly complex kinds of noise the probability entries in the matrix may change with time, but we will consider only *constant* channels where the entries remain fixed. As a further simplification we assume that noise affects all inputs equally, so that the rows of the matrix are distinct permutations (rearrangements) of the same set of probability values. Such channels are said to be *uniform from the input*. The capacity *C* of a discrete constant *N*-symbol channel that is uniform from the input can be shown to satisfy the inequality

$$C \leq \log N + \sum_{i=1}^{N} p_i \log p_i \tag{1.3}$$

where the p_i are the probability values found in any row of the matrix.

If the channel is also *uniform from the output* (the columns of the matrix are permutations of the same set of probability values) it is said to be *doubly uniform*. In this case, Equation (1.3) becomes an equality (the capacity always attains its upper bound). Notice that if all but one of the p_i are zero, every input symbol is always transformed into a particular output symbol and the channel is effectively noise free. In such a case the right hand term of Equation (1.3) becomes zero and we are left with the capacity of a noiseless channel. On the other hand, if each input symbol is transformed into all output symbols with equal probability then the right hand term becomes $-\log N$ and the capacity drops to zero (the output symbols give no information about the input symbols).

The simplest and most commonly studied doubly uniform constant channel is the binary symmetric channel, for which the matrix has the general form shown in Figure 1.4. In this channel, *p* is the probability of either symbol being transformed into the other (i.e., the probability of error). Equation (1.3) (with an equals sign since this is a doubly uniform channel) with $N = 2$ gives us the capacity of the binary symmetric channel as $C = 1 + p \log p + (1 - p) \log(1 - p)$, which ranges from 1 bit per symbol ($p = 0$) to 0 bits per symbol ($p = 1/2$).

We are finally now in a position to appreciate Shannon's two fundamental theorems for discrete communication systems as he originally stated them.

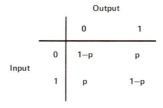

Figure 1.4.   A binary symmetric channel.

This is the fundamental theorem for a noiseless channel (Shannon's Theorem 9):

> Let a source have entropy H (bits per symbol) and a channel have a capacity C (bits per second). Then it is possible to encode the output of the source in such a way as to transmit at the average rate $C/H - \varepsilon$ symbols per second over the channel where ε is arbitrarily small. It is not possible to transmit at an average rate greater than C/H.

To prove the converse part of theorem (C/H cannot be exceeded), Shannon noted that the entropy H', of the encoded channel input (in bits/second) could not, by definition exceed the capacity of C. Dividing both sides of the inequality by H (in bits/symbol) gives the number of symbols per second $H'/H \leq C/H$. One way Shannon proved the first part of the theorem was to construct an encoding scheme based on assigning shorter symbol sequences to less frequent messages. We will not elaborate on this scheme here, since it is equivalent to the (simpler) Shannon–Fano encoding scheme described in the next chapter.

Lastly, here is the fundamental theorem for a discrete channel with noise (Shannon's Theorem 11):

> Let a discrete channel have the capacity C and a discrete source the entropy per second H. If $H \leq C$, there exists a coding system such that the output of the source can be transmitted over the channel with an arbitrarily small frequency of errors (or an arbitrarily small equivocation). If $H > C$, it is possible to encode the source so that the equivocation is less than $H - C + \varepsilon$ where ε is arbitrarily small. There is no method of encoding which gives an equivocation less than $H - C$.

(The term "equivocation" in the above theorem refers to a measure of the average amount of information lost because of noise; it is related but not identical to frequency of errors. For those familiar with joint and conditional probabilities, equivocation is actually a form of conditional entropy defined as

$$H(X|Y) = - \sum_{j=1}^{M} \sum_{i=1}^{N} p(x_i, y_j) \log p(x_i|y_j)$$

where X is an input message ensemble and Y is an output message ensemble.)

The proof of this amazing result is beyond the scope of our discussion. But we should note that, in order to obtain the performance promised, it may well be necessary to encode jointly (together) arbitrarily large groups of symbols. Also, unlike Theorem 9, the proof of Shannon's Theorem 11 does not provide a simple method for constructing the required encoding.

Bibliography

Arbib, Michael A. *Brains, Machines, and Mathematics.* McGraw-Hill, 1964.
Section 3.3 of this comprehensive and stimulating little book contains a development similar to ours in many respects but mainly building toward a proof of Shannon's second fundamental theorem.

Cherry, Colin. *On Human Communication*. Wiley, 1957.
   A wide ranging critical survey of communication disciplines. Chapter 2 contains
   a detailed history of communication theory, Chapter 5 a somewhat different
   approach to our material.

Fano, Robert M. *Transmission of Information*. Wiley, 1961.
   A systematic textbook treatment of the work of Shannon and others. Chapters
   1, 2, 4, and 5 contain an extended mathematical treatment of the material
   covered in this chapter.

Pierce, John R. *Symbols, Signals, and Noise*. Harper, 1961.
   A delightful popular treatment of communication theory and its applications to
   areas like psychology and art.

Reza, Fazlollah M. *An Introduction to Information Theory*. McGraw-Hill, 1961.
   Despite its title, a comprehensive text for engineers which includes considerable
   material on stochastic processes. Chapters 1 and 3 relate to our discussion.
   Chapter 2 is a useful condensed introduction to discrete probability theory.

Shannon, Claude E., and Weaver, Warren. *The Mathematical Theory of Communication*.
   University of Illinois Press, 1959.
   Contains Shannon's original monograph (which first appeared in two parts in
   the July and October issues of the 1948 *Bell System Technical Journal*) and
   Weaver's excellent nontechnical essay.

Exercises

1.1. Give two examples of communication systems you are familiar with, explicitly
identifying the various components as diagrammed in Figure 1.1.

1.2. Compute the entropy and redundancy of message ensembles with the following
probability distributions:
(a) 0.25, 0.25, 0.25, 0.25
(b) 1/32, 1/32, 1/16, 1/8, 1/4, 1/4, 1/4
(c) 0.3, 0.25, 0.2, 0.15, 0.1

1.3. A source independently generates two symbols with probabilities 0.7 and 0.3.
Find the source entropy for messages composed of (a) the individual symbols,
(b) all two-symbol pairs, and (c) all three-symbol triples.

1.4. For each of the following channels compute either the (exact) capacity or an
upper bound on the capacity.
(a) a binary symmetric channel with $p = 0.2$

(b)

	a	b	c
a	0.7	0.1	0.2
b	0.2	0.7	0.1
c	0.1	0.2	0.7

(c)

	a	b	c	d
a	0.6	0.1	0.2	0.1
b	0.2	0.6	0.1	0.1
c	0.2	0.1	0.6	0.1
d	0.1	0.1	0.2	0.6

2
Coding information

The creation of efficient and reliable codes was a major reason for the development of communication theory and remains one of its principal applications. The theorems of Shannon, with which we closed the last chapter, tell us that coding schemes exist which guarantee optimum transmission rates or minimum error frequencies, but not what those schemes might be. In this chapter we examine some aspects of the coding problem.

Shannon's two theorems actually relate to separate branches of coding theory. On the one hand, if noise is ignored or absent, there are effective procedures for constructing codes which maximize information transmission rates for particular message ensembles. (One such procedure was actually developed by Shannon in proving his first theorem.) The first section of this chapter treats such optimal codes. The second theorem, however, is silent on the issue of transmission rate and promises only an arbitrarily small error frequency under certain kinds of noisy conditions. Our second section will discuss codes which are designed to detect and/or correct transmission errors. The unification of these two branches of coding theory, the development of general procedures for finding *optimal error correcting codes*, is a major unsolved problem of communication theory.

In a simplified form then, the *coding theory problem(s)* can be stated as follows: given a source which generates messages, from an ensemble X of N messages with a known fixed probability distribution, and an alphabet of D symbols requiring equal time (cost) to transmit, what is the one-to-one assignment of messages to sequences of symbols that minimizes (a) the average cost of transmission or (b) the probability of transmission errors?

D is usually less than N, so that it is not possible to code every message with a single symbol. The sequences of symbols that are assigned to messages are called *code words*. The *length* of a code word is the number of symbols it contains. We will deal mainly with binary code words ($D = 2$) since most results generalize easily to coding alphabets of three or more symbols. Also, binary coding is itself of considerable importance in modern computers.

2.1 Efficient codes

In the search for code word assignments that maximize the rate (or minimize the cost) of information transmission it is necessary to establish some constraints on the kinds of codes we will accept. One obvious constraint has already been mentioned; we want a *unique* assignment of code words to messages and will not be satisfied if a code word represents more than one message. Another desirable property is that we can uniquely recover a sequence of messages from a sequence of unpunctuated code words. If we assign a set of four messages the binary code words 0, 1, 01, and 10, then the sequence 1001 could be the encoding of two, three, or four successive messages.

A code assignment which permits unique recovery of messages in sequence is called a *separable* code. One property which is sufficient (although not necessary) for separability is the *prefix property*, which requires that no code word can be obtained from another by the addition of more symbols (i.e., no code word is the prefix of another). One method of generating a set of code words with the prefix property is to use a code tree in which the exits from each node are labeled with the D code symbols. A simple binary code tree is shown in Figure 2.1. The code words are generated by tracing any path to a terminal node and using the symbols in the order encountered.

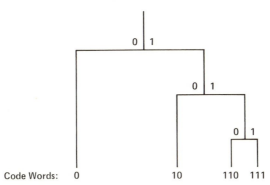

Code Words: 0   10   110   111

Figure 2.1.   A binary code tree.

Notice that the prefix property is inherent in the tree structure; no terminal node can be on a path leading to any other terminal node.

While use of a code tree guarantees a separable code it implies nothing about the code's efficiency. Code assignments which maximize information transmission rate need to take the message probabilities into account. It seems reasonable, for example, to try to assign shorter code words to more commonly occurring messages. It also makes sense to try for roughly equal transmission frequency of the various code symbols, since (for the binary case) only when $p(1) = p(0) = 1/2$ is each symbol carrying its maximum possible amount of information (1 bit). While these criteria cannot always be attained for arbitrary message probability distributions, the coding algorithms we are about to look at try to come as close as possible to a "perfect" encoding.

Before turning to these encoding methods we need some way to measure just how good a code assignment is. One indication of the rate of information transmission (under the assumption that all symbols take equal time to transmit) is the *average code word length*. To compute this value we cannot of course simply average the number of symbols in all the code words irrespective of their probabilities of occurrence. Rather, for a set of messages with probabilities p_i and respective code word lengths of l_i symbols, the average code word length is

$$L = \sum_{i=1}^{N} p_i l_i \text{ symbols.} \tag{2.1}$$

It can be shown that a lower bound for L is $H(X)/\log D$; the source entropy divided by the logarithm of the number of code symbols is the smallest possible average code word length. (Incidentally, it can also be shown that there always exists a code assignment with an average word length *less than* $H(X)/\log D + 1$.) We therefore define the *efficiency* of a code assignment to be

$$E = (H(X)/\log D)/L = H(X)/(L \log D) \tag{2.2}$$

where L is calculated as in Equation (2.1). For binary codes $D = 2$, so the efficiency is just $H(X)/L$.

The first encoding procedure we study was developed by Shannon and Fano. It is easy to use and gives quite efficient code assignments, although not always the best possible for a given set of messages. To use the Shannon–Fano algorithm for binary encoding we first list the messages in order of decreasing probability then divide the set into top and bottom groups which each contain as close to half (0.5) of the total probability as possible. Then we assign a first code symbol of 0 to all messages in one group and of 1 to all messages in the other group. This process is then repeated for successive subgroups of messages, always coming as close as possible to an equal division of the total probability in the subgroup. Each new division produces a new set of code symbols. When no further division is possible each message has been assigned a code word.

Since the algorithm is implicitly constructing a binary tree we are guaranteed that the code assignment is separable. The Shannon–Fano binary coding algorithm is illustrated in Figure 2.2. Note that for the lower second division the best that could be done was 0.2 of the probability above and 0.3 below the division.

To calculate the efficiency of the code generated in Figure 2.2 we need to

Message	Probability	Code Word
x_1	.25	0 0
x_2	.25	0 1
x_3	.20	1 0
x_4	.15	1 1 0
x_5	.10	1 1 1 0
x_6	.05	1 1 1 1

Figure 2.2.   Shannon–Fano binary encoding.

compute the average code word length; this is $2(0.25 + 0.25 + 0.20) + 3(0.15) + 4(0.10 + 0.05) = 2.45$. The entropy $H(X) = 2.42$; so the efficiency $E = 2.42/2.45 = 0.988$, which we will later discover to be the maximum attainable efficiency for this set of messages.

The Shannon–Fano procedure generalizes quite easily to coding alphabets with D symbols where $D > 2$. We simply let each division consist of $D − 1$ cuts which divide the total probability as nearly as possible into D equal portions. Then we distribute the D symbols among the resulting subgroups of messages. Figure 2.3 shows a ternary (three-symbol) code assignment for the set of messages in Figure 2.2. The average code word length in Figure 2.3 is $0.25 + 2(0.75) = 1.75$. The entropy is still 2.42; so the efficiency is $E = 2.42/(1.75 \log 3) = 0.874$ which is lower than for the binary code assignment.

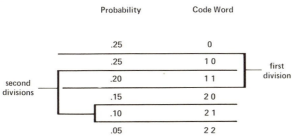

Probability	Code Word
.25	0
.25	1 0
.20	1 1
.15	2 0
.10	2 1
.05	2 2

Figure 2.3.   Shannon–Fano ternary encoding.

It turns out that there is a better ternary code assignment than that of Figure 2.3. To find it we need to use the optimum coding procedure discovered by D. A. Huffman in 1952. The Huffman algorithm is somewhat more complicated than the Shannon–Fano procedure but guarantees a set of code words with maximum possible efficiency. We again begin with the messages arranged in order of decreasing probability. For binary encoding we first combine the two least probable messages and treat them as a single message with probability equal to the sum of their individual probabilities. Now we consider the new set of $N − 1$ "messages" and again combine the two least probable ones, generating another node of the tree. Continuing in

19

this manner we are finally left with just one "message" that has unit probability; this is the top node of the tree. Now we assign 0 and 1 to the branches at each node and generate code words by tracing down to each terminal node from the top, picking up successive code symbols in the process. The Huffman algorithm for the message set we have been using is illustrated in Figure 2.4.

Notice that the code word lengths in Figure 2.4 are identical to the ones

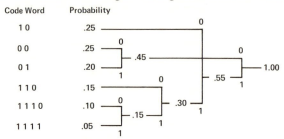

Figure 2.4. Huffman binary encoding.

we obtained with the Shannon–Fano procedure in Figure 2.2. The code word assignments are not identical because of the (arbitrary) assignment of 0 and 1 to the branches at the nodes. But the tree structure insures that this code is separable too. Thus both the Shannon–Fano and Huffman procedures produced equivalent, equally efficient codes for this set of messages.

Huffman codes for alphabets with more than two symbols are constructed in much the same way as in the example just given, except that we combine D messages at each stage. This means that the initial size of the message set must be such that we will be left with exactly D messages at the last step. To provide for this outcome we may need to augment the original message set so that it contains $D + k(D - 1)$ messages where k is an integer (since we have $D - 1$ fewer messages after each step). The extra "dummy" messages have probability zero; their ultimate code assignments are ignored. To construct a Huffman ternary code for the example we have been using, then, requires a seventh dummy message ($D = 3$, $k = 2$). The encoding is shown in Figure 2.5. Note that the average code word length (for the six "real" messages) is 1.65, giving an efficiency of 0.925 compared to 0.874 for the Shannon–Fano encoding of Figure 2.3.

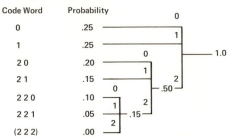

Figure 2.5. Huffman ternary encoding.

2.2 Error correcting codes

Highly efficient codes like those we have just been examining are particularly susceptible to information loss through faulty transmission. Consideration of noise in the channel leads us into an extensive domain of coding theory concerned with finding encoding/decoding procedures which allow the message recipient to determine if a transmission error has occurred (error detecting codes) and in some cases what the error was (error correcting codes). At present, unfortunately, error detecting and correcting codes tend to be complex, limited to binary channels, and quite inefficient. No simple optimal method like Huffman's is available for noisy channels.

Our discussion of error correcting codes will be confined to the type of binary codes first described in 1950 by R. W. Hamming of the Bell Telephone Laboratories. In a Hamming code, all words contain n binary digits and carry $n - k$ bits of significant information. The extra k digits provide the redundancy necessary for error detection and/or correction.

The frequently used parity check bit in modern digital computers is actually the simplest form of a Hamming code ($k = 1$). The parity bit is set to 0 or 1 in order to make the total number of 1's in a computer word always even (or always odd, since some machines employ "even parity," others "odd parity"). Although cheap, requiring only one extra bit per word, parity bit error checking is limited to the detection of single errors. No information is provided about which digit is in error if the number of 1's does not tally; it may well be the parity bit itself. Furthermore, two errors in the same word will cancel each other out and the message will appear to be error free. This is usually not a serious problem in computers, where the probability of a single error is so small that its square (the probability of a double error) is infinitesimal.

In other applications, however, we may wish to guard against two or more errors, or to know *where* an error occurred (which in the binary case amounts to knowing what error it was). To facilitate the development and analysis of more complex error detecting and/or correcting codes, Hamming defined the notion of the "distance" between two code words as a count of the number of positions in which they have different digits (or, more precisely, the sum of the 1's in their bitwise exclusive or). Thus the Hamming distance between 01010 and 00111 is 3, and between 000000 and 111111 is 6. The distance ranges between 0 and n for n-digit code words. Geometrically, Hamming distance corresponds to the number of vertices which must be traversed to go from one code word to the other when each n-digit word occupies a designated vertex of an n-dimensional hypercube. The Hamming spaces for $n = 2$ and 3 are shown in Figure 2.6. (A 4-dimensional hypercube has 16 "corners," defined by all possible binary combinations, and so on for higher dimensions.)

A code's error detecting/correcting properties depend on the minimum Hamming distance between any pair of its words, as is suggested by Figure

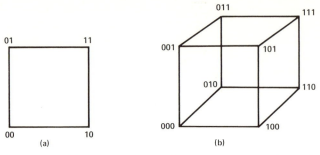

Figure 2.6. Hamming code spaces for (a) $n = 2$ and (b) $n = 3$.

2.6. Obviously if the distance is 1 a change in any digit will give another valid code word and the error will go undetected. With a minimum distance of 2 between any pair of code words we have the computer parity bit scheme and we can detect single errors. Hamming has shown the following relation between minimum distance and a code's error detecting/correcting properties:

Minimum distance	Code properties
1	No error detection
2	Single error detection
3	Single error correction
4	Double error detection
5	Double error correction

The last line of this table, for example, confirms our intuition that if 5 vertices must be traversed to get to the next nearest valid code word, two errors will lead to a vertex closer to the original code word than to any other valid one. It should also be noted that a minimum distance of 3 is adequate for double error detection if no correction is attempted. When used for single error correction, however, a minimum distance of 3 can result in "miscorrection" of double errors.

The geometric interpretation of Hamming codes is illuminating, but turns out to be of little use in practice. Given some total code word length n, how can we determine the number of check digits k required for some desired detection/correction code property? Rather than attempt a general answer to this complex question, let us confine our attention to the relatively simple case of single error correction. We need to discriminate $n + 1$ possible conditions (n single errors plus the error-free case), using 2^k parity digit combinations. To have at least one such "parity word" for each error condition, we clearly must have $2^k \leq n + 1$, or $k \leq \log(n + 1)$.

Once the number of required check digits is known it is possible to construct a series of logical functions which determine the value of each check digit for given values of the $n - k$ information digits. Again the general procedure is somewhat involved and tedious. So let us conclude with an examination of a particular single error correcting code in which $n = 7$ and $k = 3$. In this code the check digits (numbered 5, 6, and 7) must be given values which, together with the first four information digits, satisfy the following three conditions: (1) digits 1, 2, 3, and 5 have even parity; (2) digits 1, 2, 4, and 6 have even parity; and (3) digits 1, 3, 4, and 7 have even parity. Upon receipt of an encoded message we check to see if these three conditions hold. Each of the seven possible combinations of failure of the conditions (one, two, or all three at a time) will identify a distinct one of the seven digits as an error. Figure 2.7 shows the overlapping "responsibilities" for digits of

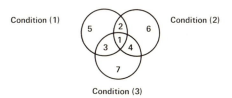

Figure 2.7.   Diagram of Hamming code for single error correction.

each of the conditions. Clearly if only condition (1) fails the error must be in digit 5 (e.g., 1111011 should be 1111111). Correspondingly if both conditions (2) and (3) fail the error is in the fourth digit (e.g., 1110111 should be 1111111). If all three conditions fail digit 1 is in error.

Bibliography

The books by Arbib, Fano, and Reza listed in the Chapter 1 Bibliography all deal with some aspects of coding theory. Reza's Chapter 4 is a particularly good treatment of the types of codes we have looked at. Other works which give special emphasis to coding are listed below.

Abramson, Norman. *Information Theory and Coding.* McGraw-Hill, 1963.
An excellent little book on both subjects. Coding is covered primarily in Chapters 3, 4, and 6.

Berlekamp, Elwyn R. *Algebraic Coding Theory.* McGraw-Hill, 1968.
An advanced text on the mathematical foundations of coding theory.

Hamming, R. W. "Error-detecting and error-correcting codes." *Bell System Technical Journal, 29,* 1950, pp. 147–150.
The original paper on Hamming codes.

Huffman, D. A. "A method for the construction of minimum redundancy codes." *Proceedings of the Institute of Radio Engineers, 40,* 1952, pp. 1098–1101.
The original paper on Huffman codes.

Singh, Jagjit. *Great Ideas in Information Theory, Language, and Cybernetics.* Dover, 1966.
An informal popularization of many of the subjects covered in the present book. Chapters I through VII treat communication theory, focusing on coding in Chapters IV and V.

Exercises

2.1. Construct a set of six binary code words that do not satisfy the prefix property but still form a separable code. Do these code words satisfy some other property that you can describe concisely?

2.2. Construct and calculate the efficiency of Shannon–Fano binary and ternary codes for each of the following message probability distributions:
(a) 1/2, 1/4, 1/8, 1/16, 1/16
(b) 1/3, 1/4, 1/8, 1/8, 1/12, 1/12
(c) 1/3, 1/6, 1/6, 1/12, 1/12, 1/12, 1/24, 1/24

2.3. Repeat Exercise 2.2 for Huffman binary and ternary codes.

2.4. Construct and calculate the efficiency of Shannon–Fano and Huffman quaternary (4-symbol) codes for the following message probability distribution: 0.30, 0.25, 0.10, 0.08, 0.07, 0.06, 0.05, 0.04, 0.03, 0.02.

2.5. Use the $n = 7$, $k = 3$ Hamming code of Section 2.2 to correct (if necessary) the following received code words:
(a) 1101001
(b) 0101100
(c) 1111111
(d) 1000000

3
Finite automata

In this chapter we consider the kinds of information processing that can be carried out by machines built from rather simple components. A *finite automaton* (or finite state machine) is a member of a class of abstract machines whose *behavior* may always be described in terms of a series of *states* occurring at successive units of *discrete time*. These machines are called finite because the set of possible states is finite. The machine is in one of these states at each time step and moves to a next (but not necessarily different) state at the next time step, a process known as a *state transition*. Time is counted in integral units beginning at $t = 0$.

Thus for a finite automaton with a set of states labelled a, b, and c we might have behavior for $t = 0, 1, 2, \ldots, 7$ consisting of the following sequence of states: a–c–c–b–a–b–c–a. Normally, however, we are less concerned with this sort of arbitrary slice of behavior than with the rules which characterize the particular automaton and determine all the possible behavioral sequences it can manifest. It is thus necessary to have some way of describing a finite automaton which reveals its behavioral potential. In this chapter we look at three rather different but equivalent notations for the description of automata: networks, functions, and formal language expressions. We will employ some basic concepts of elementary logic, particularly in Section 3.1. The reader unfamiliar with such concepts may wish to consult the first part of Section 13.1 before proceeding with this chapter.

3.1 Modular nets

A modular net is a collection of components of specified types which have been interconnected according to specified rules. One of the earliest forms of a modular net was proposed in 1943 by McCulloch and Pitts. A

McCulloch–Pitts net is built from a single type of primitive component, called a "neuron" because it somewhat resembles the cell of that name which is the fundamental building block in biological nervous systems (see Chapter 8).

A McCulloch–Pitts neuron is diagrammed in Figure 3.1 and may be seen to consist of the following three parts: (1) a single *output* line, O, which carries a binary signal (a value of 0 or 1 at each time step) to zero or more other neurons (if the line branches each branch carries the same signal);

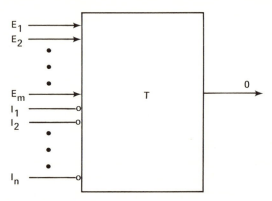

Figure 3.1. Diagram of a McCulloch–Pitts neuron.

(2) an arbitrary number of binary *input* lines which may be "excitatory" (E_i) or "inhibitory" (I_j) and are symbolized as arrows and circles respectively; and (3) a quantity known as the *threshold* which has some fixed real number as its value (in practice only nonnegative integer thresholds are used, since they suffice for the realization of any behavior).

The operation of a McCulloch–Pitts neuron is governed by the following rule:

$$O(t + 1) = \begin{cases} 1, & \text{iff } \sum_{j=1}^{n} I_j(t) = 0 \quad \text{and} \quad \sum_{i=1}^{m} E_i(t) \geq T \\ 0, & \text{otherwise.} \end{cases} \tag{3.1}$$

Equation (3.1) says that a McCulloch–Pitts neuron will have an output of 1 at time $t + 1$ if and only if at time t the sum of the excitatory inputs equalled or exceeded the threshold and there were no inhibitory inputs of 1. (Thus each inhibitory input has absolute "veto" power in this original McCulloch–Pitts version; another popular and equivalent type of neuron has an output of 1 at the next time step whenever the sum of the excitatory inputs minus the sum of the inhibitory inputs exceeds the threshold.) Note that the effects of a combination of inputs cannot be reflected in the output of a neuron until the next time step; we say that each such element has an inherent *unit delay* associated with its function.

When interconnecting McCulloch–Pitts neurons we must observe one simple rule to insure that the resulting nets are well-formed: each input line

26

can be identified with at most one output line. This condition insures that we will not encounter ill-formed connections in which two outputs somehow "join" together before entering a neuron. We may, however, have input lines which are identified with no output lines. Such inputs are called *external inputs* and their values at each time step are presumed to be supplied by some source in the net's "environment." We may also have outputs which are identified with no inputs, which we will call *external outputs*. Finally note that there is nothing in our connection scheme to prevent a neuron's output from being one of its inputs. In fact any time a neuron can affect its own input, even through a chain of intermediate neurons, we say that the net has a *cycle*, with length equal to the number of neurons on the closed path.

The *state* of a McCulloch–Pitts net at time t is just the set of all values on the output lines of its component neurons at that time. Thus a net with k neurons has 2^k possible states. These are sometimes called the internal states to distinguish them from the net's *input state* which is the set of all values on the external input lines. We also sometimes refer to the net's *output state* which is the set of values on the external output lines (and is really just a subset of the values included in the internal state). The sequence of states, or *behavior*, of a particular net is thus fully determined only when we have specified: (1) the connections and thresholds of the net itself; (2) the temporal sequence of input states coming from the environment; and (3) some designated starting or *initial state* which is the (internal) state at time $t = 0$.

Figure 3.2a shows a simple McCulloch–Pitts network containing three neurons with unit thresholds, two external inputs (labelled X and Y), one external output (O_3), and no cycles. The net has 8 internal states, 4 input states, and 2 output states. If we designate the state $O_1 = O_2 = O_3 = 0$ as the initial state and feed in the sequences shown for X and Y we obtain the sample of the behavior of the network that is shown in part (b) of the figure.

Because the net in Figure 3.2 contains no cycles its output O_3 at any time is completely determined by the previous values of O_1 and O_2, which are in turn functions only of the preceding inputs. Even the small sample of behavior in Figure 3.2b indicates that this network is actually computing a simple Boolean or logical function of X and Y. $O_3(t)$ is an exclusive *or* (or

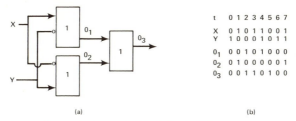

Figure 3.2. (a) A simple McCulloch–Pitts net; (b) a sample of its behavior.

27

inequivalence) of X and Y at time $t - 2$ (the output is 1 whenever X and Y had different values). To see this from the network note that the third neuron actually computes a disjunction (logical *or*) of its inputs, each of which is a conjunction (logical *and*) of one external input and the negation of the other.

A McCulloch–Pitts network can actually be designed for any logical expression. It is sufficient to show that any *complete* set of logical operators (completeness is defined in Section 13.1) can be realized by McCulloch–Pitts neurons. Logical design with these neurons quickly becomes tedious, however, and fraught with timing problems arising from the delay inherent in each component. For such reasons McCulloch–Pitts nets are now of mainly historical interest. We next look at a class of nets with equivalent computational power and more convenient primitive components.

The primitives of our *logical nets* will be of two general kinds: (1) unit delays diagrammed as rectangles with a single input and output; and (2) a set of multi-input logical function units, diagrammed as circles with the appropriate logical symbol inscribed. The delays perform no computation other than to delay the input one time step, $O(t) = I(t - 1)$. The logical function units have no inherent delay but compute instantaneous functions of their inputs, e.g. $O(t) = I_1(t)$ *and* $I_2(t)$, $O(t) = I_1(t)$ *or* $I_2(t)$ *or* $I_3(t)$, $O(t) = not\ I(t)$, and so on. The number of different logical functions we employ, and the number of inputs we allow them to have, may be chosen for maximal convenience or for minimal number of primitives, as long as we are sure to include a complete set of logical operators. In what follows we will generally use 2-input versions of the familiar *and*, *or*, and *not* operations.

Well formed logical nets can be constructed by interconnecting our primitives subject to two constraints. The first is the familiar rule from McCulloch–Pitts nets: each input line can be identified with at most one output line. The second constraint avoids logical paradoxes that can result from the use of instantaneous primitives. What, for example, would be meant by a *not* unit which received its own output as a direct input? To avoid such situations we stipulate that every cycle in a logical net must contain at least one delay.

The notions of external inputs and outputs, and of internal and input states, carry over almost completely from McCulloch–Pitts nets to logical nets. The one major difference is that the internal state must now be the set of all *delay* outputs at a given time. These outputs will be understood to be 0 at $t = 0$ unless a 1 is inscribed in the delay rectangle to signify $O(0) = 1$. Those pieces of the net which contain no delays can compute possibly quite complex logical functions in zero time. In fact a net containing only instantaneous logical primitives is called a switching or combinatorial network; it is obviously not a finite state machine since it does not have states in any meaningful sense.

Figure 3.3a shows a switching network which computes the *inequivalence* function that was built from McCulloch–Pitts neurons in Figure 3.2. If we

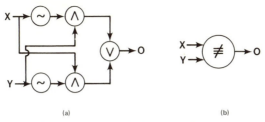

Figure 3.3. (a) An inequivalence switching net;
(b) abbreviated representation.

agree to abbreviate the switching net with the single primitive shown in
Figure 3.3b, we can then add a single delay and create the simple but interesting 2-state machine of Figure 3.4.

The machine in Figure 3.4 is the first one we have encountered which
contains a cycle. The presence of cycles in a network makes possible a sort of
indefinite memory for past inputs. More precisely, an input arbitrarily far in
the past *may* still influence the current state of a machine with cycles. Note
that in the cycle free McCulloch–Pitts net of Figure 3.2 inputs further
removed than two time steps back cannot influence the current state. Compare this situation with the net in Figure 3.4, which is called a *parity machine*
because its current state (which can only be 0 or 1, since there is a single
delay) always reflects the parity of the total number of 1's which have occurred

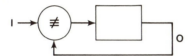

Figure 3.4.   A parity machine.

on its input line since time $t = 0$. It is easy to see that the machine starts in
state 0 and changes to a distinct new state each time a 1 appears on the
input line; thus state 1 means an odd number of 1's have been input while
state 0 signifies an even number. The behavior of this machine is therefore
a consequence of its entire history of inputs.

We can also think of our parity machine as a modulo 2 counter. Addition
of another stage and an *and* unit to this counter, as in Figure 3.5, gives us a
modulo 4 counter with 2 cycles and 4 states. The binary number represented by O_2O_1 is modulo 4 the number of 1's that have occurred in this
machine's input history. In general, we can design a machine with n cycles
that will count modulo 2^n.

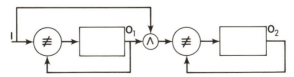

Figure 3.5.   A modulo 4 counter.

3.2 State transition functions

The second way in which we look at finite automata is a mathematical characterization in terms of sets and functions on sets. Formally we may define a finite automaton as a quintuple (I, O, S, G, F), where

I is a finite set of *inputs* (or, more precisely, input states);
O is a finite set of *outputs* (or output states);
S is a finite set of (internal) *states*;
G, the *next state function*, maps state-input pairs into states with a one time step delay, $G: S \times I \to S$ or $S(t + 1) = G(S(t), I(t))$; and
F, the *next output function*, maps state-input pairs into outputs with a one time step delay, $F: S \times I \to O$ or $O(t + 1) = F(S(t), I(t))$.

Variations of this definition are frequently encountered. For example we could add the designation of a starting state to the definition and treat two otherwise identical machines with different starting states as different automata. It will be convenient to make such a distinction in the next section. Also, when dealing only with those machines where the next output is totally determined by the next state (which we will temporarily assume to be the case) we may omit explicit mention of the set O and the function F from our definition.

In any case, the above type of definition makes it clear that the behavior of a finite automaton is a temporal sequence of states (and outputs) each of which is determined by the combination of state and input which occurred at the previous time step. The essence of this behavior is captured in the next state (or state transition) function, G. It is often convenient to represent G in tabular form, as a *state transition table* showing the next states resulting from all possible state-input pairs, or in graph form, as a *state transition diagram* in which the nodes are the individual states and the arcs show the transitions associated with the various inputs. Figures 3.6 and 3.7 show the

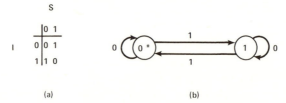

(a)   (b)

Figure 3.6.   (a) State transition table and (b) diagram for the parity machine.

state transition tables and diagrams for the parity machine (Figure 3.4) and the modulo 4 counter (Figure 3.5) respectively. Such tables and diagrams can also be constructed for the McCulloch–Pitts variety of modular nets. In Figures 3.6 and 3.7 we have indicated the starting state for the machine (all delay outputs zero) by an asterisk in the appropriate state node of the diagram. Initial states may also be so flagged in state transition tables.

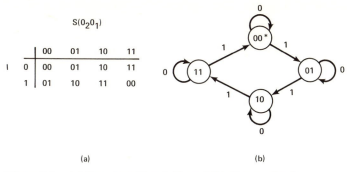

$S(0_2 0_1)$

		00	01	10	11
I	0	00	01	10	11
	1	01	10	11	00

(a)

(b)

Figure 3.7. (a) State transition table and (b) diagram for the modulo 4 counter.

In the above examples the machine's output at any time is a direct consequence of the state to which the transition has been made. Automata to which this condition applies are called Moore machines after the man who described them in the 1950's. Our original quintuple definition of automata, however, actually encompasses a more general class of machines in which outputs are associated with the *transitions* among states and may be different for different paths to the same state. Such automata are known as Mealy machines after an investigator contemporaneous with Moore. Figure 3.8 illustrates a simple Mealy machine which is not also a Moore machine. This automaton "remembers" and outputs the input which it received one time step earlier. Note that to diagram a Mealy machine we must specify both the input and the output associated with a transition, in the form input/output. Also we must display the next output function F as well as the next state function G.

Mealy machines are often more convenient to use than Moore machines, especially when we are primarily concerned with a machine's outputs and are willing to assign arbitrary labels to its states (an example is given at the end of the next section). But it should be emphasized that Mealy machines do not constitute a more powerful class of automata than Moore machines. Given any Mealy machine we can always design a Moore machine which is equivalent in that it has the same behavior. But the Moore machine will often require more states than the equivalent Mealy machine.

The automata we have been concerned with up to this point have all been so-called *deterministic* automata, in which a single next state or next output

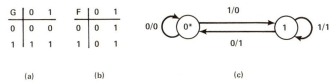

G	0	1
0	0	0
1	1	1

F	0	1
0	0	1
1	0	1

(a)

(b)

(c)

Figure 3.8. (a) Next state function, (b) next output function, and (c) state transition diagram for a Mealy machine.

31

is an inevitable consequence of the current state-input pair. If we allow a pair to lead to one of two or more next states (or outputs) we have the class of machines called *nondeterministic automata*. The study of nondeterministic automata is of considerable importance, particularly when we consider the design of physical machines with components which may sometimes fail and thus may not enter the "correct" state. If we know the probability with which each of the alternate transitions occurs, we have what is known as a *probabilistic automaton*. Although the study of probabilistic automata is beyond the scope of this book, we can illustrate this type of machine by considering a parity machine which models an actual physical device that makes correct state transitions only with probability $p < 1$. If we indicate the probability of each transition in parentheses after the input associated with the arc, a state transition diagram of such a machine is shown in Figure 3.9. In a more complicated probabilistic automaton we might want to associate different failure probabilities with each of the different transitions.

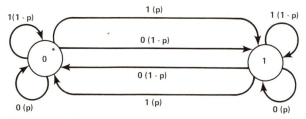

Figure 3.9. Diagram of parity machine with failure probability of $1 - p$ for all transitions.

3.3 Regular expressions

In the last section we encountered finite automata which could "remember" properties of their input sequences. This suggests characterizing machines in terms of their abilities to discriminate among inputs. In the simplest sort of case an automaton might have the ability to indicate recognition or acceptance of all input sequences satisfying some property and rejection of all other sequences. When viewed in this manner finite state machines are often termed *recognizers* (or sometimes *acceptors*).

We thus seek a simple and formal means of describing the class of sequences a particular machine can recognize. Hopefully this will also lead us to a way of describing the nature of *all* classes of sequences for which a finite state acceptor can be designed. The formal language of regular expressions constitutes such a description and is our third and final characterization of finite automata.

In what follows we will limit our consideration to binary input sequences. There is no loss of generality in so doing, since we can always use binary words to encode the elements of an input set containing more than two symbols (states). We define an *event* to be any subset of the set of all binary sequences. Thus $\{1, 0\}$ and $\{01, 100, 001\}$ are two events, containing 2 and 3 sequences respectively, as are the set of all sequences (the improper subset) and the set of no sequences, denoted ϕ. We will also want to refer to the sequence of zero length, denoted Λ.

We will call an event *realizable* if there exists a finite automaton with a designated initial state and a single binary output (again there is no loss of generality) such that when the machine is started in the initial state and receives an input sequence it (finally) emits a 1 output (signifying recognition) if and only if the sequence is a member of the event. (In an equivalent definition we could require the machine to enter some designated recognition state if and only if the sequence is a member of the event.) Our task is thus to characterize the set of all realizable events and to find a way of relating individual events to their corresponding recognizers.

Let us temporarily forget about machines and look at a way of describing certain sets of binary sequences. The descriptions are called *regular expressions* and may be recursively defined in the following three steps:

1. 0, 1, Λ, and ϕ are regular expressions;
2. If E and E' are regular expressions, then so are: (a) $E \vee E'$, (b) EE' and (c) E^*;
3. There are no other regular expressions.

The above definition requires some explanation and comment. Step 1 is called the *base* of a recursive definition and tells us what primitive components may be used to build the class of things we are defining. In this case we have four primitive regular expressions which serve to describe four primitive sets of sequences. The first three of these are just the single element sets containing the sequences 0, 1, and Λ, respectively; the fourth is the empty set.

Step 2 of the definition is called its *recursion* and gives us several ways of combining the primitive components and (recursively) the results of those combinations to construct increasingly complex regular expressions. Part (a) says that the *disjunction* of any two regular expressions is a regular expression. Where E and E' describe two sets of sequences, $E \vee E'$ describes the set containing all the distinct sequences found in either E or E'. Thus if E describes $\{01, 110\}$ and E' describes $\{\Lambda, 00, 01\}$ then $E \vee E'$ describes $\{\Lambda, 00, 01, 110\}$. Note that ϕ is the algebraic identity for disjunction: $\phi \vee E$, $E \vee \phi$, and E describe the same set. Part (b) says that the *concatenation* of two regular expressions is a regular expression. The concatenation EE' describes the set of sequences containing any one sequence of E immediately followed by any one sequence of E'. For the above examples, EE' describes $\{01, 110, 0100, 11000, 0101, 11001\}$. Note that Λ is the algebraic identity for concatenation; ΛE, $E\Lambda$, and E describe the same set.

Finally part (c) tells us that if E is any regular expression then its *closure* E^* is also. E^* describes the set of all sequences obtained by concatenating zero or more not necessarily distinct elements of E. This set is necessarily infinite (except for Λ^* and ϕ^*, which are both just Λ) and always includes Λ. For E as above, E^* describes $\{\Lambda, 01, 110, 0101, 110110, 01110, 11001, 010101, \ldots\}$. Taken together and applied over and over again, these three operations allow us to construct any valid regular expression from the primitives of Step 1.

Step 3 is called the *restriction* of a recursive definition. Although sometimes omitted, this step tells us the important fact that there does not exist any *other* way to construct regular expressions.

When dealing with complex regular expressions we will want to use parentheses to isolate subexpressions to be evaluated first, much as in algebra or computer programming languages. We will also order the basic operations in a precedence hierarchy of evaluation, to be employed when parentheses do not indicate otherwise. This hierarchy requires that all closure operations be performed before any concatenations which in turn precede any disjunction operations. With these conventions in mind, let us consider some simple regular expressions and the sets of sequences (or *regular events*) they describe. Here are six examples:

Expression	Regular event
(a) Λ	just that "sequence"
(b) $(0 \vee 1)^*$	all sequences (i.e., any number of 0's and 1's intermixed in any order)
(c) $(0 \vee 1)^* 1$	all sequences ending in 1 (including 1 itself since we may "choose" Λ for the first element of concatenation)
(d) $((0 \vee 1)(0 \vee 1))^*$	all sequences with an even number of symbols (including no symbols)
(e) $(0^* 10^* 10^*)^* \vee 0^*$	all sequences with an even number of 1's
(f) $0^* 1(0^* 10^* 10^*)^* 0^*$	all sequences with an odd number of 1's

It must be emphasized that not all sets of binary sequences can be described by regular expressions. Two examples of sets which are easy to describe in English but impossible to describe with regular expressions are (1) the set of all sequences containing n symbols where n is any perfect square, and (2) the set of sequences containing n 1's followed by n 0's, for any n. The sets of sequences which can be described by regular expressions are interesting precisely because they comprise a well defined proper subclass of the class of all events.

The result toward which we have been building can finally be stated. It was first proved by the well known mathematician Kleene. In our terminology Kleene's theorem says that an event is realizable if and only if it is regular. In other words the sets of input sequences that can be recognized by finite automata are identical to the sets of sequences that can be described by regular expressions.

This result is of great importance, and not only because it provides an especially compact and convenient way of describing finite automata. Kleene's theorem also provides our first real means of defining the *limitations* of such machines. Neither networks nor transition functions implicitly characterize what finite automata *cannot* do, whereas we have just mentioned examples of "nonregular events." The use of formal languages to identify and order the computational powers of various types of machines will be further considered in Section 4.4.

A rigorous constructive proof of Kleene's theorem demonstrates how a state transition diagram can be designed from any regular expression and how a regular expression can be derived from any state transition diagram. Both demonstrations are based on induction, on the number of symbols in the expression, for the first case, and on the number of states in the diagram, for the second.

Thus, to prove that any regular event is realizable, we first exhibit state transition diagrams recognizing all events described by expressions composed of just a single symbol. (The diagram for Λ is given as an example in Figure 3.10a below; diagrams for 1, 0, and ϕ are similarly trivial.) For the induction step, we assume the theorem holds for expressions of n or fewer symbols (excluding parentheses). An expression of $n + 1$ symbols must contain two such shorter expressions connected by disjunction or concatenation (or one shorter expression with an appended *). Diagrams recognizing the events described by the longer expressions may be constructed from the diagrams already available (by assumption) for the shorter expressions (using a "parallel connection" for disjunction, a "series connection" for concatenation, and an appended "loop" for closure). Hence a finite automaton state transition diagram can be constructed to recognize any regular event.

We can best understand the approach used in proving the other half of Kleene's theorem by restricting our attention to binary Moore type automata with two or more states. (A one-state Moore machine "recognizes" all sequences or no sequences and is rather uninteresting.) There are 32 two-state binary Moore machines (4 transition patterns from each state, 2 choices of starting state), for which we could easily show the corresponding regular expression. Six of the cases are actually given in Figure 3.10 below. With the induction base thus established for $n = 2$, it remains to be shown that any $n + 1$-state machine recognizes a regular event if all n-state machines are assumed to do so. Although the argument here becomes too involved for us to pursue in detail, the basic idea is to show that the addition of a state can cause only a few, well-defined changes in the paths through a state transition diagram. Each such change can then be associated with an alteration of an expression which preserves its regularity.

Although a more complete and careful proof of Kleene's theorem is beyond the scope of our discussion we can demonstrate some simple correspondences between machines and expressions. Figure 3.10 shows Moore type diagrams for the six regular events listed previously. (When both inputs

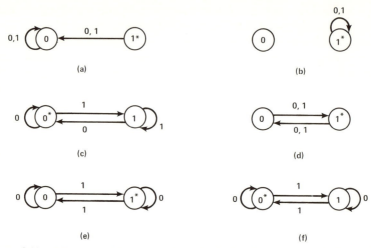

(a)

(b)

(c)

(d)

(e)

(f)

Figure 3.10. Moore machines recognizing (a) Λ, (b) all sequences, (c) all sequences ending in 1, (d) all sequences with an even number of symbols, (e) all sequences with an even number of 1's, (f) all sequences with an odd number of 1's.

cause the same transition they are shown on a single arc separated by commas.) Note that Figure 3.10f is our old friend the (odd) parity machine and that a simple switch of the all important starting state converts it into the even parity machine of Figure 3.10e.

The regular expressions for which machines are shown in Figure 3.10 were selected with some care so that they could be recognized by simple two state automata of the sort we have come to associate with a logical net containing a single delay. In finding machines for other types of regular expressions we will often want to dispense with states which are tied to particular network representations in favor of Mealy machines with transition outputs and arbitrary state labels. A simple example of this type of diagram is shown in Figure 3.11 for the regular expression 00(0 ∨ 1)* 11 describing the set of all sequences beginning with two 0's and ending with two 1's. In this diagram state a is the starting state and state f is a "recognition" state. If either of the first two input symbols is not 0 the machine

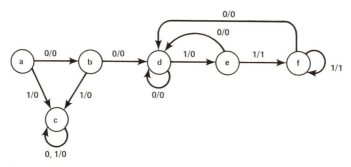

Figure 3.11. Mealy machine recognizing 00(0 ∨ 1)* 11.

36

enters state c, from which there is no return. (Time 0 outputs on Mealy transition arcs may be shown in association with Λ as an input.)

Figure 3.12 summarizes the six possible transformations among the three equivalent representations of finite automata that we have studied in this chapter. We have not explored ways to accomplish all of these transformations, for they are by no means equally straightforward. We began with simple modular nets and found it easy to derive their equivalent state transition functions (as tables or diagrams, the transformation between those

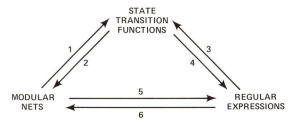

Figure 3.12.   Transformations among finite automata representations.

two forms being trivial). For more complex logical nets transformation 1 remains straightforward, although it is often useful to find the logical expressions for the delay outputs (as functions of the inputs and other outputs) to aid in filling the transition table. To go the other direction, from state transition functions to modular nets (transformation 2), is somewhat more complicated. This synthesis of networks which behave in accord with some given state transition function is known as the *state assignment problem.*

We have seen that transformation 3, from regular expressions to state transition functions, is another fairly straightforward one in simple cases. Again the reverse is more challenging; but algorithms do exist. This closing of two sides of the triangle has provided an indirect path in both directions from networks to regular expressions. In practice no one attempts the extremely difficult direct transformations (5 and 6) except in the most trivial cases.

Finally we should note the existence of another class of algorithms which we have not yet mentioned at all. Usually there are several machines (in whatever representation) which perform essentially the same computations. It is often desirable to find the *minimal* machine for the job, in terms of number of states, number of components, or whatever. Like the representation transformation algorithms just mentioned these *minimization* procedures go far beyond our needs and purposes in this book. Needless to say, the development and applications of all these techniques have been of great value not only to automata theorists but also to computer scientists and engineers.

Bibliography

Arbib, Michael A. *Brains, Machines, and Mathematics*. McGraw-Hill, 1964.
Chapter 1 contains a compact discussion of all three representations we have considered.

Arbib, Michael A. *Theories of Abstract Automata*. Prentice-Hall, 1969.
A comprehensive and mathematically sophisticated treatment of automata theory and related subjects. Chapter 3 is devoted to finite automata.

Kleene, S. C. "Representation of events in nerve nets and finite automata." In C. E. Shannon and M. McCarthy (eds.), *Automata Studies*, Princeton University Press, 1956.
The original paper on regular events.

Kohavi, Zvi. *Switching and Finite Automata Theory*. McGraw-Hill, 1970.
An excellent basic text for the engineering approach to finite automata. Emphasis is on switching algebra, logical design, state assignment, fault detection. The last chapter contains a good treatment of regular expressions.

McCulloch, W., and Pitts, W. "A logical calculus of the ideas immanent in nervous activity." *Bulletin of Mathematical Biophysics*, 5, 1943, pp. 115–133.
The original formulation of the McCulloch–Pitts model.

Minsky, Marvin. *Computation: Finite and Infinite Machines*. Prentice-Hall, 1967.
A highly readable introduction to most aspects of automata theory. Chapters 2, 3, and 4 cover state transition, McCulloch–Pitts, and regular expression representations, respectively.

Exercises

3.1. Show the McCulloch–Pitts neurons which perform the following logical operations: (a) *not*, (b) three-input *or*, (c) three-input *and*, (d) implication, (e) equivalence, (f) *nand* ("*not* (A *and* B)"), (g) *nor* ("*not* (A *or* B)").

3.2. Show the logical net and state transition table and diagram for a modulo 8 counter.

3.3. Construct the state transition tables and diagrams for the following networks:
(a) the net in Figure 3.13a;
(b) the net in Figure 3.13b;
(c) the McCulloch–Pitts net in Figure 3.2.

3.4. Give the regular expressions and state transition diagrams of the recognizing (Mealy) automata for the following binary events:
(a) set of no sequences (ϕ);
(b) all sequences with an odd number of 0's;
(c) all sequences containing at least one triple of adjacent 0's;
(d) all sequences with an odd number of symbols and ending in 00;
(e) all sequences beginning with 010 and ending with 101.

3.5. Consider a deterministic finite automaton with n states and a single binary output. For each of the following input conditions state whether the output is (ultimately) periodic and if so what the length of the period is:
(a) the machine has no external input;

(b) the machine has a single nonperiodic binary external input;
(c) the machine has a single periodic binary external input, with period m;
(d) the machine has two binary external inputs, with periods m and m'.

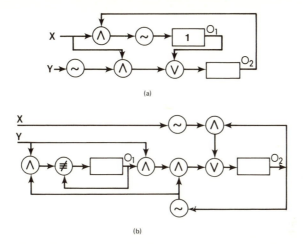

(a)

(b)

Figure 3.13.   Nets for Exercise 3.3.

4
Turing machines

In the last chapter we mentioned some sets of input sequences which could not be described by regular expressions and which therefore could not be recognized by any finite automaton. It turns out that there are more general and powerful kinds of machines which can easily recognize those events. It is thus natural to seek the limits of mechanical behavior. Can we define a type of abstract machine, no matter how impractical it might be to build, which can compute anything that we regard as computable? Are there precisely describable processes that cannot be implemented on any machine?

Many mathematicians have been concerned with finding a formal, mechanical realization of the intuitive notion of an *effective procedure* or algorithm for carrying out a given class of computations. In 1936 the British logician A. M. Turing proposed a class of machines (which now bear his name) and defended the thesis that any process which could naturally be called an effective procedure could be carried out by a Turing machine. This thesis is not subject to proof or disproof, since the notion of effective procedure is not well defined (except possibly by the thesis itself). On the other hand a good deal of credence is lent Turing's proposal by the mere fact that mathematicians have been testing their intuitions against it for four decades. No more satisfactory "definition of computability" has emerged. In this chapter we examine Turing machines, how they compute, and what they can and cannot compute.

A Turing machine can be "physically" characterized in terms of familiar components, as shown in Figure 4.1. Component A is a finite automaton just like those we studied in the last chapter, except that we sometimes wish to designate one of its states as a HALT state which causes the Turing machine to stop computing. Component T is a tape divided lengthwise into squares. Each square of the tape contains a symbol from some finite *tape alphabet*

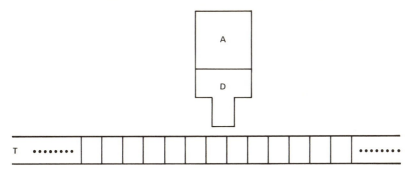

Figure 4.1. Components of a Turing machine.

of two or more symbols. One symbol in the alphabet (usually called "blank") has a special function which we consider shortly.

A Turing machine's remarkable computational power derives from the fact that its tape is effectively infinite. More precisely (and perhaps with greater comfort) we can say that the tape is indefinitely extendable in the sense that whenever more squares are needed they can automatically be added to either end of the tape. There is one important restriction on this infinite tape however. We require that at the outset of a Turing machine's computation its tape contain only a finite number of nonblank symbols. Since a Turing machine can change only one tape square per time step, we are assured that after any finite number of time steps there is still a finite number of nonblank squares on the tape.

The last component of a Turing machine is a tape control device D, which provides an interface between the automaton and tape. D can read the symbol in the tape square currently being scanned and transmit it as an input to A. D can also translate outputs from A into tape handling commands which write a particular symbol in the scanned square or move along the tape one square in either direction. We will largely ignore the detailed functioning of D in what follows. Note however that it is both an encoder and decoder of information.

4.1 Turing and Wang formulations

The operation of a Turing machine proceeds in discrete time steps. In a single step the following sequence of basic operations occurs: (1) D reads the symbol of the scanned square and sends it to A; (2) based on this input and its current state, A undergoes a state transition; (3) the output associated with this transition is decoded by D, which (a) writes a (not necessarily new) symbol in the scanned square and (b) moves along the tape one square to the left, or one square to the right, or not at all. Thus the behavior of a Turing machine is fully specified by (1) the state transition function and starting state of A, (2) the encoding/decoding operations of D, (3) the initial configuration of symbols on the tape, and (4) the location of the first scanned square.

We now look at two rather different formal notations for describing Turing machines. One convenient and concise way of exhibiting the potential behavior of a Turing machine is as a set of quintuples, where the five components respectively specify (1) the current state of A, (2) the current (input) symbol on the tape, (3) the next state of A, (4) the next (output) symbol on the tape, and (5) the direction of movement along the tape (Right, Left, or None). This quintuple notation is very close to Turing's original formulation.

As a simple example of a Turing machine in quintuple form, we can construct a machine to complement binary strings. The tape alphabet consists of three symbols, 0, 1, and blank (b). The automaton has three states denoted x, y, and h (halt), with x as the starting state. As diagrammed in Figure 4.2a the problem is to begin with the "tape head" scanning any square of a binary string delimited by blanks at either end and to finish with the head at the right delimiter of the complemented string. The table of quintuples in Figure 4.2b will cause the machine to find the leftmost binary digit and then proceed along the string to the right hand end, complementing each binary digit in turn.

The binary complementation task in Figure 4.2 can also be carried out by a finite state automaton, and a very simple one indeed. A modular net containing just a *not* element and a single delay will complement any input

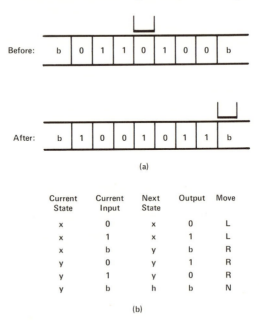

(a)

Current State	Current Input	Next State	Output	Move
x	0	x	0	L
x	1	x	1	L
x	b	y	b	R
y	0	y	1	R
y	1	y	0	R
y	b	h	b	N

(b)

Figure 4.2. (a) Example and (b) quintuples for binary complementation machine.

string. Its (Moore type) state diagram has transitions to state 1 on 0 inputs and to state 0 on 1 inputs.

Figure 4.3 shows an initial tape configuration and quintuple table for a Turing machine which checks whether a set of nested parentheses is well formed, a computation which *cannot* be done by a finite state machine. The

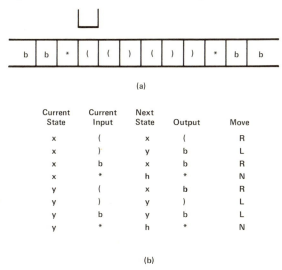

(a)

Current State	Current Input	Next State	Output	Move
x	(	x	(	R
x	)	y	b	L
x	b	x	b	R
x	*	h	*	N
y	(	x	b	R
y	)	y	)	L
y	b	y	b	L
y	*	h	*	N

(b)

Figure 4.3. (a) Initial tape and (b) quintuples for parenthesis machine.

tape for the parenthesis checking machine uses 4 symbols: blank,), (, and * to delimit the parenthesis string. The machine begins scanning at the leftmost parenthesis and in state *x*. It moves right to the first right parenthesis, erases it, then moves left to find and erase its mate. When the machine halts, if the original parenthesis string was well formed, the tape head will be over the right * and there will be only blanks between the * delimiters; otherwise, the head will be over the left *, or at least one parenthesis will remain, or both.

The similarities of the Turing machine quintuple notation to state transition tables for finite automata suggest we might adapt state transition diagrams to describe Turing machines. As long as we accept a state (halt) which has no successors (not even itself), we need only add tape movement information to the arc of a Mealy type state transition graph. Figure 4.4 shows such diagrams for the two machines we have just looked at; on each arc is noted input/output/move information.

With Turing machines of greater complexity than those we have just examined the quintuple notation becomes cumbersome and difficult to follow. In 1957 the logician H. Wang proposed a different means of describing the calculations of a Turing machine (and proved his formulation equivalent to Turing's). Wang machines, as they have come to be called, appeal especi-

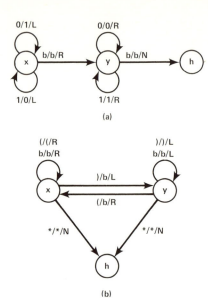

Figure 4.4.   Turing machine state
transition diagrams for
(a) complementation and
(b) parenthesis checking.

ally to computer scientists because the notation is written in the form of a program.

A Wang machine uses just two symbols on its tape (without loss of generality, as we will see later) which we can denote as 0 and 1, with 0 playing the role of a blank. There are six instructions in the programming language:

0 : write a 0 (on the square being scanned)
1 : write a 1
+ : move one square right (along the tape)
− : move one square left
∗ : stop
$t(n)$: transfer to instruction n if scanned square contains a 1

The first five instructions are self-explanatory; but note that a Wang machine need not always read, write, and perform a tape operation in that order. The conditional transfer instruction is a branch to some other instruction in the program (numbered n) when a 1 exists in the current tape square. Otherwise the next instruction in sequence is executed. An attempt to transfer to a nonexistent instruction is equivalent to a ∗ (stop) instruction.

Figure 4.5 shows a program that will cause a Wang machine to add two numbers, as shown in the example tape configurations. Since Wang machines use only two tape symbols we cannot represent delimited numbers in other than unary (or "tally") form. Thus the number four must be coded as 011110, while the number zero occurs between the two delimiters in the

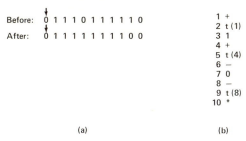

(a)   (b)

Figure 4.5.   (a) Example and (b) program for
Wang machine unary addition.

sequence 00 (i.e., *no* 1's). The addition program simply pushes the two numbers together by filling in the middle delimiter and changing the last 1 to a zero. Notice that this program adds correctly even with one or two zero arguments.

Before considering a more complicated Wang machine program let us add two "macro" instructions to our language. Since we frequently scan the tape leftwards or rightwards for the first occurrence of a zero, we abbreviate the common pair of instructions $[n: + ; n + 1 : t(n)]$ by RTZ (for (Right-To-Zero). Similarly, LTZ stands for the instruction pair $[n: - ; n + 1 : t(n)]$. Using these abbreviations Figure 4.6 shows a program which

```
Before:  0 1 1 0 1 1 1 0 0 0 0 0 0 0 0       1 +        11  1
After:   0 1 1 0 1 1 1 0 1 1 1 1 1 1 0       2 0        12  +
                                             3 RTZ      13  t (5)
                                             4 +        14  LTZ
                                             5 0        15  LTZ
                                             6 RTZ      16  1
                                             7 RTZ      17  +
                                             8 1        18  t (2)
                                             9 LTZ      19  RTZ
                                            10 LTZ      20  *
```

(a)   (b)

Figure 4.6.   (a) Example and (b) program for Wang machine
multiplication.

multiplies two numbers in unary form (and, unlike the addition program, preserves the original arguments). For arguments of m and n this program makes m consecutive copies of n digits. The routine in instructions 5–13 copies n digits and is used m times by the remaining instructions. To keep track of which copy is being made, and of which digit is being copied, the program sets to zero and later restores the argument digits.

4.2 Universal Turing machines

In this section we investigate one of Turing's most remarkable results, that there exists a single Turing machine which can perform the computations performed by any other Turing machine. This Universal Turing Machine (UTM) effectively simulates the operation of any other machine, working from a description (quintuples or Wang program, plus the initial tape configuration) of the other machine. To understand and appreciate the UTM we should first briefly consider some relations between the kinds of Turing machines we have been discussing so far and some variants or generalizations of the original Turing machine model.

We first generalize the idea of a Turing machine tape. Although the original model used a single linear tape potentially infinite in both directions, a Turing machine's capabilities are not curtailed if we consider the tape to have one end and be extensible in only one direction. To see this consider the mapping of all squares of the doubly infinite tape onto the squares of the singly infinite tape, as shown in Figure 4.7. In this figure the numbers in the doubly infinite tape squares should be interpreted as "coordinates" with

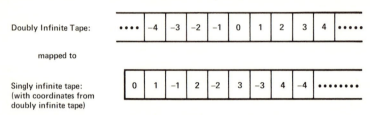

Figure 4.7.   Mapping of doubly infinite tape to singly infinite tape.

square 0 the point of initial scan. Note that the mapping essentially "folds" the doubly infinite tape by using alternate squares for each direction. Although considerable "reprogramming" of the machine might be required to accommodate the "folded" tape, there is clearly no limitation on computing power entailed.

Similar mapping arguments allow us to show that a Turing machine with a "tape" of two or more dimensions has no more computational power than a conventional machine. In fact it is easy to show that the addition of several extra tapes (of any variety) to a Turing machine does not increase its computing power (although it may compute *faster* than the original machine). In the same vein it can be shown that the presence of two or more tape heads on a Turing machine tape may accelerate computation but does not make the machine more powerful.

Finally we should mention the remarkable demonstrations by Shannon that any Turing machine with just two tape symbols, *or* with just two states, can be made computationally equivalent to any given Turing machine. The two symbol result is perhaps less surprising; we have already used it in the Wang machines. All that is required is a coding of symbols in the larger alphabet into blocks of symbols in the smaller one. Generally any reduction in tape symbols will increase the number of internal states required for a given computation. But the tradeoff goes in the other direction too. Increasing the tape alphabet allows reduction of states, in the extreme case to just two. This result becomes more believable if we think in terms of the huge number of *distinct* transitions possible in a two-state Mealy automaton with large numbers of inputs and outputs.

Incidentally, Shannon's demonstration of the state-symbol tradeoff has inspired designers of UTM's to a sort of competition to see who can produce a universal machine with the smallest product of number of states and number of symbols. Minsky has constructed a 4-symbol 7-state UTM. And it is known that no 2-symbol 2-state machine is universal. But much of the area in between is still open to competitors.

In the UTM we are about to consider we will sacrifice economy of both states and symbols in favor of ease of understanding. We will begin with a machine which is very easy to understand in principle but lacks several necessary features of a true UTM. Then we will successively impose these features. Our initial candidate for a UTM is shown in Figure 4.8. This is a 2-tape Turing machine which simulates any Wang machine T, with a singly infinite tape after being supplied its description (program), $d(T)$, on one tape and its initial tape configuration $t(T)$ on the other tape.

It is not hard to imagine what a state transition function for the machine in Figure 4.8 would look like. Each cycle of operation would require moving

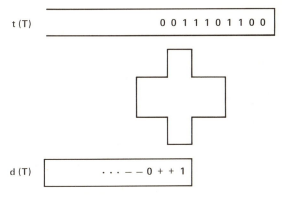

Figure 4.8.   Initial candidate for a UTM.

left along the program tape (dragging the data tape along) to fetch the next instruction. Input of the instruction would lead to one or more state transitions with outputs which would cause the proper manipulation of the data tape. Instead of quintuples we might want to employ sextuples, since there will always be one input from each tape at each time step. On the other hand a binary tape output alphabet would suffice, since it is never necessary to write on the program tape. Transfer instructions would present some difficulties but could certainly be handled by a sufficiently elaborate and clever design.

Why is the machine of Figure 4.8 not entirely acceptable as a UTM? The main reason is that it is not of the same type as the machines it can simulate. It is always fair to prove something about Turing machines by proving it about a particular class of machines which has the same computing power as any other class. But it is not fair to employ a machine of another class in the analysis. We have limited ourselves to simulating Wang machines with single binary tapes. Thus our UTM should also be a Wang machine with a single binary tape if we wish to demonstrate the existence of a UTM within a particular but complete domain of machines. But our UTM is a (sort of) quintuple machine with two tapes, one of which is nonbinary. It can hardly be called a "universal" machine if it cannot even attempt to simulate itself.

Fortunately these difficulties are easy to surmount. First we make the program tape binary by encoding the Wang instructions in the following manner: 0 as 01, 1 as 011, + as 0111, − as 01111, * as 011111, $t(n)$ as 00 followed by n 1's, and instruction label k as 000 followed by k 1's. This encoding enables us to move back and forth along the program tape and always know where instructions begin, what their labels are, and to differentiate transfer instructions (e.g., $t(2) - 0011$) from other similar encodings (e.g., 1–011). To check the effectiveness of this code we can write out the encoding of the first few instructions in the Wang program of Figure 4.5: 000101110001100100011101100011110111 ... Of course this code is neither elegant nor efficient; but then we have never considered Turing machines to be especially practical.

Now we can easily combine the two binary tapes into a single tape with the (nonexpanding) program tape first. The problem is that when the machine leaves the program tape to simulate the effects of an instruction on the data tape it will have no way of knowing where the program ends and the data starts or to what point in the program it should return. This problem is solved by using only alternate squares of the program-data tape for information. The remaining squares will all be 0 except for four: a 1 to "remember" the current instruction in the program tape, a 1 to "remember" the current square being scanned on the data tape, and two 1's together to delimit the program data boundary. If we draw these alternating work squares on a different level to make them stand out from the information squares, the final tape has the appearance shown in Figure 4.9.

We now have a UTM with a single, singly infinite binary tape. What

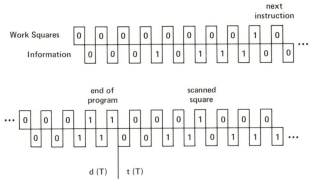

Figure 4.9. Tape for UTM.

remains is to rewrite the UTM's description as a Wang program, a monumental task that we shall not attempt here. But it should be clear that there is nothing in principle to prevent the construction of a Wang program which will suitably interpret the encoded instructions and perform the proper tape operations, all the while adjusting its work square 1's to keep track of its current position in the program and on the simulated tape. Since we know that any Turing machine can be described as a Wang program plus a singly infinite binary tape, and since that is also the structure of our machine, we have now set out the design specifications for a genuine UTM.

4.3 Computability and unsolvability

Although much too slow and cumbersome for practical purposes a UTM can perform any computation that can be done by any other Turing machine. It would be nice to be able to characterize this class of computations as neatly and precisely as the regular expressions characterized the behavior of finite automata. But if we accept Turing's thesis a UTM's potential behavior includes everything that can be computed by an effective procedure. The limitations of effective computability are the focus of a large and active area of automata theory, an area riddled with open questions and unsolved problems.

Many of the unsolved problems are in reality *unsolvable*. To clarify the sense in which we use such terms, let us consider the following possible interpretations of "unsolvable problem": (1) one for which it has been shown that no solution exists; (2) one for which a solution may exist, but none has been found; (3) one for which a solution has been shown to exist but has not been found; and (4) one for which a solution has been shown to exist and to be "unfindable." No problems of type (4) are known. Problems of types (2) and (3) may be called "unsolved"; but only those of type (2) can potentially be shown "unsolvable" in the proper sense of the term (i.e., type (1)). Computability theorists are usually concerned with reclassifying type (2) problems as type (1) or type (3) (or even actually producing a solution).

Many significant results in computability theory have thus been of the form "There is no effective procedure for computing (or deciding)..." Proofs of such results usually involve showing the nonexistence of a Turing machine to do the computation (or make the decision). A *decision procedure* is actually equivalent to a Turing machine which accepts some appropriate subset of tapes (and rejects all other tapes in finitely many steps). The tapes considered by such a *decision Turing machine* may contain any sort of information, including descriptions of Turing machines. Acceptance or rejection of a tape may be signalled by a designated output symbol.

A classic limitation on effective computability is the undecidability of the *halting problem* for Turing machines. Although all the machines we have so far considered will eventually stop computing (i.e., the automaton will enter the *halt* state), there are clearly many machines which will go into unending computational "loops." A trivial example of a nonhalting Turing machine is the one described by the following Wang program: $[1: +; 2: 1; 3: t(1)]$. Since there are Turing machines which will halt for some initial tape configurations and not for others, the halting classification actually applies to machine-tape combinations. We therefore state the halting problem as follows: Is there an effective procedure which, given *any* Turing machine and tape, can decide whether the automaton will ever enter the halt state? In other words, does there exist a Turing machine which can be given descriptions of other machines and their tapes (in a manner analogous to that for the UTM) and *always* report whether or not the machine-tape combination will halt?

To establish the nonexistence of an effective procedure for the halting problem we will show that the assumption that one exists leads to a contradiction. We therefore posit the existence of a decision Turing machine D which, given the description $d(T)$ and tape $t(T)$ of any Turing machine, will enter one state (call it YES) if the described machine halts and another (NO) if it does not. As shown in Figure 4.10 these decision states can occur just before the decision machine itself halts. (Note that a decision machine must halt, by definition.)

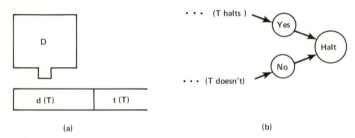

Figure 4.10.   (a) Configuration and (b) state transitions for halting problem decision machine.

We now make two strange but simple alterations to D, producing the machine D' shown in Figure 4.11. The first alteration is to have the input tape be a machine description only, and to have the machine immediately put a copy of $d(T)$ on the tape, to the right of the original (Figure 4.11a). Secondly we alter the state transition diagram of Figure 4.10b so that the YES state leads to a new state (x) from which there is no exit (and therefore no halting) as shown in Figure 4.11b.

The machine in Figure 4.11 is strange indeed. But consider what happens when the description presented to D' is of itself, $d(D')$. D' immediately copies this description and tries to decide if D' operating on a description of D' halts. If the answer is YES, D' itself enters an unending loop and does not halt. If the answer is NO, D' itself halts. Therefore if D' applied to itself halts it does not. But if it does not halt it does. This contradiction forces us to conclude that there has been an error in our argument. Since the various modifications to the original machine were clearly feasible, we must admit

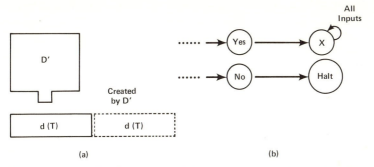

Figure 4.11.   (a) Configuration and (b) state transitions for machine D′.

that our assumption of the existence of a decision machine for the halting problem was in error. Hence there is no effective procedure for deciding if any given Turing machine plus tape will ever stop computing.

Of course the above conclusion does not mean that we cannot decide if a particular machine ever halts. We can easily demonstrate many machines which always halt (for any tape) and many others which do not. What the above argument denies is the existence of a general algorithm that can always decide if a Turing machine halts. This result is not only somewhat surprising, but also quite useful. Many other problems in computability theory have been proved unsolvable by demonstrating their equivalence to the halting problem.

4.4 Grammars and machines

The finite automata of the last chapter and the Turing machines of this one are actually the end points on a continuum of machines with increasing computational power. In the late 1950's the brilliant MIT linguist Noam Chomsky (whose contributions to linguistics will be discussed in Section 15.1) devised a formal notation which characterized this continuum of machines in terms of the types of symbol sequences they could recognize or accept.

Although we may have appeared to be using them interchangeably, recognition and acceptance are not the same thing. We have already seen that a finite automaton can recognize a regular event by assigning all inputs to the set or its complement. Acceptance is a weaker capability. A Turing machine can accept a set of inputs by identifying the correct instances (and halting) yet not always halt for the inputs in the complement. A set is thus recognizable (by some type of machine) if and only if its complement can also be recognized (by the same type of machine). (Those familiar with the terminology of recursive function theory may identify recognizable sets with recursive sets, and acceptable sets with recursively enumerable sets.)

In this section we briefly consider formal languages, the grammars which describe them, and their relations to automata. A *grammar* may be defined as a quadruple (V, T, P, S) where

V is a finite set of *variables* $(A, B, C, \ldots)$,
T is a finite set of *terminals* $(a, b, c, \ldots)$,
P is a finite set of *productions* (or rewriting rules), and
S, an element of V, is a designated *start* symbol.

Productions define permitted replacements of symbol sequences by other symbol sequences. The sequence to be replaced (which must contain at least one nonterminal symbol) appears on the left hand side of an arrow; the new sequence is on the right. Thus the following three productions

$$(1)\ S \to ABA \qquad (2)\ A \to x \qquad (3)\ B \to yy$$

can be applied successively to generate the sequence of terminal symbols $xyyx$. Five steps are involved:

S: begin with the start symbol
ABA: apply production (1) to replace S by ABA
xBA: apply production (2) to replace A by x
$xyyA$: apply production (3) to replace B by yy
$xyyx$: apply production (2) a second time

The set of all possible sequences containing only terminal symbols, which can be produced by repeated applications of a grammar's productions, is called the *language* defined by that grammar. To generate a "sentence" in such a language we begin with S and keep rewriting until we have a string of terminal symbols.

Here is a simple but interesting example of a grammar, which we will have occasion to refer to below. Let $V = \{S\}$, $T = \{a, b\}$ and $P = \{S \to aSb, S \to ab\}$. This grammar generates all strings having n a's followed by n b's. We merely apply the first production $n - 1$ times and then the second production once. Thus for $n = 3$, the generation is as follows: $S \to aSb \to aaSbb \to aaabbb$.

Grammars (and the languages they generate) are classified according to the restrictions placed on the types of rewriting rules allowed in P. Chomsky and others have identified four types of successively more restricted grammars. In a type 0 grammar any productions are allowed. A type 1, or *context sensitive*, grammar allows any production in which the number of symbols on the left does not exceed the number on the right. Thus $aBa \to aa$ and $aBa \to aba$ would both be acceptable type 0 productions; but only the latter would be a legitimate type 1 production. In general any productions of type n are also of type $n - 1$ (for $n = 1, 2, 3$).

A type 2 grammar is called *context free* and has productions which contain only a single variable on the left. The example given above is a context free grammar. A type 3, or *regular*, grammar allows only rules of the form $A \to aB$ and $A \to a$ in its so-called right linear form. Alternatively we may have a left linear grammar which allows only rules like $A \rightarrow Ba$ and $A \rightarrow a$.

The similarity of the terms regular grammar and regular expression is not coincidental. They are actually equivalent ways of describing the sets of sequences that finite automata can recognize. Thus the machines we studied in Chapter 3 can be defined in terms of type 3 grammars. For example, if we use binary values for terminal symbols, the three rules $\{S \rightarrow 1S, S \rightarrow 0S, S \rightarrow 1\}$ define the set of all sequences ending in 1, for which the state transition diagram was given in Figure 3.10.

At the other end of the machine-grammar continuum, type 0 languages can be accepted by Turing machines. (Since the acceptor machine may not halt for inputs in the complement, these languages are called *semidecidable*.) There are few interesting (and no simple) type 0 languages which are not also of some more restrictive type. Thus the parenthesis checking Turing machine in Figure 4.3 above was actually accepting (in *this* case recognizing as well) a type 2 language. Note the similarity between well formed strings of parentheses and the language generated by the context free grammar given above. We might inquire what less powerful type of machine *could* have checked parentheses.

For accepting languages of types 1 and 2 we must define two new kinds of machines. The sequences of a context free (type 2) language can be accepted by a nondeterministic finite automaton equipped with a special kind of indefinitely extendable memory known as a *pushdown store*. A pushdown store is a last-in first-out (lifo) kind of memory which is usually likened to a spring loaded stack of trays in a cafeteria. Although it can store an unlimited amount of information, a pushdown store automaton is less powerful than a Turing machine because it must discard all symbols on the stack above the one to be retrieved.

To recognize context sensitive (type 1) languages we require a nondeterministic machine known as a *linear bounded automaton*. The only difference between a linear bounded automaton and a (nondeterministic) Turing machine is that the former never uses any tape squares other than those upon which the input was placed. A linear bounded automaton is thus free to move back and forth within an arbitrarily large but not extendable memory.

Formal grammars have acquired an established place in computer science because large portions of programming languages like ALGOL and LISP can be generated by context free grammars. The development of effective algorithms to parse (i.e., deduce the structure of) ALGOL type expressions is a major concern of those who design compilers. Context free rewriting rules have also seen extensive use in the more formal aspects of natural language analysis. We will be discussing this application in Section 15.1, where we will look at an example (Figure 15.1) of how such rules can be used to generate simple English sentences.

Bibliography

The Minsky and both Arbib books in the Chapter 3 Bibliography have excellent discussions of Turing machines.

Chomsky, Noam. "On certain properties of formal grammars." *Information and Control, 2,* 1959, pp. 137–167.
The original paper on formal grammars.

Hopcroft, John E. and Ullman, Jeffrey D. *Formal Languages and their Relation to Automata.* Addison-Wesley, 1969.
A fine textbook for the formal language approach to machines.

Trakhtenbrot, B. A. *Algorithms and Automatic Computing Machines.* Heath, 1963.
Mainly devoted to the theory of algorithms, this book treats Turing machines in Chapters 8–13.

Turing, A. M. "On computable numbers, with an application to the Entscheidungs problem." *Proceedings of the London Mathematical Society, Series 2, 42,* 1936, pp. 230–265.
The original Turing paper.

Wang, Hao. "A variant to Turing's theory of computing machines." *Journal of the Association for Computing Machinery, 4,* 1957, pp. 63–92.
The original definition of Wang machines.

Exercises

4.1. If a Turing machine tape uses n symbols and its automaton has only binary inputs and outputs, describe precisely the encoding/decoding functions of the tape control device, D.

4.2. Write Wang programs for the following tasks, where all numbers are in unary form:
(a) addition of two numbers, placing the sum to the right of the arguments;
(b) subtraction of two numbers, $x - y$ with y leftmost and no larger than x, only difference preserved;
(c) as in (b) but preserve original arguments;
(d) greatest common divisor of two numbers.

4.3. Show the mappings from the tapes of the following Turing machines to a single singly infinite tape:
(a) a machine with three doubly infinite tapes;
(b) a machine with a two-dimensional tape, bidirectionally infinite in both dimensions.

4.4. Does a finite automaton with two pushdown stores have the computational power of a Turing machine? Why or why not?

4.5. Is there a decision procedure for classifying all *blank tape* Turing machines (those which start with no symbols on the tape) into those which halt and those which do not? Sketch an informal proof of your answer, making use of results given in the chapter.

4.6. Using binary values for terminal symbols, give the regular grammars for the following input sets that can be recognized by finite automata:
(a) all sequences beginning with 0;
(b) all sequences with an odd number of symbols
(c) all sequences with an even number of 1's.

4.7. For each set of production rules below, identify the type of grammar and describe the language generated:
(a) $S \rightarrow aSa$, $S \rightarrow bSb$, $S \rightarrow aa$, $S \rightarrow bb$
(b) $S \rightarrow aB$, $B \rightarrow aB$, $B \rightarrow bS$, $B \rightarrow b$
(c) $S \rightarrow aSBC$, $S \rightarrow aBC$, $CB \rightarrow BC$, $aB \rightarrow ab$, $bB \rightarrow bb$, $bC \rightarrow bc$, $cC \rightarrow cc$.

5
Cellular automata

In this chapter we focus on a relatively new and currently quite active branch of automata theory. The study of cellular automata is concerned with the behavior of systems composed of regular arrays of identical interacting components. Theoretical questions of importance in cellular automata research relate to the computational powers of such machines. Thus we might want to know how many components, how many states per component, and what sorts of interconnections among components are required to simulate the behavior of a UTM. Some of the important applications of cellular automata are in the design of parallel computers, the modelling of natural cellular systems, and the solution of systems of equations.

We may define a cellular automaton (also frequently called a cell space, a tesselation automaton, or an iterative array) as a collection of identical cells (or modules, or components) arranged and interconnected in some regular manner. The *collection* may be finite or infinite. The *cells* may be any sort of machine but are usually fairly simple finite automata, since we are interested in discovering the computational power that derives from the cellular structure. The *arrangement* of cells may be any regular organization in any number of dimensions. By far the most common arrangement locates the cells at the integral coordinate points of a rectangular (Cartesian) grid on a two-dimensional plane.

The *interconnection* of cells is usually based on some set of coordinate displacements which identify a set of cells called the *neighborhood* of any given cell. Two common neighborhoods in a Cartesian plane are (a) the four orthogonally adjacent cells, having relative coordinates of $(0, 1), (0, -1)$, $(1, 0), (-1, 0)$, and (b) the eight orthogonally and diagonally adjacent cells, having the additional relative coordinates $(1, 1), (1, -1), (-1, 1)$, and $(-1, -1)$. In general however the neighborhood defined over a cell space need not be symmetric or composed of adjacent cells.

The behavior of a cell space is determined by a *cell transition function* which maps the state of a cell and all its neighbors at time t to a new state of the cell at time $t + 1$. The state of the cell space at any given time is just the set of individual states of all its cells. If the space is not finite however we stipulate that all but a finite number of cells must be in a distinguished *quiescent* state at any given time. This quiescent state thus functions analogously to the blank symbol on a Turing machine tape. Since all cells change state synchronously in discrete time, there is a *cell space transition function* induced over the entire array by the (local) cell transition function. Finally we may sometimes wish to permit some or all of the cells in a space to be influenced by *external inputs* from the environment, which function like the external inputs to a modular net. The specification of an *initial state* of a cell space, together with the temporal sequences of any external inputs, fully determines the behavior of the space.

A simple and popular example of a cellular automaton is John Conway's simulation "game," called LIFE because of analogies to population dynamics in a society of living organisms. The LIFE cell space is a two-dimensional Cartesian array of cells with an 8-cell neighborhood of the second type mentioned above (orthogonally and diagonally adjacent cells). Each cell may be in one of two possible states, occupied ("alive") or empty ("dead," quiescent). The cell transition function is defined by four rules: (1) an occupied cell with exactly two or three occupied neighbors remains occupied ("survives") at the next time step ("generation"); (2) an occupied cell with four or more occupied neighbors becomes empty ("dies" from "overcrowding") at the next time step; (3) an occupied cell with fewer than two occupied neighbors "dies" from "isolation"; and (4) an empty cell with exactly three occupied neighbors becomes occupied (is "born") in the next generation (otherwise it remains empty). Figure 5.1 shows the Conway transition function graph where state 1 is occupied, state 0 is empty, and the arcs are labelled with the number of occupied neighbors.

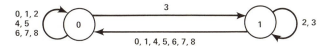

Figure 5.1.   LIFE transition function.

The behavior (pattern of occupied cells) of the LIFE space is surprisingly varied and interesting for so simple a transition function. Conway and others have devised initial configurations of occupied cells which lead to intricate and fascinating patterns of activity. One of three long range outcomes usually occurs: the "society" dies out (e.g., three consecutive cells on a diagonal will disappear in two time steps); a stable pattern is reached and activity ceases (e.g., a square array of four cells); or the pattern develops a regular oscillation (e.g., three cells in a horizontal row will alternate indefinitely with three in a vertical column). But some initial configurations have as yet unknown fates, having been tracked for hundreds of generations without reaching any of the above outcomes.

5.1 Von Neumann's machines

In the late 1940's the brilliant applied mathematician John von Neumann turned his attention to automata theory. His interests in universal and self-reproducing machines led to the development of a cellular automaton with the computational power of a UTM, the ability to construct arbitrary machines within the cell space, and the capacity for self-reproduction. Before considering his contributions we should characterize more precisely what it means for a cellular automaton (or any machine) to be universal in the three ways of interest to von Neumann.

The first kind of universality is *computation universality*. To show that a machine has this power we need to demonstrate that it can simulate any Turing machine (or just a UTM). To show this for a cellular automaton we seek an *embedding* of Turing machine features in the structural and functional aspects of the cell space. A second and more powerful kind of universality is *construction universality*; our machine must be able to *build* any other machine when supplied with its description. For a cellular automaton we require the means to embed an arbitrary configuration of states and connections. Note that construction universality implies computation universality since, even if the universal constructor does not have universal computation ability, it can build a machine that does.

A third kind of universality is inherent in a machine with the power to reproduce itself. More is implied than the trivial kinds of "self-reproduction" manifested by processes like crystal formation. What von Neumann and others have usually sought is a computation/construction universal machine with self-reproduction capabilities. And we do not consider a machine truly self-reproducing unless its "offspring" also have that capability.

It is not at all obvious that such a machine can be designed. One of von Neumann's first contributions was to show how the existence of self-reproducing machines followed logically from the assumed existence of a *universal constructor*, denoted A in Figure 5.2a. A can take a description of any other machine and build it. In particular we can give A its own decription, $d(A)$, and construct another A. Now A is not self-reproducing because the new machine differs from the original in that it lacks a copy of its own description. We therefore consider a second machine B which simply makes a copy of any description given to it (Figure 5.2b). Now we combine A and B with a control device C which accepts any description tape, passes it to B for copying, to A for construction, and finally inserts the tape copy into the new machine. As shown in Figure 5.2c, the A-B-C complex, which we call D, can accept a description of A and produce A with a tape of its own description.

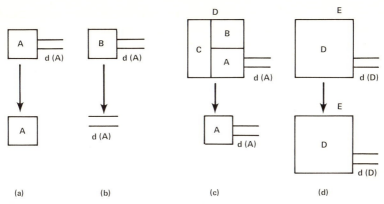

Figure 5.2. Steps in the design of a self-reproducing machine.

Finally we denote by E the machine D operating on its own description, $d(D)$. E is self-reproducing since it causes another E to be produced, which is in turn capable of producing another E, and so on. This argument shows that the existence of a universal constructor is logically sufficient for the design of a self-reproducing machine. Although we do not really know how to build the latter machine in any detail, we can proceed to design cellular spaces with universal computation/construction properties and have some confidence that such automata will also be capable of manifesting self-reproduction.

Von Neumann actually proposed two approaches to the design of a universal constructor (and hence a self-reproducing machine). In an informal *kinematic model* he envisioned a machine with sufficient computational power and the ability to join together the sorts of components of which it itself was constructed. Descriptions of machines could be encoded as suitable linear sequences of elementary building blocks. When given the description of some machine and provided with an unlimited supply of "spare parts" the kinematic constructor could build the described machine. If also endowed with the ability to copy any description, the constructor would be self-reproducing in the manner shown above (Figure 5.2).

Von Neumann's self-reproducing cellular automaton was worked out with much more rigor and detail than his kinematic model. His original description of the complete design consumes more than 150 pages and can obviously not be treated in depth here. But let us examine the general nature of the von Neumann cellular system.

The cells of the von Neumann cell space occupy the integral coordinate points of a bidirectionally infinite (Cartesian) plane. A cell's neighborhood is the set of four orthogonally adjacent cells. Each cell is a 29 state finite automaton with a designated quiescent state. The remaining 28 states are used for computation, for transmission of information along binary communication paths in the array, and for construction of desired state configurations in designated regions of the array.

There are four pairs of "ordinary transmission states" to handle the transmission of a pulse (active state) or not (inactive state) in each of the four possible directions permitted by the neighborhood. Ordinary transmission states also function as logical *or* modules, since they pass (with unit delay) a signal received from *any* of the three directions in which they do not transmit. Four "confluent" states compute a logical *and* of all ordinary transmission signals directed to them and propagate the result in all other directions (with a two time step delay, hence the four states). Four pairs of "special transmission states" carry signals in a manner identical to ordinary ones; but these signals cause the "destruction" (conversion to the quiescent state) of all ordinary transmission and confluent states they reach. This arrangement is required because it is often necessary to destroy a constructed component or transmission line after it has served its purpose (special transmission states can be destroyed by ordinary ones). Finally there are eight "sensitized states" which are arranged in a binary tree with the quiescent state at the top node and (the inactive forms of) all other states at the terminal node. This provision allows a particular quiescent state to undergo a series of transitions terminating in a desired state, under control of an input sequence. Thus the sequence 10001 constructs an inactive upward-pointing ordinary transmission state.

Von Neumann next shows how to use his intricate state transition function to embed the following sorts of constructions in his cell space: various computational·"organs" (e.g., pulsers, decoders), an arbitrary finite automaton, the tape of a Turing machine, a Turing machine itself, a constructing arm for building arbitrary state configurations, and finally a universal constructor. The details of this analysis are often tedious and messy. But the inarguable conclusion is that there can be embedded in the 29-state von Neumann cellular automaton a computation and construction universal machine which is self-reproducing.

Several other investigators, mainly at the University of Michigan, have developed or refined von Neumann's system. The original description was actually completed by Arthur Burks after von Neumann's death. James Thatcher has presented a more elegant set of embedding techniques using von Neumann's original 29 states. And Edgar Codd has devised an 8-state cellular automaton equivalent to von Neumann's. Rather than attempting a detailed study of even the more elegant refinements of von Neumann type cell spaces, however, we turn next to a radically different type of universal cellular automaton.

5.2 Arbib's machine

Michael Arbib has developed a model in which no attempt was made to keep the number of states small. Although his cells have some 2^{335} potential states their operation is easily understood, especially by those familiar with digital computers. In this section we take a fairly detailed look at Arbib's universal self-reproducing cellular automaton.

Like von Neumann's cells, Arbib's "basic modules" are arrayed on a Cartesian plane and communicate with their four orthogonal neighbors (denoted u, d, l, and r for up, down, left, and right). The components of an Arbib module are diagrammed in Figure 5.3. There are four pairs of lines to carry signals to and from neighboring modules. Since quite complex signals will have to pass over these lines in a single time step we must consider them to have very large symbol alphabets (or to be cables of binary lines). The module also has a one-bit "weld" register associated with each neighbor (Wu, Wd, Wr, Wl), the function of which will be explained shortly. Internally

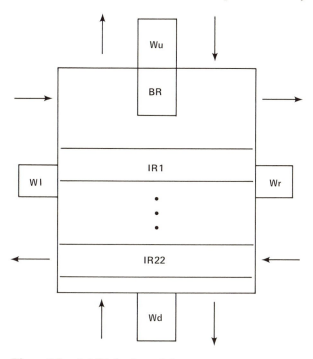

Figure 5.3. Arbib's basic module.

the module contains "instruction registers" ($IR1$ through $IR22$) and a "bit register" (BR). The bit register is useful when we wish to regard the module as having only two significant states. The instruction registers can hold a "program" of up to 22 15-bit words (the reasons for these particular numbers will become apparent later). The module is considered to be in the quiescent state when the 335 bits in all 27 registers are set to 0. Arbib intentionally conceals a very complex state transition function in the form of instruction sequences and (unspecified) circuitry for communication with a module's neighbors.

One of the things an Arbib module can do is dump the contents of all its registers into the corresponding registers of a neighbor (erasing the neighbor's previous state but not changing that of the "dumping" module). When this occurs we will say the module has "moved" left, right, up, or down (as the case may be). When a module moves it carries along (causes to move in the same direction) all modules to which it is *welded*. Two modules are welded if either of their opposing weld bits is 1. We may thus have an entire collection of modules welded together, a collection referred to as a *co-moving set* because if any member of the set moves in a particular direction all the other modules do the same.

The concept of a co-moving set of modules is quite useful for embedding things like Turing machine tapes. But conflicts can arise if two cells in the same set simultaneously attempt to move in different directions, or if two nonwelded cells simultaneously attempt to move into a common third cell. Arbib provides a complex set of conventions to resolve such conflicts. Fortunately, the conventions are not required in the development of a universal self-reproducing machine, since no movement conflicts arise.

The behavior of an Arbib module is governed by the sequence of commands in its instruction registers (and the inputs it receives from its neighbors). We now describe Arbib's instruction code (programming language), using a slight modification of his notation. In this description A will denote any direction (u, d, l, or r) and b a bit value (0 or 1). We will use k and k' to stand for any of the 22 instruction registers, but k'' will also include the bit and weld registers. The instruction forms thus entail about 4,000 different individual instructions. We also allow any instruction I to be prefixed by [A], which will mean that the module is ordering its direction A neighbor to execute I. We thus have a total of some 20,000 distinct instructions. Since 20,000 is between 2^{14} and 2^{15} we now know why the instruction registers hold 15-bit words. The instruction formats, together with examples and explanations, are shown below.

Format	Example	Explanation
weld Ab	weld $u1$	set weld bit in direction A to b
move A	move r	move in direction A
emit Ak''	emit lWd	send the contents of k'' in direction A
place Ab	place $d0$	set BR of direction A neighbor to b
store Ak, k'	store $u19, 12$	store contents of k in k' of direction A neighbor
branch Ak, k'	branch $r4, 6$	transfer to instruction k if input from direction A is 0, to instruction k' if it is 1; if A and k' are omitted the branch is unconditional, e.g. branch 20.
halt	halt	stop executing instructions (overridden by execute orders from neighbors)
[A]I	[l] weld $r0$	have direction A neighbor execute I, where I may be any of the above

To embed an arbitrary Turing machine in the Arbib cell space we use a slight variation on the Wang formulation introduced in the last chapter. These modified Wang machines will have no instruction labels in their programs: transfer instructions will be of two forms, $t + n$ and $t - n$, meaning branch forward or backward n instructions if the scanned square contains a one. (Note that this "relative" addressing would also be a useful simplification in describing machines to the UTM of the last chapter.) The Wang machine tape can be embedded in the Arbib cell space simply by using a linear string of co-moving cells with each cell representing a tape square marked with the bit contained in the cell's *BR*. Whenever more tape is required at either end another quiescent cell can be welded on.

An arbitrary Wang program can be embedded by encoding it on another simulated tape, using one cell for each instruction other than the transfers. To encode a $t \pm n$ instruction will require $1 + n \pm 1$ cells for purposes of counting right or left to the appropriate instruction. The instruction registers of the program tape cells will contain a sequence of commands particular to the Wang instruction being simulated.

Finally, to coordinate the embedded program and data tapes, we require a two-cell control head situated between them, as shown in Figure 5.4. Control cell *C*1 interprets and executes all Wang program instructions except the transfers. Control cell *C*2 handles the rather messy business of

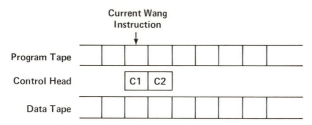

Figure 5.4. An embedded Wang machine.

branching within the Wang program. We will not provide further details about transfer instruction encoding or cell *C*2, except to note that the latter requires a 22 instruction program and thus determines the number of instruction registers required in (every) Arbib module.

The program tape cells for the nontransfer Wang instructions all contain the following commands in the first 3 instruction registers: store d, 4, 6; [d] branch 4; halt. The program cell thus stores its *IR*4 in *C*1's *IR*6 and then tells *C*1 to branch to its own *IR*4. The program cell's *IR*4 (the instruction transferred to *IR*6 of *C*1) will contain a command particular to the Wang instruction being simulated: place d1 for a 1 instruction, place d0 for a 0 instruction [d] move l for a $+$ instruction, and [d] move r for a $-$ instruction.

The commands in *C*1's *IR*s first move the program tape to the next instruction cell and then activate that cell's program. After receiving the appropriate command in its *IR*6, *C*1 assures that the square below is welded into the data tape and then executes the tape operation called for by the Wang instruction. Finally C1 completes the cycle by branching back to its own *IR*1. Here is the 7 instruction C1 program:

> *IR* 1. [*u*] move *l*
> 2. [*u*] branch 1
> 3. halt
> 4. [*d*] weld *r*1
> 5. [*d*] weld *l*1
> 6. (loaded by program tape cell)
> 7. branch 1

The capacity to embed an arbitrary Turing machine shows that the Arbib cell space is computation universal. To demonstrate construction universality we must show how to build any desired configurations of cells in specified states. Arbib gives the (straightforward) instruction contents of three successive program cells which, operating together with C1, will load with specified contents all registers of the (formerly quiescent) cell above the program cell above C1. Finally this constructed cell can be moved in any desired direction (along with any previously built cells to which it is welded), making room for construction of another cell. It is thus possible to place an arbitrary configuration of cells in the construction area above the program tape.

Given a computation/construction universal space, von Neumann's argument says that a self-reproducing machine can be embedded. Arbib shows tedious but straightforward methods for encoding module command programs so that they can be interpreted by other modules. This makes it possible for a machine processing its own description to build a copy of itself processing its own description. The components of Arbib's self-reproducing machine are shown in Figure 5.5 with the same labels (*A, B, C, D*) used in the original von Neumann argument. The tape copier, *B*, first constructs a copy of *d*(*D*) in the construction area and then temporarily moves it out of the way. The universal constructor, *A*, then builds machine *D* (i.e., *A + B + C* with control head) from its description. Finally *C*

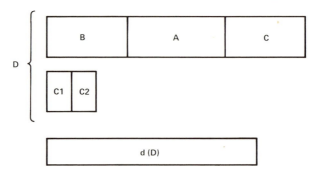

Figure 5.5.   Arbib's self-reproducing machine.

properly positions the copy of $d(D)$ under the control head of the new machine D, yielding a replica of the original machine-tape configuration.

Bibliography

Arbib, Michael A. *Theories of Abstract Automata*. Prentice-Hall, 1969.
Chapter 10 contains a general discussion of cellular automata and full treatment of Arbib's model.

Burks, Arthur W. (ed). *Essays on Cellular Automata*. University of Illinois Press, 1970.
A collection of many key papers in the field, including Burks' summary and Thatcher's revision of the von Neumann model.

Codd, Edgar F. *Cellular Automata*. Academic Press, 1968.
Detailed description of an 8-state cell space equivalent to von Neumann's original model.

Gardner, Martin. "Mathematical games." *Scientific American*. October, 1970, pp. 120–123.
The first of many such columns which discuss Conway's "LIFE" game and related topics.

von Neumann, John. *Theory of Self-Reproducing Automata*. Edited and completed by Arthur W. Burks. University of Illinois Press, 1966.
An extensive collection of von Neumann's thoughts on automata, including a complete development of the original 29-state model.

Exercises

5.1. Explore the behavior of the following starting configurations for LIFE:

(a) 0 0 0 0 0
   0 1 0 0 0
   0 1 1 1 0
   0 0 0 0 0

(b) 0 0 0 0 0
   0 0 1 0 0
   0 1 1 1 0
   0 0 0 0 0

(c) 0 0 0 0 0
   0 0 1 0 0
   0 0 0 1 0   (the "glider")
   0 1 1 1 0
   0 0 0 0 0

(d) 0 0 0 0 0 0 0 0
   0 0 1 0 0 1 0 0
   0 0 1 1 1 1 0 0
   0 1 0 0 0 0 1 0   (the "Cheshire cat")
   0 1 0 1 1 0 1 0
   0 1 0 0 0 0 1 0
   0 0 1 1 1 1 0 0
   0 0 0 0 0 0 0 0

5.2. Program a LIFE simulation for a machine and language of your choice.

5.3. For the Wang machine with program [+, 1, −], scanning the leftmost square of the tape 1 0 1 0 0 ...:
  (a) show the complete embedding as an Arbib machine (except for the program in C2);
  (b) trace the execution of the module instructions shown in (a).

Part II
Biological Information Processing

In the next five chapters we turn our attention to how living systems process information. We begin with the basic organizational unit of life, the cell. After looking at some of the general features common to most living cells we focus on the large biological molecules specialized for encoding information—proteins and nucleic acids. In the DNA of a cell's chromosomes we will find stored all the information required by the organism. The way in which this information is coded and the way in which it is translated into other molecular structures are treated in some detail. Then we examine how biological function may be modified to suit changing circumstances. Even in the simple bacterium we discover adaptive abilities rivaling those designed by man. Genetically coded information not only regulates the life cycle of an organism but also provides for continuity of species. Chapter 7 looks at how and with what evolutionary consequences information is transmitted from generation to generation, both in primitive unicellular organisms and in higher animals.

The modification and (presumed) augmentation of information transmitted over many generations of these higher animals has resulted in the evolution of nature's most sophisticated information processing machine, the human brain. Chapters 8 and 9 examine neural information processing, beginning with a brief look at the structure of the human nervous system. Each of the billions of neural cells in that system is a specialized and sophisticated electrochemical communication device. Interconnected in ways that are not yet fully understood, these neurons carry virtually all the messages that enable us to perceive, remember, and think about our world. After looking at neural coding and signals we turn to how information crosses the interface between organism and environment. Rather than attempting to study any significant portion of the numerous input–output systems, we first examine a few general principles underlying motor function and sensory organization, then focus on the vertebrate visual system where extensive research has uncovered many basic principles of operation.

In Chapter 10 we reintroduce artificial information processing as we look at how computers have been programmed to simulate some of these biological systems. We study simulations of visual information processing, of the neural mechanisms which may underlie learning and memory, and of a complete living cell. Not all of these simulations have achieved equal success. And the ultimate goal of simulation, a predictive research tool, has seldom been attained. But as more is learned through work of the sort we will examine, so does the biologist find that his debt to the computer scientist is increasing.

I want to emphasize that the genetic and neural systems we study in these chapters are by no means the only biological information processing systems. There are some fascinating communication and control mechanisms in the endocrine system, for example. And the more that is learned about embryological development the more its informational aspects become apparent. But since we cannot talk about everything in one book I have selected the systems which I have found most intriguing from the standpoint of a computer scientist.

6
Biochemical coding
and control

In this and the next chapter we consider the informational aspects of biological organization and function at the cellular level. Before we begin with some general background material about biological cells, we should appreciate that this understanding of cell structure and operation has been acquired slowly, at a rate limited by the state of laboratory technology. It was not until the 19th century that improvements in light microscopy allowed biologists to observe that all living matter was composed of cells with essentially similar structures. Only with the advent of the electron microscope in the 1940's did most details of internal cellular structure become accessible. And the contemporary cell biologist's impressive battery of laboratory techniques is being continually augmented.

6.1 Biological cells

The smallest and most primitive unit of living matter is the virus. Some biologists even question whether viruses should be called living since they lack almost all the usual features of biological cells and cannot reproduce outside a host cell. True biological cells are either *plant* cells or *animal* cells. When a choice presents itself we will usually discuss only features common to animal cells. We will not, for example, consider the complex process of photosynthesis peculiar to plant cells. All animal and most plant cell types belong to the class of *eukaryotes*. The *prokaryotes*, bacteria and one type of algae, lack certain features (nuclear membrane, structurally differentiated cytoplasm) that we will shortly describe as typical of cells.

Perhaps more fundamental than the plant/animal or prokaryotic/ eukaryotic distinctions is the fact that some cells are *unicellular organisms* while others are components of multicellular organisms. Unicellular organisms (bacteria, algae, protozoa) must carry out all the functions essential to their existence within the boundaries of a single cell. Most cells in multi-cellular organisms, on the other hand, are specialized for some particular biological task. Some major groups of specialized cells are the following: epithelial cells, which provide external covering; connective cells, which provide structural framework; fat cells, which store energy; receptor cells, which receive information about the organism's environment; effector cells, which operate on the organism's environment; and conductor cells, which transmit information within the organism. The last three cell types, particularly the neuron conductor cells of higher animals, will be the focus of Chapters 8 and 9.

With all the above diversity of cell types there is obviously no such thing as a "typical" cell. Nevertheless, Figure 6.1 is a generalized diagram showing many of the features typically associated with most (animal) cells. A number of cautionary remarks are required for proper interpretation of Figure 6.1. First, not all of the features shown in this diagram would be found in a given 2-dimensional cross section of a 3-dimensional cell. Secondly, not all features are drawn to scale. The mitochondria, for example, have actually about 1,000 times the cross-sectional area of the ribosomes, which cannot be resolved with the light microscope. Thirdly, even the microphotographs from which the generalized diagram of Figure 6.1 is derived may contain artifacts not characteristic of living cells but introduced by the complex series of steps required to prepare tissue for the microscope. After the cell has been removed from its natural environment and killed, it must be hardened with a fixative and sliced into very thin sections. Finally various chemical stains are required to make features of interest visible.

As suggested by the labelling of Figure 6.1, a cell has three major components: the outer membrane, the cytoplasm, and the nucleus. The *outer membrane* defines the external boundary of the cell and acts as a selective filter governing the interchange of material between the cell and its environment. Actually a complex structure consisting of layers of molecules, the membrane allows easy passage to water and other small molecules and ions. In a phenomenon known as *passive transport* such substances flow in or out of the cells in accord with their concentration gradients and, in the case of charged ions, as a function of local electrical potentials. The membrane's nature can be altered so as to permit free flow of a substance to which it was formerly impermeable. In Chapter 8 we shall see that such a phenomenon is the basis for transmission of information by nerve cells. Finally, there are some substances which cannot passively cross the membrane but are carried into or out of the cell by energy consuming *active transport* processes.

The *cytoplasm* is the locus of most of the cell's metabolism, the place where energy and raw materials are converted into products the cell needs. In addition to a fluid matrix the cytoplasm contains several different kinds of integral structures with their own limiting membranes, called *organelles*. Among the most prominent organelles are the *mitochondria* which house

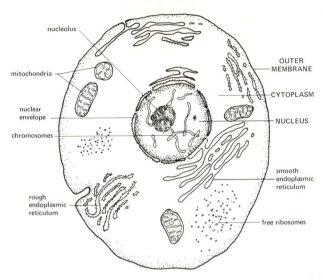

Figure 6.1.   Generalized diagram of an animal cell.

complex structures participating in the cell's major energy producing re-action, known as oxidative phosphorylation. In plant cells photosynthesis takes place in organelles called chloroplasts.

Also found in the cytoplasm is an intricate network of membrane bound channels, called the *endoplasmic reticulum*. These channels, which are often continuous with the external and/or nuclear membranes, give the cell a larger interface with its environment and are used for internal circulation of materials and as a source of other internal membranes. When these channel membranes are densely covered with ribosomes we speak of "rough" (as opposed to "smooth") endoplasmic reticulum. The *ribosomes* themselves are small but complex structures that are the sites for synthesis of an im-portant class of informational molecules called proteins. The ribosomes on rough endoplasmic reticulum produce mostly those proteins which the cell exports to its environment by "dumping" them into the channel network. "Free" ribosomes, on the other hand, synthesize the proteins required internally by the cell.

The (eukaryotic) cell's third major component is a *nucleus* which is bounded by its own membrane (actually a double-walled envelope, with gaps or "pores" to allow passage of material in both directions). The nucleus contains *chromosomes*, the structures which house the DNA that is the cell's permanent information repository. (Small amounts of DNA are also found outside the nucleus, in mitochondria and other self-replicating organelles.) Throughout most of a cell's division cycle the chromosomal material is widely distributed throughout the nucleus in the form of thin fibers known as chromatin. The chromatin condenses into the chromosomal form shown in Figure 6.1 just before the cell divides (about which more will be said later).

71

Also seen in the nucleus is an organelle called the *nucleolus* which is the site of synthesis of ribosomal constituents.

Despite its internal complexity the cell is still only the elementary component in the organizational hierarchy of multicellular organisms. A localized group of cells with a common functional property is called a *tissue* (e.g., muscle tissue, connective tissue). A localized combination of several tissues integrated to perform a particular function is called an *organ* (e.g., heart, liver). Finally, a distributed collection of organs which cooperate in some biological task is called a *system* (e.g., circulatory system, nervous system).

We now consider the major biochemical constituents involved in the functioning of most cells. At least two-thirds of a cell's volume is usually water, a condition with a number of important consequences. When most molecules are in solution there is a fairly uniform distribution of material throughout the cell. Biochemical reactions can thus proceed at reasonable rates (although we shall soon see that enzymes are also necessary). Molecules in aqueous solution can also take advantage of weak attractive forces (bonds) in order to form molecular complexes. An important and frequent form of weak bond is the *hydrogen bond*, in which two atoms (usually oxygen or nitrogen) have a common attraction to a hydrogen atom. Since electrolytes disassociate in water, the presence of positively and negatively charged inorganic ions is a last important consequence of the cell's aqueous medium. The inorganic composition of cellular fluid is actually quite close to that of seawater, the principal ions being sodium (Na^+), potassium (K^+), calcium (Ca^{++}), iron (Fe^{++}), magnesium (Mg^{++}), chloride (Cl^-), phosphate (PO_4^{-3}), and sulphate (SO_4^{--}).

Most of a cell's organic constituents fall into one of the four main classes of biological molecules. *Carbohydrates* contain carbon (C), hydrogen (H), and oxygen (O), usually in ratios of about $1:2:1$. These molecules are used for construction (e.g., cellulose in plant cell walls) and as a readily available form of stored energy. In this latter role carbohydrates can be classified into monosaccharides (simple sugars, like glycose, $C_6H_{12}O_6$) and polysaccharides (starches like glycogen which is composed of glucose building blocks and is the principal means of carbohydrate storage in animals). *Lipids* or fats (also composed mainly of C, H, and O) serve as a more permanent and less accessible form of energy storage and as an essential component of membranes. Although both carbohydrates and lipids play major roles in a cell's structure and metabolism, they are much less involved in information processing functions than the two remaining kinds of biological molecules, *proteins* and *nucleic acids*.

6.2 Informational macromolecules

Proteins are very large molecules, containing C, H, O, nitrogen (N), and sometimes sulphur (S), which may comprise more than half of a cell's non-aqueous substance. A protein is composed of one or more *polypeptide chains.* Each chain is a sequence of up to a thousand *amino acids* linked together by *peptide bonds*. The names and abbreviations of the 20 amino acids commonly found in proteins will be given below (Figure 6.5) in connection with the genetic code. All amino acids have the general structure shown in Figure 6.2a. The side group ranges in complexity from a simple hydrogen atom to ring and chain structures involving nearly 20 atoms. Figure 6.2b shows how removal of water (H_2O) from the opposing amino (NH_3^+) and carboxyl (COO^-) ends of two simple amino acids results in a peptide linkage.

The ordering of the amino acids on its polypeptide chains is only part of a protein's structure. Hydrogen bonds, disulfide (S–S) bonds, and other forms of attractions among a protein's constituent amino acids (and between its component polypeptide chains) cause it to assume an intricate three-dimensional configuration. A cell uses its proteins in two major ways, both of which depend on the molecules' three-dimensional structures. In the cell membrane, ribosomes, and elsewhere proteins are structural building

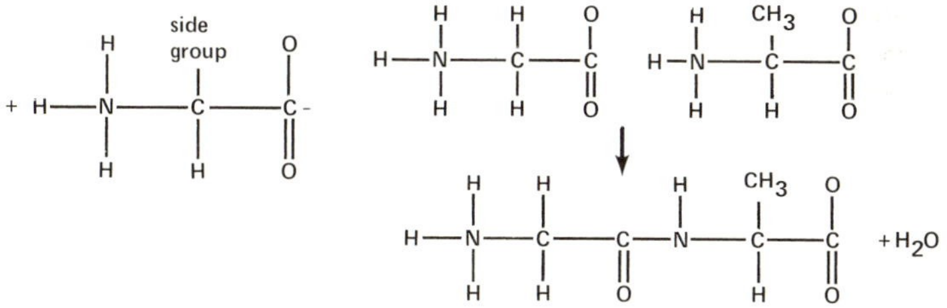

Figure 6.2.   (a) General form of amino acids; (b) formation of peptide linkage between glycine (left) and alanine (right).

blocks. But most kinds of proteins are *enzymes,* molecules whose shapes control the rate of biochemical reactions in a manner we will soon consider. The determination of a protein's amino acid sequence, to say nothing of its three-dimensional structure, is a challenging laboratory task which has so far been successfully completed for relatively few molecules.

The other class of biological molecules with important informational properties are the *nucleic acids.* Like proteins, nucleic acids are constructed from small building blocks. A particular nucleic acid molecule will contain from a few thousand to many million *bases,* selected from a set of four distinct bases and sequentially arrayed along a linear backbone of alternating sugar molecules and phosphate groups.

When the sugar molecule in the backbone is the five-carbon *ribose* we have a *ribonucleic acid,* or RNA, molecule. Removing an oxygen from ribose yields *deoxyribose,* the sugar component of *deoxyribonucleic acid,* or DNA. RNA and DNA also differ slightly in the set of bases attached to their sugar-phosphate backbones. Both use the two double-ring *purines, adenine* (abbreviated A) and *guanine* (G), and the single-ring *pyrimidine, cytosine* (C). But the other pyrimidine is *thymine* (T) in DNA and *uracil* (U) in RNA. As a last bit of essential terminology we will denote a sugar-base combination

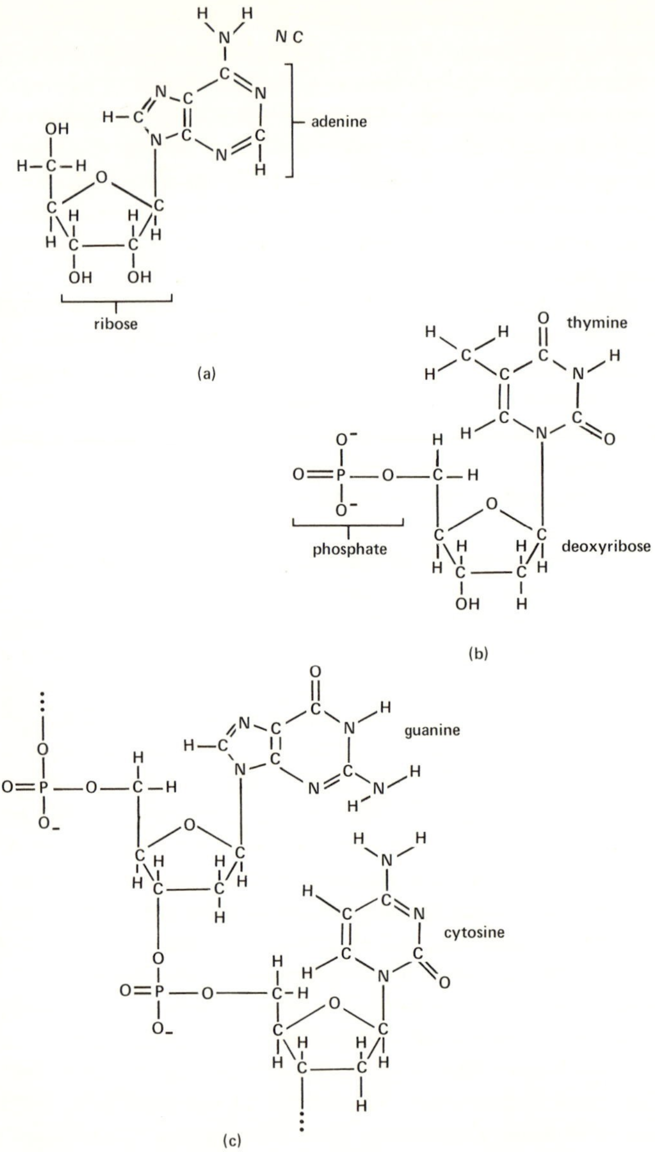

Figure 6.3. (a) Ribonucleoside; (b) deoxyribonucleotide;
(c) 2-base DNA fragment.

as a *nucleoside* and a sugar-base-phosphate combination as a *nucleotide*.
Figure 6.3 shows the structure of adenine ribonucleoside (properly called
adenosine), of thymine deoxyribonucleotide (properly called deoxythy-
midine-5′-phosphate), and of a fragment of DNA containing guanine and
cytosine bases. For most of our future purposes we will be able to dispense
with chemical structures or long names and use letter sequences like

CGGTCA to describe the ordering of bases in a nucleic acid.

The role of nucleic acids in a cell's functioning cannot be overstated. Long DNA molecules in the chromosomes specify in their base sequences nearly all the information required for the cell's biochemical reactions. Yet this information cannot be decoded without the assistance of several types of RNA molecules and proteins which help translate the DNA base sequence into the amino acid sequences of proteins. That process is the subject of the next section. We conclude this one with a few remarks about some of the basic metabolic processes that go on inside a cell.

Metabolism refers to the set of all chemical reactions occurring in the cell. Our concern is primarily with *intermediary metabolism*, the reactions involved in the transformation of elementary food molecules into essential biochemical building blocks. In addition to raw materials, water, and oxygen, the reactions in these biosynthetic pathways require two components: energy and catalysis by enzymes.

Most energy generation in animal cells is a consequence of complex series of reactions involving oxidation (addition of oxygen or removal of hydrogen) and reduction (reverse of oxidation) steps. These reactions may be thought of as a complicated equivalent of the direct oxidation of glucose by combustion: $C_6H_{12}O_6 + 6O_2 \rightarrow 6CO_2 + 6H_2O$ + heat. Heat energy is of little use to the cell and is difficult to store. So instead the energy produced in the stepwise degradation of glucose is converted to convenient and stable forms like high energy molecular bonds. The most frequent means of storing energy is the *phosphorylation* of adenosine diphosphate (ADP). ADP is just adenine plus ribose plus *two* linked phosphate groups (cf. Figure 6.3). Phosphorylation refers to the addition of phosphate which changes ADP into ATP (adenosine triphosphate). The third phosphate group is attached to ADP by a high energy bond. The energy can be released to do chemical work when the bond is broken and ATP reverts to ADP. In many biosynthetic reactions ATP donated phosphate is temporarily bound to some molecular component and then released, providing the energy required to bind the component to a growing macromolecular structure. ADP molecules can be reused after rephosphorylation.

Despite these clever indirect arrangements for storage and use of energy, most cellular reactions would still proceed far too slowly for life to endure were it not for biological catalysts. The class of proteins called *enzymes* can increase the speed of reactions by many orders of magnitude and, like other catalysts, are not consumed in the process. Most enzymes are specific for particular reactions and function by weakly binding the reaction components (called *substrates*) into positions especially favorable for the making or breaking of bonds. We now see why the 3-dimensional configuration of a protein is so important. The region of enzyme structure which is tailored to the shape of the substrate(s) is called the *active site* of the enzyme.

In a favorable environment the intermediary metabolism we have just considered will cause a cell to grow. But this increase in volume cannot continue forever because the cell's surface area (and hence its contact with environmental food sources) increases as the square of its radius, while its volume increases as the cube. Cells must therefore divide to sustain an increase in the volume of a tissue (or of a colony of unicellular organisms). The division process is called *mitosis* and proceeds in a complex series of steps. For our purposes the important thing about mitosis is that a complete copy of the cell's genetic information, which has been duplicated by chromosome replication, is apportioned to each new cell. Thus the two new daughter cells will carry the same DNA base sequences as the parent cell did. (Another kind of cell division, which is the basis for sexual reproduction, will be considered in the next chapter.)

6.3 The genetic code

In this section we look more closely at the structure of DNA and how it specifies the amino acid sequences of a cell's protein molecules. DNA usually occurs as two strands of base sequences coiled around each other in a sort of double spiral staircase. The elucidation of this *double helix* structure earned James Watson, Francis Crick, and Maurice Wilkins the 1962 Nobel Prize in Medicine and Physiology. The two strands of the double helix tend to stay together because of hydrogen bonds between the bases on the two strands. Since such bonds form easily only between A and T or between G and C, the base sequence on one strand (e.g., AGGCTA) is always matched

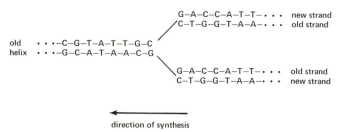

Figure 6.4.   Semiconservative replication of DNA (coiling of helices not shown).

by a *complementary base sequence* (e.g., TCCGAT) on the other. Although the double helix thus carries no more information than either of its strands, base pairing is of fundamental importance not only to protein synthesis (as we will see shortly) but also to DNA replication.

Figure 6.4 schematically depicts the process by which a DNA double helix produces two exact copies of itself during chromosomal replication prior to cell division. Note that each strand serves as a template for a new complementary strand. The new strands are strung together from available DNA nucleotides with the aid of a special enzyme called DNA polymerase and the use of energy derived from conversion of ATP to ADP. Each new double helix consists of one old and one new strand, a so-called *semi-*

conservative replication which is the now accepted choice among several proposed models of DNA duplication. Since replication of (eukaryotic) chromosomes proceeds bidirectionally from a number of initiation sites, Figure 6.4 actually depicts only a single *replicating fork.*

As soon as DNA became firmly identified as the self-replicating repository of all primary genetic information the question arose as to how this information regulated the cell's operation. Since almost all biochemical reactions are controlled by enzymes, it is sufficient for the DNA nucleotide sequence to determine the amino acid sequences of the cell's proteins. The classical concept of a *gene* as the fundamental unit of inheritance can now be identified with a string of DNA bases. Since a gene with about 1,500 bases provides sufficient information for the construction of a protein with about 500 amino acids, it seems likely that about 3 bases constitute the code word (or *codon*) for each amino acid. Other considerations reinforce this conclusion. There are 64 3-base codons but only 16 2-base ones (insufficient for the 20 amino acids) and 256 4-base ones (a wasteful superabundance).

The (correct) assumption of a triplet code still leaves open several questions about its structure. Since only 20 of the 64 triples are required, is the code redundant or are there many triples which do not code for anything ("nonsense" triples)? Is the code overlapping, with a given base participating in more than one code word, or not; and, if not, is there "punctuation" between codons? And finally, even when satisfied with respect to all these issues we must still inquire about the actual mapping or encoding used.

Vast experimental programs in numerous laboratories throughout the world began to yield evidence on the nature of the genetic code about 1960. By the end of the decade most of the answers were in: the genetic code is a nonoverlapping, nonpunctuated, redundant code in which all but three triples code for amino acids. These three "nonsense" triples are in fact "stop" or chain terminating signals, indicating the end of the polypeptide has been reached. A particular amino acid may be specified by one to six different triplets with greatest variation in the third base. For reasons which will become clear shortly codons are usually expressed not as DNA base triples but as the complementary triples that would appear in an RNA molecule (uracil (U) replaces T as the complement of A). Inspection of the code as presented in Figure 6.5 shows, for example, that glycine has the four codons GGX and alanine the four codons GCX, where X may be any of the RNA bases. Tyrosine is coded by UAU and UAC, while methionine is specified only by AUG. The stop codons are UAA, UAG, and UGA. Nor are such encodings species specific. One amazing property of the genetic code is its apparent *universality*, at least for all organisms whose codons have been studied.

Elucidation of the genetic code unfortunately tells us almost nothing about how the information is *used* to build proteins. This must be a rather indirect process since most DNA resides in the nucleus while protein syn-

First Position (Read Down)	Second Position U	C	(Read Across) A	G	Third Position (Read Down)
U	phe	ser	tyr	cys	U
	phe	ser	tyr	cys	C
	leu	ser	stop	stop	A
	leu	ser	stop	trp	G
C	leu	pro	his	arg	U
	leu	pro	his	arg	C
	leu	pro	gln	arg	A
	leu	pro	gln	arg	G
A	ile	thr	asn	ser	U
	ile	thr	asn	ser	C
	ile	thr	lys	arg	A
	met	thr	lys	arg	G
G	val	ala	asp	gly	U
	val	ala	asp	gly	C
	val	ala	glu	gly	A
	val	ala	glu	gly	G

Figure 6.5. The genetic code. Amino acids are abbreviated as follows:

ala—alanine;
arg—arginine;
asn—asparagine;
asp—aspartic acid;
cys—cysteine;
gln—glutamine;
glu—glutamic acid;
gly—glycine;
his—histadine;
ile—isoleucine;

leu—leucine;
lys—lysine;
met—methionine;
phe—phenylalanine;
pro—proline;
ser—serine;
thr—threonine;
trp—tryptophan;
tyr—tyrosine;
val—valine.

thesis is carried out by ribosomes in the cytoplasm. Extensive research has revealed a two stage process involving two forms of information bearing RNA molecules. Stage one, *transcription*, uses base pairing to build a complementary image of the DNA gene in the nucleotides of a *messenger RNA* (*m*-RNA) molecule. True to its name the messenger molecule then leaves the nucleus and, after some processing, functions during stage two, *translation*, as a template for the proper sequencing of amino acids. Translation is accomplished with assistance not only of ribosomes but also of a whole class of small *transfer RNA* (*t*-RNA) molecules which are responsible for the proper pairing of *m*-RNA codons and amino acids. We now consider these incredibly complex transcription and translation processes in somewhat more detail.

Transcription begins when the DNA double helix separates locally allowing the template strand to base pair with RNA nucleotides. Although the template strand is always the same one (the complement strand would code for a different and probably useless protein) the mechanism insuring this selection is unknown. The properly ordered RNA nucleotides are chained together into an *m*-RNA molecule with the aid of ATP donated energy and the enzyme RNA polymerase. Synthesis of *m*-RNA always proceeds in the same direction, often from a "promoter" region on the

DNA, where RNA polymerase must make its first attachment, to an identified stopping point. Initiation and termination of transcription are only beginning to be fully understood and apparently require participation of a number of small proteins called "factors." Transcription is a relatively fast process by biological standards, with the capacity to synthesize a 1,000-nucleotide m-RNA molecule in as little as one second.

Transcription is actually used for more than building templates for protein synthesis. All forms of RNA, including the t-RNA's used in translation and the RNA component of the ribosomes, must be constructed by base pairing with templates found in segments of chromosomal DNA.

Once the m-RNA molecule has made its way out of the nucleus and into the vicinity of ribosomes, translation of nucleotide triplets into amino acids can commence. Ribosomes are complex composites of protein and RNA which appear to have several active sites that guide the translation process. The other key to effective translation is the set of t-RNA molecules which are bound to their "proper" amino acids by a class of powerful enzymes which recognize correct pairings. Another part of the t-RNA is specialized to form base pairs with an m-RNA triplet. The three distinct t-RNA bases corresponding to the amino acid it recognizes are called the *anti-codon* because of their complementarity to the m-RNA codon. Given a supply of t-RNA's with amino acids attached, the ribosome moves along the m-RNA molecule, pairing codons with anti-codons and initiating the formation of peptide bonds between the properly sequenced amino acids. Each successive t-RNA actually carries along the entire polypeptide built to that point, as shown in Figure 6.6. Like transcription, translation always proceeds in only one of the two possible directions.

The initiation of translation is a complex process involving ribosomal

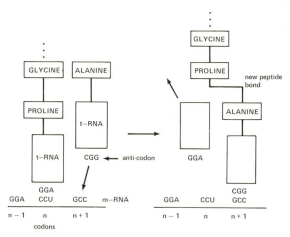

Figure 6.6. Schematic diagram of translation. Alanine is added to growing polypeptide chain as ribosome moves (left to right) along m-RNA.

constituents, at least three protein factors, and special use of "initiating codons" which elsewhere code normally for amino acids. Recognition of stop codons also involves special proteins called release factors. Translation may require from a few seconds to as much as several minutes for the synthesis of a complete protein. But unlike transcription translation can occur in "parallel" with several ribosomes operating at different points along the *m*-RNA and carrying various stages of completion of their individual copies of the protein molecule.

It should finally be mentioned that transcription and translation may proceed simultaneously in prokaryotes, where there is no nuclear membrane barrier to prevent ribsomes from working on partially completed transcripts. Note that this "multiprocessing" depends critically on the fact that both transcription and translation proceed in the *same* direction. Translation initiating codons are always transcribed *first*.

6.4 Biochemical control processes

Since cell division confers a multicellular organism's entire DNA endowment on the daughter cells, every cell contains the information for all proteins required anywhere in the organism. Thus there must be some means of shutting down production of inappropriate or unnecessary substances. A liver cell should produce just those enzymes needed for liver cell reactions. This complex problem of *differentiation*, in which cells specialize by (permanently) "turning off" large portions of their DNA, is beyond the scope of our discussion.

But unicellular organisms face similar control problems, although of a more dynamic nature. Even though a bacterium may eventually require all of the reactions ultimately specified in its DNA, there will be times when products are available in the environment and need not be synthesized, or when enzymes are not required because it is not yet time for certain processes (e.g., those associated with cell division). In this section we examine two common feedback control mechanisms (not limited to unicellular organisms) which permit dynamic adjustment of biochemical reactions. Although both of these processes control reactions through their enzymes, the first affects the enzyme's *function* and the second its *synthesis*.

One way to reduce production of an abundant product is by *allosteric inhibition*. In this process the product reduces the effectiveness of an enzyme required for its own production. The process is termed allosteric ("shape changing") because the product combines with the enzyme, changing its shape and making its active site nonfunctional (or less functional) in recognizing the proper substrates. Such enzymes are called allosteric proteins. If, as is usually the case, the product in question is a result of a long reaction pathway, allosteric inhibition may inhibit the effectiveness of an early enzyme and thus reduce the concentrations of the (unnecessary) intermediate products as well. Such a situation, also frequently called *end-*

product inhibition, is illustrated in Figure 6.7 where end-product F alters enzyme ab and reduces conversion of A to B. With higher concentrations of F more molecules of ab will be inhibited and the reduction in F synthesis will be larger. As F is used up (or becomes unavailable in the environment) the feedback control mechanism causes more to be produced.

From the standpoint of strict biological efficiency one disadvantage of allosteric inhibition is that the cell continues to expend energy producing an enzyme that is not required. It would be more economical to control the

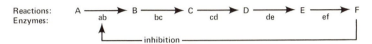

Figure 6.7.   Diagram of end-product inhibition.

synthesis of the enzyme itself. A classic example of this sort of process is the synthesis of the enzyme beta-galactosidase in the human intestinal bacterium *Escherichia coli. E. coli* (for short) is a much studied organism that feeds preferentially on glucose. But beta-galactosidase helps break down lactose type sugars (galactosides) into glucose.

One of the amazing things about *E. coli* is that it contains essentially no beta-galactosidase when in an environment where glucose is the principal carbon source, but rapidly synthesizes several thousand molecules of the enzyme when switched to a lactose environment. Careful analysis has shown that the enzyme's *m*-RNA template is also absent when the bacterium is in the glucose environment. This indicates that in the absence of lactose (or, more generally, galactosides) there is inhibition of the *transcription* phase of beta-galactosidase synthesis. (Interference with translation instead may occur in essentially similar control processes, particularly in higher organisms.)

Phenomena like that just described are called *enzyme induction* control processes. Substances like lactose, which appear to increase the synthesis of enzymes required for their own processing, are called *inducers*. Enzymes like beta-galactosidase are called *inducible enzymes*. In the early 1960's the French biochemists Jacob and Monod developed the *operon* model as explanation of enzyme induction and related phenomena. The operon model is most easily understood with reference to the (simplified) section of *E. coli* DNA schematically depicted in Figure 6.8. The three genes at the right of the DNA segment produce *m*-RNA templates for beta-galactosidase and two other enzymes which are also associated with processing of lactose type sugars (and which are also induced by lactose). Separated from these three genes by an *operator* is the *promoter* region where RNA polymerase must make its initial attachment to the DNA in order to synthesize the templates. Finally (just to the left of the promoter region, although in general it need not be nearby) we have a *regulatory gene* which encodes the structure of a protein called a *repressor*.

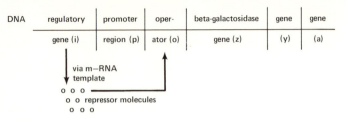

Figure 6.8. A portion of the *lac* region of the *E. coli* chromosome, showing the major regions involved in the operon model of enzyme induction.

As suggested by Figure 6.8 repressor molecules can interact with the operator. Specifically they can attach to the operator and prevent the movement of RNA polymerase down the DNA and the attendant linking of RNA nucleotides, thus preventing effective transcription of genes (z), (y), and (a). The term *operon* was devised by Jacob and Monod to apply to any such group of genes under coordinate control of a single promotor/operator combination. Enzyme induction occurs when lactose molecules enter the cell, undergo some modification to produce an effective inducer, and combine with repressor molecules to inactivate them (in an allosteric manner). Since inactive repressors cannot interfere with *m*-RNA synthesis the cell can now make templates for the enzymes which process lactose. (Actually a single *m*-RNA molecule with internal stop and start codons provides templates for all three enzyme molecules.)

This explanation of enzyme induction is in fact only one of two complementary aspects of the operon model. In inducible systems of the sort we have just looked at the natural (uncombined) repressor is active. Combination with the inducer inactivates it and induces enzyme production. In a *repressible system* on the other hand the natural repressor is inactive. Combination with an environmental *co-repressor* activates it and represses enzyme production. This latter kind of system is actually much more like end-product inhibition than is enzyme induction. Repression of enzymes allows prevention of transcription to reduce production of abundant substances. The real difference between repression and end-product inhibition is that the latter modifies enzyme function while the former affects enzyme availability.

A final question about the operon model is what, if anything, controls synthesis of the repressor? If the answer should turn out to be *another* repressor (i.e., the regulatory gene is part of another operon), we will find ourselves on the brink of an infinite regression of repressors of repressors of ... It has never been suggested however that *all* proteins are under genetic feedback control. Many, including repressors, appear to be synthesized in fixed amounts regardless of environmental conditions (so-called *constitutive* synthesis). Of course a constitutive enzyme's effectiveness may still be under control of nongenetic mechanisms like end-product inhibition.

Bibliography

Gatlin, Lila L. *Information Theory and the Living System.* Columbia University Press, 1972.
An intriguing analysis of biochemical coding in terms of communication theory concepts.

Goodenough, Ursula, and Levine, Robert P. *Genetics.* Holt, Rinehart and Winston, 1974.
A good, up-to-date introductory text with an excellent treatment of molecular aspects.

Haynes, Robert H., and Hanawalt, Philip C. (eds.). *The Molecular Basis of Life.* Freeman, 1968.
A good selection from two decades of highly readable *Scientific American* articles.

Kornberg, Arthur. *DNA Synthesis.* Freeman, 1974.
A readable compendium of his own and other research on replication and related topics.

Lehninger, Albert L. *Biochemistry.* Worth, 1975 (2nd edition).
A comprehensive, "up to the minute" text on the molecular basis of cell structure and function, by one of the field's leading investigators.

Lerner, I. Michael. *Heredity, Evolution, and Society.* Freeman, 1968.
A wide ranging text for nonbiologists, with considerable emphasis on human genetics and social issues.

McElroy, William D. *Cell Physiology and Biochemistry.* Prentice-Hall, 1971 (3rd edition).
A compact text, part of the publisher's modern biology series.

Reiner, John M. *The Organism as an Adaptive Control System.* Prentice-Hall, 1968.
An excellent systems theory approach to biological function, emphasizing genetic coding and regulation processes.

Rosenberg, Eugene. *Cell and Molecular Biology: An Appreciation.* Holt, Rinehart, and Winston, 1971.
A good short introductory text for nonbiologists. Contains excellent microphotography.

Srb, Adrian M., Owen, Ray D., and Edgar, Robert S. *Facets of Genetics.* Freeman, 1970.
Another fine *Scientific American* collection.

Watson, James D. *The Double Helix.* Atheneum, 1968.
An exciting nontechnical account of the discovery of the structure of DNA and the race for the Nobel prize.

Watson, James D. *Molecular Biology of the Gene.* Benjamin, 1970 (second edition).
An ideal combination of introductory text and reference work by one of the field's leading researchers.

Wolfe, Stephen L. *Biology of the Cell.* Wadsworth, 1972.
A good introduction to cell biology, with an extensive collection of microphotographs.

Wooldridge, Dean E. *The Machinery of Life.* McGraw-Hill, 1966.
A pleasant popular treatment from the viewpoint of a physical scientist.

Exercises

6.1. Show the chemical structure of a fragment of an RNA molecule with bases adenine, guanine, and cytosine in that order. Identify the guanine ribonucleoside (guanosine) and the cytosine ribonucleotide (cytidine-5′-phosphate) in the fragment.

6.2. For the 15 nucleotide DNA sequence GTCACGATACGATCG find (a) the corresponding sequence on the complementary DNA strand, (b) the complementary m-RNA sequence that would result from transcription, (c) the t-RNA anti-codons, and (d) the amino acid sequence that would result from translation of the m-RNA.

6.3. Assuming that RNA can occur in a two-stranded, base-paired form, indicate the type of nucleic acid and whether it could be two-stranded for each of the following samples (numbers shown are percentages of each nucleotide in the sample):

	A	G	T	C	U
(a)	30	20	30	20	0
(b)	25	25	0	25	25
(c)	40	10	10	40	0
(d)	5	5	5	85	0
(e)	30	30	0	10	30

6.4. For the amino acid sequence ser-arg-val-ala-leu-gly
   (a) Compute the number of distinct DNA base sequences that could have produced the polypeptide;
   (b) Show a sequence from those in part (a) that has the largest possible *base ratio*, i.e. (frequency of A + T)/(frequency of G + C), in the DNA double helix.

Note: The following two exercises assume familiarity with Part I of this book.

6.5. Analyse and evaluate the genetic code with respect to (a) separability, (b) efficiency, and (c) error detection/correction properties; (d) indicate what sort of information would be needed about amino acids and/or nucleotides to construct an optimal genetic code.

6.6. Write a comparative discussion of biological cells and cellular automata.

7
Genetic information transmission

  In the last chapter we were primarily concerned with the role of genetic information in the day-to-day life of the cell. We noted in passing that mitosis transmits the cell's entire complement of genetic information to the new generation of cells. In this chapter we examine more closely this transmission of genetic information to subsequent generations. We will touch both extremes of the time scale, from the replication of viruses and bacteria (a matter of minutes) to the evolution of new animal species (a matter of millenia). And we will discover that exact preservation of genetic information down through the generations is not always a good thing. New genes and new combinations of old genes may improve a species' adaptation to its changing environment. Most of the genetic recombination mechanisms we will study have the introduction and maintenance of genetic variety as their primary function.

7.1 Recombination in viruses and bacteria

  As the smallest repositories of genetic information, viruses may contain as few as three genes (about 3,000 nucleotides). Viral genetic material may be either DNA or RNA and single or double stranded in either case. Although the electron microscope has revealed that viruses come in a variety of shapes and sizes, they usually consist only of a protein or protein-lipid shell protecting a single chromosome. Such primitive biochemical machinery does not endow viruses with an independent existence. They cannot multiply without entering a host organism and subverting its biochemical factory to their own ends.

  Among the most studied and best understood viruses are those which infect bacteria and are known as *bacteriophages*. The best understood

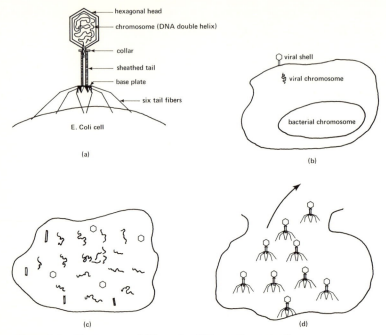

Figure 7.1.   Structure and life cycle of T-even bacteriophage.

bacteriophages are those which infect the much studied *E. coli* cell, particularly the closely related group of "T-even" bacteriophages (individually
designated T2, T4, T6). Figure 7.1a shows the structure of a T-even virus,
as it enters the first stage of its life cycle by attaching to the wall of an *E. coli*
cell.

After the tail fibers of the virus are firmly attached to the host cell the
viral chromosome is injected (Figure 7.1b). This chromosome begins to use
host energy and enzymes to produce both copies of itself and its own *m*-RNA
and enzymes (one of which breaks down the circular *E. coli* chromosome
into useful components). Shortly there appear the protein subunits of the
viral shell among the many copies of the viral chromosome (Figure 7.1c).
Finally the shells are assembled around some of the chromosome copies,
the bacterial cell breaks open (*lyses*), and 200 to 1,000 new bacteriophages
are released. The entire process takes about half an hour and involves
complex timing and sequencing controls which are still largely mysterious.

The life cycle just described is the typical result of *all* infections by viruses
of the so-called *lytic* type (causing cell lysis). The T-even bacteriophages
however are actually of a more flexible type called *lysogenic* viruses. Lysogenic viruses do not always follow the course of events shown after Figure
7.1b. In some cases the viral chromosome is incorporated into the bacterial
DNA, a situation in which it is termed a *prophage*. Prophages may be carried
along and replicated as part of the bacterial chromosome for many generations, until some chance event releases one and the lytic cycle is resumed.

We will shortly discover that lysogenic viruses provide an important means of recombining *bacterial* genetic material.

But how does viral recombination occur? How, in other words, can two slightly different strains of virus exchange mutually substitutable genes which code for proteins that produce different biochemical traits? Such interchanges of genetic material normally occur when two genetically distinct viruses simultaneously infect a single host cell. During chromosome duplication new chromosomes containing segments from both of the original types are created, leading to new viral strains. Such *phage crosses* are an instance of the general recombination mechanism called *crossing over* which we will look at in more detail later in this chapter.

Viral recombination is important not only for maintenance of genetic variety but also as a laboratory technique which helps the biologist to identify the positions of genes on the viral chromosomes. The tendency of two or more genetic traits to cross *together* is an indication of how closely positioned they are on the chromosome. Exhaustive studies of phage crosses have produced a relatively complete *genetic map* of the T4 virus, with more than 50 specific genes identified as to position and function.

While recombination increases variety among different strains it can obviously not be the primary source of different genes at a given chromosomal position. No amount of recombination could have produced a new strain from the presumed "original" T4 virus. The ultimate source of all genetic variety is *mutation*.

As a result of radiation, chemicals, and other causes there may occur in a gene random substitutions of one nucleotide for another, called *point mutations*. Mutations with more radical effects on protein function can result from insertions of extra nucleotides or the deletion of one or more nucleotides, both possible consequences of faulty DNA duplication. Insertion and deletion mutations are called *frame shift mutations* because they change the reading frame during translation and can produce an entirely different amino acid sequence in some portion of the polypeptide.

"*Nonsense*" *mutations* arise when stop codons are created by point or frame shift mutations. In such cases the protein may be much shorter than its intended length. Although mutations are frequently lethal, some inevitably produce new viable strains of virus, from which recombination by crossing over can then produce many new chromosomal arrangements. Like crossing over, mutation is a general phenomenon in all organisms and one to which we shall return.

Bacteria are much more complicated than viruses. Yet their basic reproduction mechanism, mitotic fission, provides for no increase in genetic variety other than that caused by mutation. In the last several decades, however, biologists have discovered three recombination mechanisms used by bacteria. The first of these, called *transformation*, was observed in the late 1920's when it was discovered that heat-killed cells of a virulent strain of pneumococci could kill mice only if injected along with live cells of a nonvirulent strain. The explanation of this phenomenon was eventually discovered to be substitution into the live bacterial chromosome of small pieces of the killed cells' DNA (about 1/200th of the original chromosome). There is usually a quite low frequency of transformed cells (from 1 to 10 %), making transformation of less genetic significance, and of less practical use in mapping bacterial genes, than the two remaining recombination mechanisms.

About the time the transformation mechanism was becoming understood investigators discovered that bacteria had a form of sexual recombination (*conjugation*). The presence or absence of a transmissible piece of genetic material called the F (for fertility) factor determines whether a bacterium is a donor (F^+) or recipient (F^-) cell. When the F factor exists independently of the donor cell's chromosome it will occasionally be transmitted across the cytoplasmic bridge between conjugating F^+ and F^- cells, changing the recipient cell into a donor cell in a sort of bacterial sex-change operation. But this involves no significant genetic recombination.

Integration of an F factor into a donor cell's chromosome produces an Hfr (for high frequency recombinant) donor cell. When conjugation occurs with this cell as donor a substantial portion of its chromosome may enter the recipient. This process has proved invaluable to genetic mapping, since the donor chromosome always breaks at the F factor and enters the recipient cell as a linear string (F factor last). Thus when conjugation is interrupted after some specified time interval an incomplete sequence of genes (always starting at the same point) will have been donated and therefore be capable of recombining (by crossing over) with the recipient chromosome. This procedure has contributed so much to the now virtually complete genetic map of *E. coli* that the map is calibrated in terms of minutes of conjugation. Note that only transfer of the complete chromosome, requiring some 89 minutes, will result in donation of the integrated F factor and allow conversion of the recipient into an Hfr donor.

The third type of bacterial recombination (*transduction*), not discovered until the early 1950's, requires the participation of a lysogenic virus. Sometimes when a previously dormant prophage is induced to break free it may generate new "viruses" which carry small pieces of the bacterial chromosome. The viruses may subsequently "infect" bacteria of another strain. The genetic material from the first strain can then recombine with the chromosome of the second strain. Since any genes carried by so small a piece of donor chromosome must be very close together transduction experiments have made a considerable contribution to the fine details of genetic maps.

In closing we should mention that an F factor can break free of an Hfr chromosome and carry other genetic material with it, much the way a prophage can. Subsequent donation of the "loaded" F factor also permits recombination with recipient chromosomal genes. This phenomenon of "sex-duction" has so much in common with transduction that it has led to the unifying concept of an *episome*. An episome is any self-replicating fragment of genetic material, like the F factor or the viral chromosome, that can exist either independently or as an integral part of the cellular chromosome.

7.2 Recombination in higher organisms

Bacteria have become the geneticist's favorite experimental subjects because of their relative genetic simplicity, their short life cycles, and their typically large numbers of easily differentiated genetic variants. The study of recombination in sexually reproducing higher organisms is usually complicated not only by the absence of these features but also by multiple paired chromosomes and a special type of cell division for reproductive purposes.

In bacteria and other *haploid* organisms each gene is represented only once. If, as is sometimes the case for well-fed bacteria, there are two or more copies of the chromosome, all the copies are identical. Most higher organisms are *diploid*, possessing pairs of *homologous* chromosomes with opportunity for different genes at pairs of corresponding "gene positions." From now on we refer to a gene position as a *locus* (and therefore speak of homologous loci) and the nucleic acid sequences that can functionally substitute for each other at a given locus as *alleles*. Man, for example, has 23 pairs of homologous chromosomes. At the homologous loci that determine his ABO blood group he may have any two (not necessarily distinct) alleles from the set A, B, O. When both alleles at a given locus are the same we say the organism is *homozygous* at that locus; when the alleles differ the term is *heterozygous*.

In simple two allele systems it is frequently the case that one allele (A) is always manifested as a physical trait whether it is present in homozygous or heterozygous context, while the physical effects of the other allele (a) cannot be observed unless it is homozygously present. In such a case we say A is *dominant* and a is *recessive*. If we call an organism's physical traits its *phenotype*, and its actual genetic structure its *genotype*, then at a simple dominant locus of the sort just described there are 3 distinct genotypes (AA, Aa, aa). But of these the homozygous dominant and the heterozygous genotypes manifest a single phenotype, while the homozygous recessive manifests a second.

In sexually reproducing diploid organisms a fertilized cell (zygote) is the result of the union of two haploid *gametes*, one from each parent. These gametes are produced from their diploid precursor cells by a form of cell division called *meiosis*. In meiotic reproduction homologous chromosomes first pair up and align side by side before DNA replication. The duplicated homologues are then distributed to opposite sides of the cell and a (first) cell division occurs. The resultant daughter cells then divide again, producing *four* haploid gametes.

Meiotic division provides a major means of genetic recombination in higher organisms. First, because the homologous chromosomes *do* separate, an offspring receives one allele from each parent at all its loci. Second, because the set of chromosomes distributed to a gamete is a *random* combination (of one member from each pair), different offspring receive different collections of alleles from a given parent. Although the biological basis of these two recombination mechanisms was revealed relatively recently, the underlying principles were first expressed in the 1860's by the European monk Gregor Mendel as his "laws" of *segregation* and *independent assortment*.

If the above description of meiosis were the whole story then the four resultant gametes would always consist of two identical pairs, the members of each pair having the same random selection of the original homologues. But, as shown in Figure 7.2, after replication and before separation one set of complementary homologues has the opportunity to exchange DNA segments. This phenomenon of *crossing over*, which we have already seen in

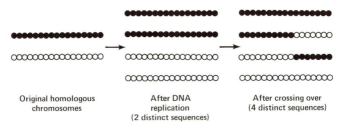

Figure 7.2.   A diagram of crossing over as it occurs during meiosis.

viral and bacterial chromosomes, allows production from a single precursor cell of gametes with four distinct sets of alleles. Crossing over is an important recombination mechanism because it allows recombining of alleles which would otherwise be irrevocably linked to their respective homologues. Crossing over also assists in the mapping of individual chromosomes since the tendency of two loci to cross together is an indication of their physical proximity.

The recombination mechanisms of segregation, independent assortment, and crossing over would contribute little to genetic variety if there were not available a fairly wide selection of alleles for most loci. And, just as for viruses and bacteria, the only source of *new* alleles (and hence the ultimate source of genetic variation) is *mutation*. Mutation in higher organisms differs from that in unicellular organisms in two important ways. First, from the standpoint of genetic information transmission across generations of higher organisms we are primarily concerned with mutations occurring in gamete cells or their precursors. *Somatic* mutations do not affect offspring genotypes. Second, in diploid organisms lethal mutations often survive for many generations because they are recessive alleles whose effects can be masked by normal dominants.

The frequencies of natural mutations are dependent on the organism and locus in question and may range up to 50 mutations per 100,000 gametes at a given locus. Estimates for man range from 0.5 to 15 mutations per locus

90

per 100,000 gametes. Even this small a frequency leads to a rather high probability of at least one mutation among all the loci in an individual. But we should not omit mention of two compensating factors, although consideration of either one in any detail is beyond the scope of our discussion. First, there is an ingenious set of genetic control mechanisms which can suppress the effects of a deleterious mutation, often by way of natural selection for an accidental but compensating mutation. And second, there exist special enzymes which can repair defective nucleotide sequences in DNA molecules.

7.3 Populations and evolution

In this section we consider the effects of genetic transmission and recombination mechanisms on large numbers of organisms over long periods of time. We begin by giving precise meaning to the term *population*. A population is *not* all organisms of a particular "type." Such a group is called a species and will be considered later. Nor is a population all the organisms in a particular geographical region. Such a collection is called an ecosystem and will not be considered in our discussion. A population (or more technically a *deme*) is rather a sort of intersection of species and ecosystem. More precisely a population is "the community of potentially interbreeding individuals at a given locality," in which "all members share in a single gene pool" or common collection of alleles.

The quoted phrases in the above definition are due to the renowned population biologist Ernst Mayr, who offers this sobering observation about the genetic role of an individual in a population.

The individual is only a temporary vessel, holding a small portion of the gene pool for a short time. It may contribute one or two new genes, or somewhat increase the frequency of certain genes in the gene pool, yet in sum its contribution will be very small indeed. It is the entire effective population that is the temporary incarnation and visible manifestation of the gene pool. Here is the proving ground of new genes and of novel gene combinations. The continued interaction of the genes in a gene pool provides a degree of integration that permits the population to act as a major unit of evolution.

The composition of a (diploid organism) gene pool for any given locus can be characterized in terms of both gene (allele) frequencies and genotype (allele pair) frequencies. We will restrict our discussion to a simple two allele locus with no dominance (so there are three observable phenotypes, one for each genotype). If we take a large random sample of N individuals and discover n_1 individuals of type AA, n_2 of type Aa, and n_3 of type aa, we can divide the n_i by N to get respective genotype frequencies x, y, z (where $x + y + z = 1$). To compute the frequency of gene A we note that our sample contained $2n_1 + n_2$ such genes and divide this by the total number of genes ($2N$), giving a frequency $p = [n_1 + (n_2/2)]/N = x + (y/2)$. Similarly gene a has frequency $q = y/2 + z$ (and $p + q = 1$).

Under a number of restrictive assumptions to be discussed shortly, we can now show the remarkable result that after one generation of random mating the genotype frequencies will become p^2 (for AA), $2pq$ (for Aa), and q^2 (for aa), regardless of the initial values of x, y, and z. To see this note that the three genotypes produce the nine male–female matings shown in Figure 7.3a, involving six distinct mating combinations (if we ignore which genotype is from the male parent and which is from the female).

It is easy to compute not only the frequency of each mating combination (assuming they occur at random) but also the apportionment of this frequency among the possible offspring genotypes for the combination. This

		females		
		AA (x)	Aa (y)	aa (z)
m AA (x)		x^2	xy	xz
a				
l Aa (y)		xy	y^2	yz
e				
s aa (z)		xz	yz	z^2

(a)

mating	frequency	AA	Aa	aa
			offspring frequency	
AA-AA	x^2	x^2		
AA-Aa	$2xy$	xy	xy	
AA-aa	$2xz$		$2xz$	
Aa-Aa	y^2	$y^2/4$	$y^2/2$	$y^2/4$
Aa-aa	$2yz$		yz	yz
aa-aa	z^2			z^2
Total	$(x+y+z)^2$ = 1	$(x+y/2)^2$ = p^2	$2(x+y/2)(z+y/2)$ = $2pq$	$(z+y/2)^2$ = q^2

(b)

Figure 7.3. (a) Mating frequencies and (b) mating-class offspring frequencies for Hardy–Weinberg equilibrium population.

is shown in Figure 7.3b together with the summed frequencies for each column. The most complicated calculation is for the Aa–Aa mating where offspring AA, Aa, aA, and aa will occur with equal likelihood, making the proportion of offspring genotypes $1:2:1$. Since the mating has frequency y^2 we allocate $y^2/2$ to the heterozygous offspring and $y^2/4$ to each of the homozygotes. The totals show that the offspring genotype frequencies, as well as offspring gene frequencies, depend only on the gene frequencies (and not on the genotype frequencies) of the previous generation. The offspring population is said to be in *equilibrium* because the new genotype frequencies will perpetuate indefinitely. Such an equilibrium is often named after the mathematician Hardy and the physician–geneticist Weinberg, who independently discovered the above principle in 1908.

Although natural populations may well attain Hardy–Weinberg equilibrium for a simple trait represented at a single locus, the "law" is by no means universally obeyed. The above calculations were based on a number of assumptions in addition to that of a simple two-allele nondominant locus. In fact, the calculations can easily be extended to more than two alleles. And the nondominance assumption was required only for easy identification of genotypes. But the *other* assumptions are both necessary and unrealistic to varying degrees.

First of all, we assumed that mating was random, at least with respect to the locus in question. But frequently the locus (or others strongly linked to it) will control the expression of physical traits which make mating more likely between similar genotypes (so-called assortative mating) or between dissimilar genotypes (disassortative mating). Second, our frequency calculations are statistically valid only for a very large population, which may not exist. Another problem with small populations is the tendency for the gene pool to become *fixed* for only one of a group of alleles, as a consequence of random events whose effects would be insignificant in a larger sample. Third, we must assume that none of the alleles in question confers a differential advantage for survival, mating, or fertility on organisms possessing it (i.e., there must be no natural selection pressures). Finally we have ignored probable alterations to the original set of alleles because of mutation or of migration into the population by individuals carrying new alleles (or having quite different allele frequencies).

The fact that there can be departures from Hardy–Weinberg equilibrium in actual populations does not vitiate the above analysis however. Population geneticists have developed useful mathematical formulations by beginning with the equilibrium assumption and calculating the effects of various complicating factors. To give just one example, it can be shown that if allele A mutates to allele A′ at rate u, and if allele A′ mutates back to A at rate v, then the frequency of A will tend toward an equilibrium value of $v/(u + v)$.

Perhaps the most complex and fascinating departures from Hardy–Weinberg equilibrium are those attributable to *natural selection*. In 1859 Charles Darwin's *The Origin of Species* introduced the notion of "survival of the fittest" and revolutionized Western man's concept of the natural world. Darwin recognized that the fantastic diversity of contemporary organisms is a consequence of the differential value in different environments of the variety of genotypes originating from mutation and recombination. In 1929 the statistician R. A. Fisher published in *The Genetical Theory of Natural Selection* a formal treatment of Darwin's ideas. Fisher's "Fundamental Theorem of Natural Selection" established that the rate of increase in the "fitness" (survival potential) of a population is proportional to the genetic variance in fitness among the population's individuals. This result underscores the importance of genetic variability as a basis of evolution.

Modern biologists recognize three major types of evolution (although

Darwin dealt effectively with only the first), all of which involve the notion of a *species* as a collection of potentially interbreeding populations. *Phyletic evolution* is the improvement of a single line of development over time. The transition from one species to its successor is gradual; and two of the species never coexist. The second type of evolution is (primary) *speciation*, in which one species splits into two or more contemporary species, usually consequent on geographic isolation. Finally there is *hybridization* (secondary speciation) in which a new species is formed from the interbreeding of two existing species. Hybridization is probably the rarest of the three forms of evolution and of greater importance in plants than in animal species.

As a final topic we might speculate briefly about the evolution of the contemporary genetic mechanisms themselves. It is improbable that primordial cells employed any system as sophisticated as the DNA-RNA-protein mechanism. There is some suggestion that RNA may have been the first primary genetic material since it is capable of self-reproduction (and does so in RNA viruses). The evolution of DNA could have been a consequence of natural selection favoring its greater stability, as could the development of the double helical structure. It also seems that the genetic code has evolved in the direction of greater error resistance. Thus the contemporary redundancy scheme permits greatest variation in the third base of a codon, the position that is most often subject to translation error.

With the evolution of genetic material and the perfection of the genetic code, further selectional advantages were possible with respect to the organization and transmission of genetic information. The most significant of such developments was probably the evolution of the chromosome. But mitotic and meiotic fission mechanisms, as well as development of the numerous forms of recombination in sexual and asexual reproduction are also of evident importance. A recent fascinating speculation is that organelles like mitochondria and chloroplasts, which contain and perpetuate the DNA required for some of their own proteins, may have evolved from primitive bacteria-like parasites which entered into an effective symbiosis with the precursors of contemporary eukaryotic cells.

Bibliography

Many items in the Chapter 6 Bibliography are also relevant to the material in this chapter, in particular the books by Goodenough and Levine, Lerner, Rosenberg, Srb, and Watson (*Molecular Biology of the Gene*). Works which focus more specifically on genetic information transmission and evolution are listed below.

Darwin, Charles. *The Origin of Species*. Originally published 1859, available as a Mentor paperback, 1958.
   Together with his *Descent of Man* a pair of classic treatises on evolution.

Dobzhansky, Theodosius. *Genetics of the Evolutionary Process*. Columbia University Press, 1970.
   A recent work by the famed pioneer of evolutionary biology.

Fisher, Ronald A. *The Genetical Theory of Natural Selection*. Dover, 1958 (second revised edition).

A sophisticated mathematical treatment of Darwin's ideas.

Mayr, Ernst. *Populations, Species, and Evolution*. Harvard University Press, 1970.

A revision and abridgement of his classic work on speciation, *Animal Species and Evolution*.

Mettler, Lawrence E., and Gregg, Thomas G. *Population Genetics and Evolution*. Prentice-Hall, 1969.

A compact text, part of the publisher's modern genetics series.

Exercises

7.1. Given the following DNA base sequence GTAGTACTAGTATTATATCGTCGT determine the *m*-RNA transcript and resulting polypeptide: (a) for the sequence as shown; (b) after a double mutation which deletes the C from position 7 (counting from the left) and inserts a G after position 16 (of the original sequence); (c) after a double mutation which deletes the T from position 5 and inserts an A after position 19.

7.2. Treatment of *E. coli* bacteria with a mutagenic chemical can produce mutant strains in which the eighth amino acid of the enzyme tryptophan synthetase changes from gly to either arg or glu. Further treatment of the arg-carrying mutant causes either reversion to gly or mutation to ser, ile, or thr. Further treatment of the glu-carrying mutant causes mutations to val and ala, as well as reversion. Assuming each change in amino acid results from exactly one base substitution, deduce the codons present in the original and various mutant strains.

7.3. For a two-locus diploid system with alleles A and a at the first locus and B and b at the second:
   (a) show the relative proportions of all offspring genotypes that could result from the mating of two parents both heterozygous at each locus;
   (b) if A dominates a but there are 3 distinct phenotypes at the second locus, show the distribution of the genotypes in (a) into phenotypic equivalence classes;
   (c) as for (b) but assume that B dominates b as well.

7.4. Carry out the Hardy–Weinberg calculations of Figure 7.3 for the following sets of x-y-z frequencies:
   (a) 0.6, 0.2, 0.2;
   (b) 0.4, 0.4, 0.2.

7.5. Write a computer program for a machine and language of your choice which simulates the dynamics of a hypothetical population which always contains 20 haploid individuals with 10 2-allele loci (so an "individual" can be represented as a 10 bit binary number). For each new generation all 20 individuals are simultaneously replaced with offspring of the current 20 individuals. Offspring are generated by random selection (with replacement) of 10 matings. Each mating produces two new individuals. In some cases these will be identical with the parents. But with a fixed probability p a single crossover of the parents may occur at some randomly selected locus boundary. Try to determine the effects of different values of p by starting with a population containing a few distinct types of individuals and watching the genetic variability for several generations.

8
Neural information transmission

The long term evolutionary systems of genetic information transmission considered in the last chapter have culminated in the development of internal communication systems which animals can use for short term adaptation to their environments. Even the most primitive nervous system is a remarkably complex network of specialized cells, called *neurons*. In this and the next chapter we will examine some of the ways in which nervous systems process information. We will focus exclusively on vertebrate and especially on mammalian systems. Our discussions of neural structures will typically be in terms of the human nervous system.

In this chapter we begin with a survey of some of the major structural divisions and components of the nervous system. Since neuroanatomy is a huge subject in itself we can hope to do no more than acquire a rough appreciation of the milieu in which neural information processing transpires. In the second section we look somewhat more closely at the neurons which mediate such processing and at the ways they interconnect through specialized structures called *synapses*. Finally we are in a position to appreciate the nature of the signals which traverse neurons and synapses, the subject of the third section of this chapter.

8.1 Neural architecture

The brain and spinal cord together constitute the *central nervous system* (CNS), which will be the main focus of our discussion. But in order to appreciate what the CNS does we also need to know a little about the *peripheral nervous system*. The central nervous system communicates with the organism's external environment (and internal milieu) through cables of fibers known as *nerves*. As with almost all neural structures these nerves occur in bilateral pairs, subserving equivalent functions on the two sides of the body. The 12 pairs of *cranial nerves* connect the brain with sensory organs, like the eyes and ears, and with muscles in the head and neck areas. The 31 pairs of *spinal nerves* carry information to and from the spinal cord, which in turn relays messages to and from the brain. As we shall see in Chapter 9, the spinal cord itself also processes information, integrating sensory and motor (muscle) functions into reflex activities.

Within the central nervous system it is convenient to distinguish two major types of regions. One kind of area has primarily an information transmission function and may be thought of as consisting of bundles of communication lines (we will later call them axons) quite similar to the nerves in the peripheral nervous system. In the CNS such bundles are called *tracts*. Tracts may vary in length from a few millimeters to more than a meter. The second kind of region is concerned mainly with information processing and contains mostly nerve-cell bodies and associated connections (synapses). These data processing centers are called *nuclei*. The terms "gray matter" and "white matter" correspond quite closely to the nucleus and tract regions of the brain respectively. Neural tissue is normally grayish-pink in color; but fibers in tracts tend to be enveloped in whitish fatty sheaths.

Figure 8.1 presents a schematic view in cross-section of the human CNS. Only major structures have been identified; and we shall have no more than a few words to say about many of those. As already mentioned, the spinal cord functions in relaying information between the periphery and the brain. For this purpose numerous ascending and descending tracts are arrayed around the outer edge of the cord. Toward the middle of the cord is the spinal

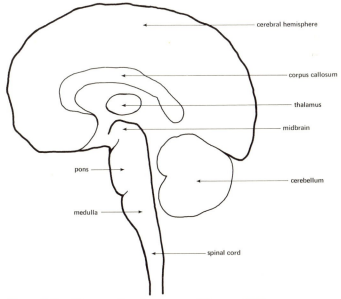

Figure 8.1.   Cross-sectional diagram of human CNS.

gray matter, which contains a number of nuclei whose synapses mediate reflex functions (see Section 9.1). The *medulla* marks the beginning of the *brain stem* (a term applied to all brain regions except the cerebral hemispheres and cerebellum) and is essentially an upward continuation of spinal tracts together with expanded and additional nuclei (some connected with cranial nerves). The brain stem expands even more at the level of the *pons*, a region of further upward continuation of spinal tracts and increasing numbers of cranial nerve nuclei.

The brain stem regions above the pons are incredibly complex. We will need to know about only two of them. The *midbrain* contains important nuclei for auditory and visual input. The *thalamus* is a collection of more than 20 nuclei (per side) and serves as the ultimate way-station for information entering or leaving the cerebral hemispheres. Some thalamic nuclei process information from a variety of sensory and/or motor systems and are diffusely connected to many cerebral regions. Other thalamic nuclei, such as the lateral geniculate nucleus of the visual system (discussed in Section 9.3), serve specific and relatively well understood functions.

The *cerebellum* is a complex structure at the back of the brain just below the cerebral hemispheres. An area subjected to much recent study, the cerebellum functions in motor coordination, acquisition of motor skills, and related tasks. Unfortunately, the scope of our discussion precludes further consideration of cerebellar structure or function.

The *cerebral hemispheres* that encapsulate much of the upper brain stem are the most prominent features of the human brain. The size and development of these hemispheres distinguish man from all other animals. The underside of each hemisphere is paved with tracts which interconnect distant regions. Of particular note is the *corpus callosum*, a wide band of fibers which provides most inter-hemispheric information transmission.

The outer covering, or cortex, of the cerebral hemispheres is a region of gray matter averaging 2.5 millimeters in thickness. This *cerebral cortex* is tightly folded in against itself, presumably to increase its "surface" area without a corresponding increase in head size. Nearly two thirds of the cortical surface is buried inside the folds, which are known as *fissures*. While many of the smaller fissures are variable from brain to brain, the larger ones form quite visible and reliable landmarks on the surface of the hemisphere. On the basis of such landmarks the cortex has been arbitrarily divided into four *lobes*, as shown in Figure 8.2.

The complexity and variability of the cortical landscape, with respect to layers and types of cells as well as distribution of fissures, have long been a source of theories about the localization of particular sensory, motor, and intellectual functions in specific cortical regions. Today it is generally believed that much of the cortex is relatively nonspecific, participating in a variety of brain functions in concert with other, perhaps remote, regions. On the other hand there are certainly some regions with well established roles, in particular the primary areas for reception of auditory, visual, and som-

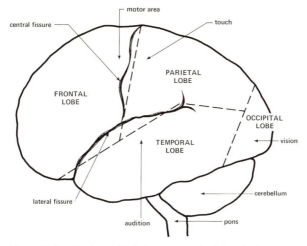

Figure 8.2.   Surface of left human cerebral hemisphere.

aesthetic (touch) sensations. These regions, together with an established area of motor control, are shown in Figure 8.2.

In closing this section, we should note that attempts to localize man's higher brain functions, like learning, memory, language, and problem solving, have met with mixed success. Of special interest, however, is the well established finding that language functions are mediated mostly by one hemisphere (usually the left). Clearly bilateral symmetry of form does not always imply the same for function.

8.2 Neurons and synapses

With respect to the cellular components of CNS tissue, neurons are actually in the minority. More numerous are the various kinds of *glial cells*, whose functions include provision of metabolic support, sheathing of neural processes, and a scavenger role. But since only minor and speculative information processing functions have been attributed to glial cells, we will not discuss them further. The true computational elements of the nervous system are the *neurons*.

Although neurons come in an incredible variety of shapes and sizes they share two properties not (simultaneously) possessed to any significant extent by other cell types. First, neurons are *excitable*; they respond to specific forms of stimulation with measured amounts of specific activity. Second, neurons have *processes*; the cytoplasm and external membrane are drawn out into projections of small diameter but often astounding length. Excitability and processes clearly underlie the neuron's information processing ability. Excitability allows the change of state in response to signal that is inherent in all computation. And processes permit the transmission of information over distance.

Although there is no such thing as a "typical neuron," Figure 8.3 portrays some of the physical features common to many of the forms taken by this cell type. Traditionally the neuron has been considered to have three components. *Dendrites* are processes specialized for reception of incoming signals. Dendritic processes may be numerous and highly branched but frequently do not extend any great distance away from the cell. The cell body or *soma* is where incoming information is integrated. The neuron's nucleus and most of its metabolic machinery, which is not significantly different from that of other active cells, also lie in the soma. The *axon* is a process specialized for transmission of information from the cell to other neurons. The region where axon and soma come together is called the *axon hillock*.

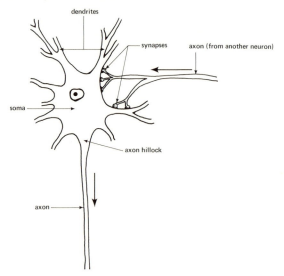

Figure 8.3.   Common features of neurons, with arrows showing information flow.

The overgeneralization inherent in this simple picture of the neuron must be stressed. There are, for example, neurons with no distinguishable axons, neurons with only a single process, and a host of specialized shapes whose significance is only beginning to be understood. It should also be noted that the distribution of neuronal types varies considerably in different regions of the CNS.

Structural variety also characterizes neural interconnections. One neuron influences the activity of another through a specialized structure called a *synapse*. One common form of synapse is shown in Figure 8.4. As can be seen, the presynaptic neuron and the postsynaptic neuron do not actually make physical contact at the synapse. Rather there is a narrow (about 10^{-8} meters) *synaptic cleft* separating the two membranes. The *presynaptic membrane* is part of a terminal specialization of the presynaptic neuron's axon, called an end-foot or *synaptic knob*. The *postsynaptic membrane* is a

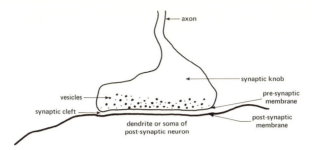

Figure 8.4.   One form of (chemical) synapse.

specialized region of the postsynaptic neuron's dendritic (or somatic) membrane. Synapses can be classified as *axodendritic* or *axosomatic* (or even axoaxonic, though these are rare) according to the location of the postsynaptic membrane on the postsynaptic neuron. Up to several thousand synapses may impinge on a single neuron, creating neural networks of incredible complexity.

As we shall discover in the next section, information processing events within a neuron are of a fundamentally electrochemical nature. By contrast, transmission of information across a synapse is a purely chemical phenomenon. (Electrical synapses do exist, but are rare in higher animals.) The *synaptic vesicles* shown in the presynaptic terminal in Figure 8.4 are spherical storage depots, each containing a few thousand molecules of a chemical called a *transmitter substance*. Signals arriving at the synaptic terminal trigger the release of the contents of the vesicles. The transmitter molecules then diffuse across the synaptic cleft and make contact with specialized receptor sites in the postsynaptic membrane. Although these receptors are poorly understood, the contact is assumed to alter the properties of the postsynaptic membrane, with consequences which we will study in the next section.

Once the transmitter substance has done its job, it must somehow be inactivated. A permanent alteration in the postsynaptic membrane would be of no use in information transmission. Three mechanisms are known to operate in transmitter inactivation: (1) passive diffusion out of the synaptic cleft; (2) chemical destruction by an enzyme; and (3) reuptake through the neural membranes. Which of these mechanisms predominates at a given synapse appears to depend on the nature of the transmitter. Although it is generally believed that only one transmitter substance is employed at a given synapse, it should be emphasized that only a few of the probable half-dozen or more chemical transmitters have as yet been unambiguously identified.

8.3 Neural signals

To understand the nature of the signals transmitted by neurons we need to know something about the distribution of charged ions across the neural membrane. In its inactive or "resting" state, the membrane is quite permeable to K^+ and Cl^-, but less so to Na^+. Each species of charged ion attempts to flow across the membrane in a direction which both equalizes its concentration on the two sides (flow with a concentration gradient) and equalizes the net charge on both sides (flow with a charge gradient). Since all these demands cannot be met simultaneously, the various forces come into a stable equilibrium situation in which the potential across the membrane is around 60 mV (millivolts), with the inside of the cell negative relative to the outside. At equilibrium there is considerably more K^+ inside the cell than outside, while the reverse is true for Na^+ and Cl^-. All neural signals are based on changes in membrane properties which give rise to ionic flows that temporarily modify the membrane potential.

Potential changes caused by transmitter substance acting on the postsynaptic membrane take one of two forms, depending on the type of receptors in the membrane. At *excitatory* synapses there is a sudden influx of Na^+ ions, reducing the potential and *depolarizing* the membrane (i.e., reducing the polarity). This *excitatory postsynaptic potential* (abbreviated EPSP) lasts for several msec., as the membrane potential gradually returns to its equilibrium value. At *inhibitory* synapses a combination of Cl^- influx and K^+ efflux *hyperpolarizes* the membrane, producing an *inhibitory postsynaptic potential* (IPSP) with a time course much like that of the EPSP. The magnitude of postsynaptic potential changes varies from a few mV to as much as 30 or 40 mV, depending on the amount of transmitter present and the duration of its effectiveness. Figure 8.5 depicts representative graphs of EPSPs and IPSPs.

By the way, it is not strictly accurate to speak of excitatory and inhibitory

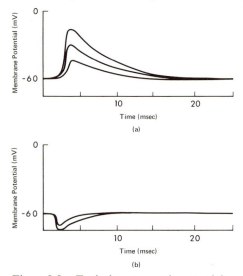

Figure 8.5.   Typical postsynaptic potentials.
(a) EPSPs, (b) IPSPs.

synapses, only of excitatory and inhibitory *effects* at synapses. Although rare in higher animals, synapses have been identified in invertebrates where a single identified transmitter substance mediates either an excitatory or an inhibitory effect, depending on the frequency of the presynaptic signal. This finding implies the existence of at least two classes of postsynaptic receptors at such a synapse. The true complexity and information processing power of the postsynaptic membrane will probably not be fully appreciated for some time.

At a given time postsynaptic potentials of both types may be present at hundreds or even thousands of synapses on a single neuron. These potentials passively spread along the dendritic and somatic membrane (losing amplitude in the process) and interact with each other. Thus the effects of an EPSP can be virtually eliminated by a nearby IPSP of sufficient strength (*spatial summation*). And two potentials of the same sign will enhance each other if they occur closely spaced in time at a single synapse (*temporal summation*). As a consequence of all these interactions the somatic membrane is constantly monitoring the integrated net effect of all PSPs impinging on the neuron in the recent past. If this net effect is depolarizing (it need not be), and if the magnitude of this depolarization measured at the axon hillock exceeds a value known as the neuron's *threshold*, then a signal will be sent down the axon. Threshold potentials are usually reached with about 10 to 20 mV of depolarization but may vary considerably from neuron to neuron and over time for a given neuron.

The electrical signals which travel in axons are impulse or spike-like in character and are called *action potentials*. A typical action potential is diagrammed in Figure 8.6. The rising or depolarizing phase is a consequence of massive influx of Na^+; recovery is accomplished by extrusion of K^+. This is clearly a situation that cannot by itself go on for long, lest the axon become saturated with Na^+ and lose all its K^+. Compensation is provided by an active transport mechanism which is constantly working in the background. This so-called "sodium pump" carries Na^+ out of the cell and K^+ back in. Despite the pump's presence however, a period of intense activity

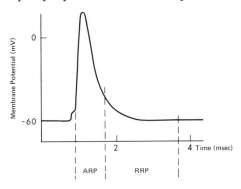

Figure 8.6.   An action potential.

can create a sufficient ionic imbalance to interfere temporarily with an axon's activity.

Although it somewhat resembles a large EPSP, the action potential is a fundamentally different electrochemical event. First of all, action potentials are of essentially fixed amplitude, usually reaching a value of 5 to 10 mV positive, whereas PSPs are of variable size. Thus information cannot be carried in the amplitude of an action potential. We will shortly examine how information *is* coded. A second difference relates to propagation. Where PSPs spread passively across the cell membrane, suffering a decrement in amplitude in the process, action potentials propagate nondecrementally, retaining their initial amplitude all the way down the axon. The speed of this propagation ranges up to a few meters/second, being faster in axons of larger diameter.

Action potential propagation is really a wave phenomenon; nothing physical moves down the axon. Thus an action potential occurring at a given point on an axon provides (through passive spread) suprathreshold de-polarization of the axon tissue immediately in front of it, generating a new action potential at that point. This is why propagation is nondecremental. Although the tissue immediately behind the wave front (where the action potential has "just been") also receives such stimulation, action potentials still travel only in the "forward" direction. Such unidirectional propagation is achieved because the threshold becomes effectively infinite during the rising and about the first half of the falling phase of an action potential. No further spikes can be induced during this *absolute refractory period* (abbrevi-ated ARP in Figure 8.6). Since the tissue just behind the wave front will be in this absolutely refractory state, unidirectional conduction of impulses is assured.

After the end of the ARP there is another period during which the threshold is elevated but returning to its normal ("resting") value. During this *relative refractory period* (RRP), a larger depolarization is required to evoke an action potential, the requirement being largest at the beginning of the RRP.

Let us now return to the axon hillock and imagine a situation in which a depolarization just equal to the resting threshold is maintained there. An action potential will be generated in the axon only after its predecessor's RRP has elapsed, giving a "firing frequency" of no more than a few hundred impulses per second. If we now increase the sustained depolarization in the hillock to a level somewhat above threshold, action potentials will be initiated near the ends of RRPs, giving a somewhat greater frequency of firing. Finally, let us increase the depolarization to a level so high that action potentials will be initated at the ends of ARPs. This situation will produce the maximum firing rate of around 1,000 impulses per second.

It is now clear how the neuron encodes information about stimulus magnitude in action potentials of uniform size. Encoding of information in the frequencies of pulses is known to engineers as *pulse frequency modulation*

(PFM for short). This discussion should not be taken as ruling out even more sophisticated encodings at given times or places in the nervous system. But it is clear that all such encodings will be based on the PFM principle of variation in the temporal distribution of pulses.

We should note the important roles in neural function we have just discovered for each of the refractory periods. Although the ARP and RRP could be regarded as unfortunate limitations placed on neural information transmission by the "weaknesses" of biological tissue, we have seen that the former assures unidirectional conduction and the latter provides for PFM encoding. These two properties are at the core of a neuron's information transmission abilities.

We close this section with a word about "spontaneous" activity in the nervous system. Although the discussion to date has implied that a neuron fires only in response to sufficient input stimulation, many cells appear to be active in the absence of input. Such spontaneous activity can probably be attributed to a threshold which varies close to the resting potential value and sometimes crosses it, generating an impulse. Many organisms possess a sophisticated type of spontaneous neural activity in the form of *pacemaker* cells. Such neurons (or sometimes groups of neurons) generate rhythmic outputs which can be useful in governing rhythmic biological activities like respiration.

In this chapter we have examined the information processing capacities of neurons without much regard for how these capacities are applied in actual neural systems. In the next chapter we will remedy this omission by looking at some of the ways in which information is passed to and from an organism's environment.

Bibliography

Cooke, Ian, and Lipkin, Mack (eds.). *Cellular Neurophysiology: A Source Book.* Holt, Rinehart, and Winston, 1972.
> A collection of early research papers by pioneer investigators of neural function.

Deutsch, Sid. *Models of the Nervous System.* Wiley, 1967.
> Mathematical characterizations of a variety of neural functions.

McLennan, Hugh. *Synaptic Transmission.* Saunders, 1970.
> A thorough technical monograph summarizing current knowledge about neural interconnections.

Mountcastle, Vernon B. (ed.). *Medical Physiology, Volume 1* (13th edition). Mosby, 1974.
> An exhaustive reference work for medical scientists, covering nearly every aspect of human neurophysiology.

Schmitt, Francis O., and Worden, Frederic G. (eds.). *The Neurosciences: Third Study Program.* Wiley, 1974.
> An outstanding collection of recent original papers dealing with many aspects of neurophysiology and molecular biology. The two earlier volumes (*The*

Neurosciences: Second Study Program, ed. by Schmitt, 1970; *The Neurosciences: A Study Program*, ed. by Quarton *et al.*, 1967; both Rockefeller University Press) are also excellent.

Shepherd, Gordon M. *The Synaptic Organization of the Brain*. Oxford University Press, 1974.
A fine treatment of modern concepts of neural function, organized by brain regions, at a reasonably introductory level.

Stevens, Charles F. *Neurophysiology: A Primer*. Wiley, 1966.
An excellent short introduction to basic concepts, although now somewhat out of date.

Thompson, Richard F. (ed.). *Physiological Psychology*. Freeman, 1971.
A good collection of *Scientific American* articles from the 1950's and 1960's, with an emphasis on the behavioral manifestations of neural function.

Wooldridge, Dean E. *The Machinery of the Brain*. McGraw-Hill, 1963.
A readable but rather dated introductory treatment, from the viewpoint of a physical scientist.

Exercises

8.1. Compare the organization and data-transmission aspects of the nervous system with those of modern digital computers.

Note: The following two exercises assume familiarity with Part I of this book.

8.2. Discuss the adequacies and inadequacies of McCulloch–Pitts "neurons" (Chapter 3) as models of biological neurons.

8.3. Consider neural encoding of information from the viewpoint of communication theory. Discuss redundancy, reliability, efficiency, and the like.

9
Neural input–output

The tremendous information processing potential of central neural structures would be useless to an organism unable to make contact with its environment. Such contact is provided, on the one hand, by sensory systems which feed information about environmental energy states to the CNS and, on the other hand, by motor systems which enable the CNS to act on the environment. In practice it is difficult to identify the boundaries between sensory or motor systems and central processing systems. Thus the input–output systems we consider in this chapter will have important components *within* the CNS as well as communication channels to and from it.

Sensory and (to a lesser extent) motor systems are considerably better understood than the central neural systems mediating such higher functions as emotion, language, or abstract thought. This better understanding has arisen from a variety of factors. First, input–output systems are more accessible to the laboratory probes of the neurophysiologist. Second, sensory and motor systems can be studied experimentally in a wide range of organisms, many of which lack some or all of the higher functions. Finally, the behavioral correlates of sensory and motor events are much easier to observe, measure, and understand than those associated with higher functions.

Our discussion will deal only briefly with motor systems, mainly in connection with the one relatively well understood complete sensory–motor system, the spinal reflex arc. In the second section we will look at the variety of sensory systems operative in higher animals and some common features uniting them. Finally, the third section will treat in some detail the extensively studied vertebrate visual system.

9.1 Reflex and motor systems

Spinal reflex systems were first systematically studied before the turn of the century, notably by the British physiologist Sir Charles Sherrington. Many of Sherrington's original findings remain basic to the modern theory of reflex function. A spinal reflex is any integrated sensory–motor event in which all central processing is carried out in the spinal cord. If any of the input information is relayed to the brain, it typically gets there after the reflex activity is completed. The knee jerk elicited by the doctor's hammer is a simple spinal reflex. To understand such reflexes we must know something about the organization of the spinal cord and about how nerves are connected to muscles.

Vertebrate skeletal muscles (those which control movements of bones around joints) are made up of long fibrous cells which contract when suitably stimulated. This stimulation usually comes from *motoneurons*, which have cell bodies in the spinal cord and send axons to groups of muscle fibers (typically several hundred per axon). Action potentials in the motoneuron axon trigger the release of a chemical transmitter which acts to produce muscle contraction. The *neuromuscular junction* operates much like an excitatory chemical synapse.

Muscles also have sensory organs. One type, known as the *muscle spindle*, is embedded among muscle fibers and causes firing of its sensory nerve fibers whenever the muscle is subjected to stretch. Another type of receptor is the *Golgi tendon organ*, located at the junction of muscle and bone. Tendon organs cause their sensory nerve fibers to fire whenever the muscle contracts. The nerve fibers from both types of sensory organs have cell bodies located in clusters or *ganglia* outside the spinal cord; but the axons continue on and enter the cord. The sensory and motor nerve fibers innervating skeletal muscles are among the many types of fibers in the cable of a spinal nerve, as shown in Figure 9.1.

Information from muscle sensors is passed to higher (brain) centers; and such centers have connections to the motoneurons. But it is the circuits completed within the spinal cord that mediate reflex activity. Two such circuits are depicted in Figure 9.1. In the "knee-jerk" or *stretch reflex*, stretch in the muscle causes contraction via a two-neuron reflex arc with a single excitatory synapse. The spindle receptors thus serve as input to a feedback control system that can maintain the muscle at a given length in the presence of increasing tension.

The tendon organ receptors participate in the three-neuron *lengthening reflex*. Here an *interneuron* is interposed between the receptor and motoneuron portions of the arc. And since the second synapse is inhibitory the reflex response to increased muscle tension will be a lessening of contraction. This feedback control system thus allows maintenance of fixed muscle tension through alteration in muscle length.

The system of spinal reflexes initiated by muscle receptors is really much

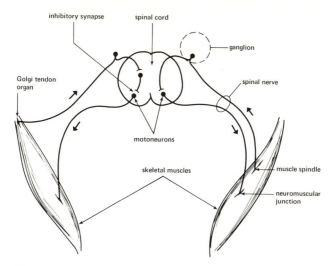

Figure 9.1. Muscle innervation and reflex pathways.

more complicated than our discussion has suggested. For one thing, there are actually two types of spindle receptors, participating in somewhat different reflex functions. And spindle activity is further complicated by special motoneurons which stretch spindles exclusively. Furthermore, reflexes are mediated by connections within the spinal cord to motoneurons of different (but related) muscles, on the same or opposite side of the body.

It should also be noted that spinal reflexes can be initiated by receptors outside of the musculature. The withdrawal of a limb from a painful stimulus is a good example of a reflex involving skin receptors. Finally, we should not leave the subject of reflex activity with the impression that all the body's reflex systems are in the spinal cord. Eye movements, for example, are partly controlled by a brain-stem reflex system.

Despite the sophistication and complexity of reflex systems there is obviously much more to the story of motor control. While we may maintain our balance and coordinate our walking by reflex, activities like speech and painting and kicking a football clearly require some sort of central, voluntary motor control. Although central systems for initiation and control of movement are becoming better understood, much remains obscure with respect to their organization and function. Our discussion must be limited to a few general observations.

Man and other mammals appear to possess two somewhat independent central motor systems. The more clearly demarcated of these was originally dubbed the *pyramidal system* because of the wedge-shaped bulges ("pyramids") formed in the medulla by fibers descending to the spinal cord. A more modern view defines the pyramidal system as all aspects of motor control originating in the primary motor area of the cerebral cortex, just in front of the central fissure (see Figure 8.2). Neurons affecting muscles in different regions of the body are arranged in this cortical region in a clear and orderly fashion, a form of *somatotopic organization* we shall encounter in sensory systems as well. The axons of the pyramidal neurons descend in a single spinal tract and synapse directly with motoneurons. The pyramidal system appears to be the more recently evolved motor system and probably vital only for finely coordinated movements.

The *extrapyramidal* motor system is really a set of systems unified only by their discovery after the pyramidal system. Originating in the cerebellum and various cortical and brain stem regions, the extrapyramidal system descends the spinal cord in numerous tracts. Widespread involvement of the extrapyramidal system in initiation and control of movement is suggested by the variety of serious motor disorders that can result from injury to various parts of the system.

9.2 Sensory systems

We have far more than "five senses." In addition to the sensory systems for vision, audition, olfaction, and gustation, there are receptors in muscles (see previous section) and joints, and a variety of specialized receptors in the skin for sensing touch, pressure, pain, and temperature. There is also the vestibular apparatus for our "sense of balance" and even receptors in blood vessels which monitor pressure and carbon dioxide concentration. We clearly cannot treat even a fraction of this host of sensory systems in any detail. Our discussion in this section deals with generalities. A specific system is examined in the next section.

All cells will "respond" in some fashion if exposed to sufficient intensities of various forms of energy. What makes receptors different is that they are *designed* to respond to a particular form of energy, often at very low levels of intensity, and convert it into neural signals. The form of energy for which a receptor is specialized may be mechanical (e.g., touch, pressure), chemical (e.g., olfaction, gustation), or electromagnetic (vision).

Receptors are sometimes responsive to the "wrong" form of energy. Thus certain types of pressure on the eyeball will create sensations of light flashes (quite possibly accompanied by pain from nonvisual receptors). The important point is that the perceived sensation is still a visual one. It cannot be overemphasized that the mode of sensation is a function of the destination of neural signals in the brain and not of the form of the impinging energy. Identical arrays of action potentials in the auditory and optic nerves create different sensations by virtue of their different locations.

Receptors can be grouped into three classes according to the complexity of their conversion of energy to neural signals. The simplest receptor type is the free nerve ending, found in the skin and various other locations. In sensing touch or pain, free nerve endings respond to mechanical deformation with depolarization, which in turn produces action potentials in the axons of which they are extensions. Specialized nerve endings, also found primarily in the skin, have tissue coverings or capsules of various sorts surrounding the nerve ending. These capsules make the ending especially sensitive to certain types of mechanical (or thermal) energy and can be a factor in the adaptation of receptors (discussed below). The most complex receptors are nonneural cells or structures, like the muscle receptors described in the preceding section or the retinal receptors discussed in the next. These highly specialized receptors respond to energy with a membrane potential change which is communicated to the associated neuron through a synapse-like structure.

Regardless of receptor type, we refer to the potential change that precedes the actual neural signal as a *receptor potential*. Stimulus intensity is thus converted first to receptor potential magnitude which is in turn expressed in neural signals, typically as a frequency of action potentials. Action potential frequency is often an approximately logarithmic function of stimulus intensity, a relation which is useful for encoding large ranges of intensity while maintaining high sensitivity to intensity differences at low levels of stimulation. In most cases it appears that the logarithmic transformation occurs in the generation of receptor potentials, followed by an approximately linear conversion of receptor potential to neural signal.

Another important feature of receptor potentials is their tendency to *adapt* to constant levels of stimulation. Since the most important information an organism can acquire from its environment is often related to changes in stimulus intensity, many receptors become less active during periods of constant stimulation. On the other hand, some types of receptors show relatively little adaptation.

Before turning to a specific sensory system, we should give more precise meaning to the term and conclude this section with three general observations about such systems. A sensory system can be defined as an information channel beginning with a group of homogeneous receptors and ending in a higher brain center, usually the cerebral cortex. A first observation about such systems is that they are not passive information transmission channels. We have already seen how incoming information is processed right at the receptor level, through logarithmic transformations and adaptation. In addition there may be several "substations" en route to the cortex. These nuclei further transform the signal often by subdividing its components and selecting or enhancing those of particular use to the organism.

Secondly we should note that a sensory system is not often a unidirectional channel. Information also flows down from higher centers to intermediate nuclei or even to the receptor level. Such *centrifugal control* mechanisms can be fundamental to the processes by which the organism attends selectively to an aspect of a sensory signal or to one of several active sensory channels.

Finally, sensory systems are rarely independent of complementary motor systems. Recognition of an object by touch is quite difficult without activity in the hand. And vision becomes all but useless without the several types of eye and head movements which support the sensory activity. In summary, a sensory system is a bidirectional communication channel which contains intermediate data processing and is closely integrated with motor activity.

9.3 The visual system

The vertebrate visual system originates with receptor cells in the retina of the eye. Light reaching these receptors has already been gathered and focused by the pupil and lens system of the eyeball; but we will not be concerned with those structures.

The two kinds of receptor cells in the human retina have been named *rod* and *cone* cells in a rough characterization of their appearances. Rods and cones differ in numbers, distribution in the retina, and responsiveness to light energy. The approximately 125 million rods in a human retina tend to be distributed around the outside edge, while the 7 million cones are concentrated in the central region which processes what the viewer is looking directly at. Rods are very sensitive receptors (capable of being excited by as little as a single quantum of light) which adapt rapidly and to a large degree. Cones adapt very little by comparison and are far less sensitive. Color vision is mediated entirely by cones, which occur in three classes, each maximally sensitive to a different frequency of light.

Rod and cone cells are hyperpolarized by light. This receptor potential is a consequence of a reversible chemical change. In human rods the photopigment rhodopsin is rapidly bleached by light, forming another chemical compound which is only slowly reconverted to rhodopsin. These processes account for the high sensitivity and adaptation of rods. Three other photopigments function in a similar manner for the three classes of cone cells.

As shown in Figure 9.2 there are a variety of neural cells present in the retina along with the receptor cells. The rods and cones are physically located at the back of the retina and make synapse-like connections with *bipolar cells*. Typically, many receptor cells project to a given bipolar cell (*convergence*) and a given receptor projects to many bipolar cells (*divergence*), although cones in the very center of the retina appear to have "private" bipolar-cell lines. Convergence and divergence are very general principles of neural organization and in the retina represent an early opportunity for processing the visual input. Bipolar cells do not support action potentials but communicate via depolarizing or hyperpolarizing signals with *ganglion cells*. The bipolar-ganglion cell interface is also characterized by convergent and divergent connections. Further opportunities for retinal information processing are provided by the *horizontal* and *Amacrine* cells, which laterally interconnect retinal elements at the receptor–bipolar and bipolar–ganglion interfaces respectively. The ganglion cell axons (which *do* carry action potentials) are gathered together into a cable which exits the retina as the *optic nerve*.

Visual pathways from the optic nerve to the cerebral cortex are shown

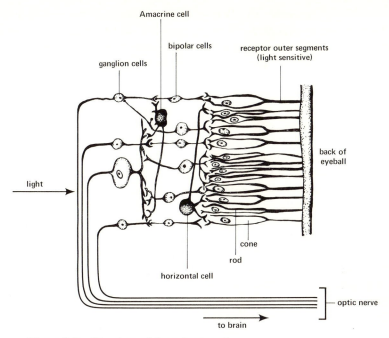

Figure 9.2.   Structure of the primate retina.

VISUAL FIELDS

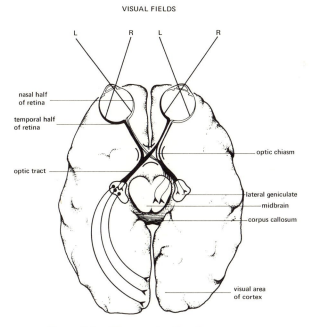

Figure 9.3.   Human visual pathways.

113

in Figure 9.3. The optic nerve fibers from the inside (nasal) half of each retina cross to the other side of the brain in the *optic chiasm*, where they join with the uncrossed fibers from the other side to form the *optic tracts*. Note that at this point the right optic tract carries all information from the right half of each retina and hence from the left visual field. Optic tract fibers make connections with some midbrain nuclei (where they serve as input for eye-movement reflexes), but mainly terminate in the *lateral geniculate nuclei* of the thalamus. New fibers, the axons of lateral geniculate neurons, then project to the primary visual cortex in the occipital lobe. Intercommunication between visual regions in the two hemispheres is mediated by the corpus callosum. At all levels of the visual system, cells and fibers maintain an organization such that adjacency in the pathways reflects adjacency in the retina. Compare this *retinotopic map* with the somatotopic organization of motor cortex mentioned in Section 9.1.

With the above sketch of the visual system connections as background, we are now in a position to appreciate some results from the numerous experimental studies that have been undertaken to discover how the visual system processes information. By information processing in this context we will mean any neural operations which *transform* the neural signals received from the previous level in the system.

An important and useful concept in sensory information processing is that of the *receptive field*. The receptive field of any visual system cell body or axon is the entire set of retinal receptors whose activation or deactivation can influence the firing pattern in the neuron. Because of anatomically localized convergence and divergence, visual receptive fields tend to be fairly small circumscribed regions on the retina. Light stimuli impinging on the retina outside this region will not affect the cell in question. It should be clear that the concept of a receptive field is not limited to visual information processing but is equally useful in other sensory systems.

Much of the following data on visual receptive fields was collected in relatively recent times with the use of modern techniques of single unit recording. These techniques permit the insertion of a very fine microelectrode into a nerve cell or axon without significant damage. The electrical behavior of the neuron can then be recorded while various light stimuli are played over the retina. In this manner the receptive field can be located and more refined stimuli used to characterize its effect on the cell.

One of the first discoveries about visual information processing was that very few cells respond to sustained light stimuli in their receptive fields with sustained trains of neural impulses. Much more characteristic are the so called ON response, a brief burst of intense firing just after the light is turned on, and OFF response, a burst just after the light is turned off but no activity in the presence of light.

Early studies of the cat retina also showed that a ganglion cell does not give a uniform response throughout its receptive field. The typical field is found to be roughly circular and 1 or 2 millimeters in diameter. In the central region of the field small spots of light elicit ON responses, while in the annular surrounding region an OFF response is produced. Complementary to these so-called ON-center receptive fields are a roughly equal number of cells with OFF-center (and ON-surround) characteristics. This arrangement seems designed to signal not only temporal changes in stimulation, by means of the transient nature of the responses, but also spatial contrasts (light–dark edges in the visual field). Thus with uniform illumination of the entire receptive field the ON and OFF responses tend to cancel each other out and the cell is quite passive.

Much of our current understanding of receptive field organization in higher levels of the visual system comes from the cat and monkey studies carried out over the past 15 years by Harvard investigators David Hubel and Torsten Wiesel. Only highlights of their findings can be mentioned here. In the monkey's lateral geniculate nucleus, Hubel and Wiesel identified three classes of cells. In addition to ON-center fields much like those of ganglion cells, two groups of geniculate neurons are differentially sensitive to the *color* of the stimulating light (monkeys, unlike cats, have color vision). Type I fields give an ON-center response to one color (e.g., red) and an OFF-surround response to a spectrally opponent wavelength (green). Type II fields also give opposite responses to opponent colors but over the entire field (no center-surround distinction). It would thus appear that a great deal of preliminary processing of color information is done at the lateral geniculate level.

In the visual cortex Hubel and Wiesel discovered a hierarchy of increasingly complex receptive fields. We consider only the simplest variety. All of these so-called simple cortical neurons respond to edges, slits of light, or dark bars in the receptive field, with an especially pronounced response when the stimulus is in motion. An important characteristic of these "edge detectors" is sensitivity only to stimuli of a particular *orientation* (e.g., vertical). An edge even a few degrees from this preferred angle has a markedly reduced effect on the cell.

Many cortical cells examined by Hubel and Wiesel responded to stimuli from either eye and had receptive fields with closely corresponding positions in the two retinas. Often the response to one of the two eyes had a greater effect ("ocular dominance"). Findings from this kind of research have recently been incorporated into a theory of the role of binocular disparity in depth perception.

An important aspect of Hubel and Wiesel's research was the discovery of the spatial organization of cortical neurons. Superimposed on the fairly coarse retinotopic map is a fine grid of columns orthogonal to the cortex, within each of which all cells are responsive to the same orientation. Superimposed on the retinotopic and orientation grids is a third organizational scheme (of intermediate coarseness) in which all cells in a column have approximately the same ocular dominance. Thus the seemingly uniform visual cortex appears to contain at least three levels of two-dimensional organization. Similar types of columnar arrangements have been demonstrated in many other cortical regions, suggesting an underlying organizational principle in the cerebral cortex.

Hubel and Wiesel also did some of the first studies on the question of whether visual receptive field properties develop with exposure to visual stimuli or are "prewired" into the organism and present at birth. In the kitten responsive units quite similar to those of adult cats can be found a few days after birth, before the animals open their eyes. On the other hand, experiments in which kittens were deprived of normal visual experience early in life showed severe abnormalities in receptive fields. These findings indicate that many aspects of visual receptive field organization are genetically specified but also require proper stimulation for normal development. Recent findings of other investigators suggest that the "critical period," during which exposure to visual stimuli is essential for normal development, may be only a matter of hours in length, at a precisely programmed point in the organism's maturation.

No discussion of visual information processing would be complete without mention of a classic earlier study on a lower organism. In the 1950's Lettvin, Maturana, McCulloch, and Pitts investigated "what the frog's eye tells the frog's brain." They were able to correlate five types of receptive field organization in the frog's retina with anatomical findings of five classes of ganglion cell dendritic field organization. The receptive fields of the frog retina are actually much more complex than those of cat, monkey, or man. For example, there is a class of ganglion cells responsive to small, dark, convex, moving boundaries (the frog's "bug detector"). This relative sophistication of retinal fields is attributable to the frog's more complex and highly organized retina.

It would however be wrong to conclude that the frog's visual abilities exceed those of man, for the frog has comparatively little by way of higher brain centers for processing visual information. In fact, the relative simplicity of the mammalian retina seems to reflect an evolutionary "decision" to defer complex information processing to more powerful and flexible higher centers. Such a principle extends to other aspects of neural information processing. Thus a mollusc may demand sophisticated multimodal performance from each of its limited number of synapses. But man can afford to use simpler devices and derive computational power from the fact that that there are trillions of them to work with.

Bibliography

Virtually all of the items in the Chapter 8 Bibliography contain material relevant to this chapter as well. The entries below are confined to relevant historical works on neural input–output.

Granit, Ragnar. *Receptors and Sensory Perception.* Yale University Press, 1955.
    A classic series of lectures by one of the field's pioneers.

Hubel, David H. "The visual cortex of the brain." *Scientific American*, November, 1963, pp. 54–62.
A readable introduction to the early work of Hubel and Wiesel.

Lettvin, J. Y., Maturana, H. R., McCulloch, W. S., and Pitts, W. H. "What the frog's eye tells the frog's brain." *Proceedings of the Institute of Radio Engineers, 47*, 1959, pp. 1940–1951.
The classic paper.

Sherrington, Charles. *The Integrative Action of the Nervous System.* Yale University Press, 1906 (2nd edition, 1947).
A compendium of his extensive research on reflex systems.

Exercises

9.1. Discuss how you might determine the number of synapses in a reflex arc. Assume you know the speed of conduction in the nerve fibers and the time required for information transmission across a synapse.

9.2. Apply, where appropriate, the generalizations about sensory systems at the end of Section 9.2 to the input devices and channels of a modern digital computer.

9.3. Indicate how the concept of a receptive field might be applied to sensory systems other than vision.

10
Computer simulation models

In this chapter we consider three representative efforts in the study of biological information processing through models embodied in digital computer programs. The theory and art of computer simulation are vast topics which we cannot discuss explicitly. Furthermore, each of the models we will look at is of at least the scope of a Ph.D. dissertation. Thus even our examples will be treated in a fairly superficial and qualitative way. The reader who has the opportunity to work his way through one of these dissertations will find it a rewarding, though difficult and sometimes frustrating, task.

The three computer models will take us back down the biological scale from the point reached at the end of the last chapter. We first consider a model of visual information processing in which the primitive components are groups of neurons. We then refine the focus to look at a network model which attempts to simulate faithfully the operations of individual neurons. Finally we examine a model of intracellular operations, an attempt to simulate the biological processes that occur inside a living bacterial cell.

The terms "effort" and "attempt" in the above paragraphs should not be taken as pejorative. All three models have been successful in the achievement of at least some of their goals. Yet the current "state of the art" in computer simulation of biological information processing is such that few models do everything expected of them or cause much excitement among laboratory biologists. We shall return to the question of what it means for a model of this type to "succeed" in the context of the third model, whose authors have made some cogent observations on the subject.

10.1 Kabrisky's vision model

For his doctoral thesis in 1964 at the University of Illinois, Matthew Kabrisky proposed a model for visual information processing in the human brain. On the basis of a variety of anatomical and physiological studies, including the columnar organization findings of Hubel and Wiesel discussed in the previous chapter, Kabrisky decided to view computation in the visual cortex as occurring in relatively isolated spots. His *basic computational element* (BCE) is therefore intended to model a piece of cortical tissue about half a millimeter in diameter and containing up to about 350 neurons. The individual neurons do not figure in the model since the behavior (output) of a BCE is governed by transformations applied to its collective input. The input and output are single numerical values, which should be regarded as proportional to the average firing frequencies on the BCE's input and output lines respectively.

The output (denoted Q) of a BCE at any given time (t) is a function (F) of its input (P) and of two memory parameters, SS (for slow storage) and SF (for fast storage). SS is a function (H) of the preceding values of SF, which is in turn a function (G) of the history of all element's input and memory quantities. SF and SS represent Kabrisky's attempt to acknowledge the short- and long-term aspects of visual memory. The basic equations relating the parameters just identified are given below.

$$Q(t) = F(P(t), SF(t), SS(t)), \quad \text{where}$$

$$SS(t) = H(SF(t), SF(t-1), SF(t-2), \ldots), \quad \text{and} \tag{10.1}$$

$$SF(t) = G(SF(t), SF(t-1), \ldots, SS(t), SS(t-1) \ldots,$$

$$P(t), P(t-1), \ldots).$$

The F, G, and H functions in the above equations can be arbitrary mappings but in the actual computer implementation are simple weighted sums. In order that a BCE communicate with its four neighbors (on a Cartesian grid), Kabrisky introduced coupling coefficients to make a BCE's actual input a weighted sum of its own input and that of its neighbors. Neighboring SF and SS values also enter into the calculation of $SF(t)$ in Equation (10.1). Kabrisky considered a plane of coupled BCE's to be capable of receiving a two-dimensional pattern of inputs and transmitting a version of this pattern altered on the basis of memory data. He sketched the ways in which stacks of BCE planes could "recognize" familiar patterns even when presented at different input regions (translation) or with differing sizes (scaling). Limited computing facilities unfortunately allowed Kabrisky to simulate only a single 10-by-10 plane of BCEs and test its performance on very simple patterns.

The BCE used in the computer implementation of Kabrisky's model is shown in block diagram form in Figure 10.1. Where numbers are shown in the boxes of this figure they are the actual values used for adjustable parameters in the model. Thus for the experiments Kabrisky reported, all coupling coefficients were fixed at 0.25 (after some preliminary experimentation). Not shown in the figure is the further flexibility of permitting coupling co-

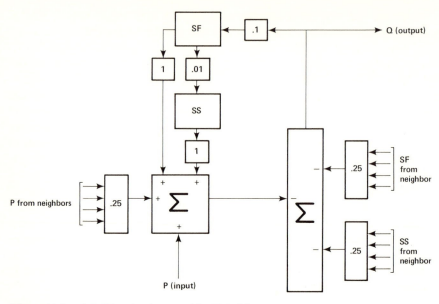

Figure 10.1.   A BCE as implemented by Kabrisky.

efficients from different neighbors to vary independently; this option was not used in the implementation.

A pattern is input to the 10-by-10 array of elements like that in Figure 10.1 by fixing a subset of P values, say in 3 adjacent rows of the array, at some large number like 50 while holding the rest at 0. Initial presentation of a pattern results in large (negative) Q values over the entire array. As the pattern is "learned" the outputs approach zero. After "teaching" the network a given pattern, Kabrisky would present others more or less closely related to it and examine the degree to which the test patterns were "recognized" (i.e., how small in magnitude were the average Q values they initially evoked).

The results of Kabrisky's experiments showed the expected better recognition of patterns which had suffered less translation or scaling from the original one. Before attaching too much significance to Kabrisky's pattern recognition algorithm, however, we should note that his results can be achieved with a much simpler strategy. An "algorithm" which simply counts the number of inputs that differ between the test pattern and the original pattern will virtually duplicate the differences in "recognizability" found by Kabrisky.

The above comment should not be taken as a fundamental criticism of Kabrisky's model. His proposal incorporated a number of still current ideas about brain organization and information processing, in a form very convenient for computer simulation. His actual implementation was just too limited to provide a test of the model's capacities. And as a pattern recognition device *per se*, the implementation could not compare in power or flexibility with systems designed specifically for such a task. We will be discussing such systems in Part III of this book.

10.2 Finley's cell assembly model

The title of Marion Finley's 1967 University of Michigan doctoral thesis says it all: "An Experimental Study of the Formation and Development of Hebbian Cell-Assemblies by Means of a Neural Network Simulation." We can clearly not appreciate Finley's model until we know what a "Hebbian cell assembly" is.

In 1949 the well known McGill psychologist D. O. Hebb published a theory about how the brain changes when new information is acquired. Hebb argued that learning caused the creation and strengthening of small networks of neurons tightly interconnected by strongly excitatory synapses. He called these networks *cell assemblies*. Hebb felt that such cell assemblies developed after many presentations of a given stimulus because the neural pathways activated by those presentations came to have "stronger" synaptic connections. Essentially, Hebb said that whenever one neuron frequently participated in causing the firing of a second neuron, then the synapse connecting the first neuron to the second would grow in effectiveness. We need not be concerned with the many ramifications and subsequent refinements of cell assembly theory, since Finley's model dealt primarily with the basic aspects just described.

Finley was actually not the first investigator to attempt simulation of cell assembly formation. He was in fact building on the earlier work of Rochester, Holland, Haibt, and Duda. Working with the relatively primitive computing equipment of the early 1950's, these investigators were able to demonstrate rudimentary cell-assembly-like properties in rather large networks of simulated neurons. Unfortunately, computing constraints precluded simulation of the neurons' individual spikes, requiring the adoption of a frequency characterization of neuronal behavior. With a larger and faster computer available, Finley undertook more refined, systematic, and extensive studies than were possible for his predecessors.

Finley's simulated neurons were affected by excitatory and inhibitory synaptic inputs, had thresholds and refractory periods, were subject to "fatigue" effects after concentrated activity, and could fire (or not) at each time step of the simulation. The behavior of a single neuron is summarized in Finley's "fundamental equation," which says that a neuron will fire at time $t + 1$ iff

$$R(t) + F(t) \leq \sum_i S_i(t)d_i(t) + I(t). \tag{10.2}$$

The left hand side of the above equation represents the neuron's threshold at time t; this is broken down into the threshold (R) based on short-term (refractory) effects and a fatigue factor (F) which can elevate the overall threshold after periods of sustained activity in the neuron. The right hand side of Equation (10.2) summarizes the inputs to the neuron at time t. $S_i(t)$ is the "weight" or value at time t of the synapse from neuron i to the neuron in question. The synapse value is 0 for no connection and positive or negative for excitatory or inhibitory connections. If the synapse carried a signal (was active) at time t, $d_i(t) = 1$; otherwise it is 0. $I(t)$ represents any "external" input (from the model's environment) the experimenter may wish to apply to this neuron at time t.

For maximum flexibility of simulation each component of Finley's fundamental equation is actually a function with several adjustable parameters. Without going into all the details, we can illustrate this idea with the *threshold function, V*, which maps the *recovery state, r*, of the neuron into threshold (R) values.

$R(t) = V(r(t))$, where $r(t)$: is 0, if the neuron fired at time t;
is $r(t-1) + 1$ if the neuron did not; and
never exceeds r_{max}.

The recovery state is thus just a count of the number of time steps that have elapsed since the neuron last fired (up to some maximum value, after which it no longer matters). A typical shape for the threshold "curve" (actually a table of discrete values) is shown in Figure 10.2. In addition to the shape of the curve itself, the experimenter may adjust the parameters r_a, the duration of the absolute refractory period, r_b, the end of the relative refractory period,

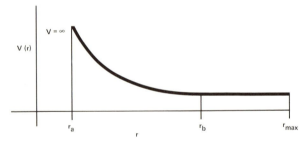

Figure 10.2.   A threshold curve in Finley's model.

and r_{max}. Some typical values used by Finley in his experiments were $r_a = 3$, $r_b = 16$, and $r_{max} = 64$. Similar functions and parameters were adjustable in the relations governing changes in fatigue and synapse value. The latter was structured to reflect Hebb's theory of enhancement of synapse effectiveness with use.

Given a full set of parameter and functional specifications for his simulated neurons, Finley still had to connect them into a network with specified initial synapse values. Connections within a typical Finley network of several hundred neurons could be determined by one of two schemes. In the *uniform random* connection scheme, each pair of neurons participating in a synaptic connection was randomly selected, until some desired density of connections was reached (e.g., an average of 12 inputs per neuron). In the *distance biased* connection scheme, synapses were also randomly determined but were formed only with neurons in a region of the network physically close to the neuron receiving the input.

Before interesting experiments can be carried out with neural networks like Finley's, an extensive period of "parameter tuning" is usually necessary. The network's initial behavior typically either degenerates rapidly to no activity or begins to oscillate in wide, regular fluctuations of neuron firing. A considerable amount of Finley's early work was thus devoted to the design of networks which would display reasonably "steady state" behavior for long periods of time.

It is difficult to convey the massive scope of Finley's experimental program in a few sentences. He began with simple networks having uniform random connections and no external inputs, inhibitory synapses, or fatigue effects. By successively introducing additional features Finley demonstrated that stable and interesting network behavior required inhibition, fatigue, and distance-biased connectivity. Such results are particularly satisfying since physiological neural information processing does appear to make use of these features.

Finley then applied periodic external input stimulation to a carefully selected subset of neurons in the "tuned" network. After several thousand time steps of simulation, there arose small collections of neurons with mutually excitatory interconnections in which activity would "cycle" around closed circuits. Such cycles may be regarded as essentially equivalent to Hebbian cell assemblies. In his last series of experiments, Finley was able to demonstrate partial formation of a second "cell assembly" in response to a second periodic stimulus which alternated with the first and was applied to a different set of input neurons. And there was some suggestion of the inhibitory interrelations between the two assemblies that are predicted by Hebb's theory.

Constraints on time and computer resources forced Finley to curtail his experiments earlier than he would have liked. Nevertheless his simulation studies did demonstrate the viability of a number of major features of cell-assembly theory.

10.3 Weinberg's *E. coli* model

For his doctoral thesis, also at the University of Michigan, Roger Weinberg undertook the imposing task of simulating a complete living cell at a reasonable level of detail. This research has subsequently been extended along a number of lines by Weinberg and several co-investigators.

The bacterium *E. coli* was selected for simulation because of its relative simplicity and the large amounts of laboratory data available to serve as a check on the simulation. At the outset Weinberg established two categories of success criteria for his simulation. First the model should be *realistic*. Simulation data should accurately reflect *E. coli*'s growth rates in a number of environments. And, ideally, the model should be able to predict the organism's behavior in new environments, to generate data which could be verified in the laboratory. Secondly the model should be *useful*. Simulation results should assist in answering current biological questions and should be able to provide information about aspects of *E. coli* behavior difficult to study in the laboratory.

Despite the impressive speed and capacity of modern computers, it was clearly not possible for Weinberg to simulate individually each of the more than 3,000 types of molecules found in *E. coli*. He therefore assigned molecules to about 20 *chemical pools* which were interconnected by a metabolic network. The 12 primary chemical pools and the flows of materials among them are shown in Figure 10.3. Additional pools not shown arose from the subdivision of both the protein and *m*-RNA pools into enzyme groups

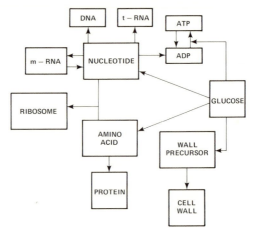

Figure 10.3. The major chemical pools in Weinberg's model.

responsible for specific classes of reactions, such as all enzymes responsible for production of amino acids from carbohydrate (glucose) precursors.

To model the cell's life cycle the simulation progresses through a series of uniform time steps, each corresponding to about one second of actual time. During each time step the contents of all the chemical pools are updated in accordance with a series of equations. Thus the amount of new DNA created in a given time step is a function of the supply of available nucleotides, ATP, and enzymes. In this form the model simulates fairly well the passive growth of an *E. coli* cell as it acquires nutrients from the (simulated) environment.

But we know that *E. coli* is a highly adaptive cell which makes just the necessary amounts of various substances and is able to adjust its metabolism to environments with different supplies of raw materials (see Section 6.4). To endow his simulated cell with adaptive behavior Weinberg incorporated allosteric (end-product) inhibition and enzyme repression. We also know that an *E. coli* cell does not grow forever but eventually divides. Weinberg's model included a mechanism for simulating the DNA replication that precedes mitosis.

To test the performance of his model, Weinberg chose three simulated environments. In the *minimal medium* cells were supplied only with glucose, oxygen, and a few essential salts and minerals. In the *enriched* environment cells were also provided with a supply of amino acids, making synthesis of these compounds unnecessary. In the *broth* environment there was the further addition of nucleosides, providing the cells with ready-made building blocks for nucleic acids. If the adaptive mechanisms functioned properly, cells in the richer environments would not waste metabolic energy synthesizing substances available in the environment, and would therefore grow faster.

Weinberg's experimental results are impressive. In all three environments he obtained good agreement with laboratory data for the growth rates of the cell as a whole and of the individual chemical pools. He also accurately simulated the expected times to cell division for the three environments (50, 28, and 25 minutes respectively). And adjustment of enzyme function by allosteric inhibition corresponded closely to laboratory measurements.

In closing this chapter we should briefly mention two extensions of Weinberg's original single-cell model to populations of *E. coli*. The first extension was a model of the behavior of a growing colony of cells. The reader familiar with Chapter 5 of this book will appreciate the fact that this colony model was derived by using Weinberg's program as the state transition function in a general purpose cell space simulation system, also developed at Michigan. Preliminary experimental results with this implementation suggested the possibility of modeling differences between normal, controlled colony growth and cancer-like explosion of cell numbers.

The other extension of the original model was to evolving populations of *E. coli* cells. By representing enzyme functions as "genes" on a "chromosome" the investigators could simulate the effects of various genetic operators (mutation, recombination, and the like) on the biological fitness ("adaptedness") of successive generations of interbreeding *E. coli* cells. Preliminary results from this work verified the importance of recombination to the evolutionary process and demonstrated the potential for remarkable increases in the average population fitness after relatively small numbers of generations.

Bibliography

Brender, Ronald R. *A Programming System for the Simulation of Cellular Spaces.* Technical Report, Department of Computer and Communication Sciences, University of Michigan, Ann Arbor, January, 1970.
  The general-purpose package mentioned in Section 10.3.

Finley, Marion. *An Experimental Study of the Formation and Development of Hebbian*

Cell-Assemblies by Means of a Neural Network Simulation. Technical Report 08333-1-T, Department of Communication Sciences, University of Michigan, Ann Arbor, March, 1967.
His doctoral thesis.

Goodman, E. D., Weinberg, R., and Laing, R. A. "A cell space embedding of simulated living cells." *Bio-Medical Computing, 2,* 1971, pp. 121–136.
Weinberg's model applied to a colony of cells.

Hebb, D. O. *The Organization of Behavior.* Wiley, 1949.
The original proposal of cell-assembly theory.

Kabrisky, Matthew. *A Proposed Model for Visual Information Processing in the Human Brain.* University of Illinois Press, 1966.
A slight revision of his doctoral thesis.

Rochester, N., Holland, J. H., Haibt, L. H., and Duda, W. L. "Tests on a cell-assembly theory of the action of the brain using a large digital computer." *IRE Transactions on Information Theory, IT-2,* 1956, pp. 80–93.
The early work on cell-assembly models.

Weinberg, R., and Berkus, M. "Computer simulation of a living cell." *Bio-Medical Computing, 2,* 1971, pp. 95–120 (Part I), 167–188 (Part II).
The original Weinberg model plus some additional discussion.

Weinberg, Roger, Flanigan, Larry K., and Laing, Richard A. *Computer Simulation of a Primitive, Evolving Eco-System.* Technical Report 03296-6-T, Department of Computer and Communication Sciences, University of Michigan, Ann Arbor, September, 1970.
Weinberg's model used in a simulation of evolutionary adaptation.

Zeigler, Bernard P., and Weinberg, Roger. "System theoretic analysis of models: Computer simulation of a living cell." *Journal of Theoretical Biology, 29,* 1970, pp. 35–56.
A study in the proper ways to simplify natural systems for tractable computer simulation.

Exercises

10.1. Discuss the common features and major differences in the approaches to simulation of natural systems adopted by each of the investigators discussed in this chapter.

10.2. Making as many simplifying assumptions as possible, program a small scale simulation of a neural network, using a language and machine of your choice.

Part III
Artificial intelligence

Marvin Minsky of MIT's Artificial Intelligence Project has defined his subject as "the science of making machines do things that would require intelligence if done by men." The next several chapters explore a variety of research efforts devoted to achieving this goal. Clearly if a machine is to behave in an intelligent manner it must be able to observe and comprehend its environment. So we begin with the subject of pattern recognition and consider examples of both pattern classification and the more complex problem of scene analysis.

Games have long been a natural domain for artificial intelligence research. After developing some of the formalisms required to program game playing in a computer we study an early but very successful checker playing program. We also talk about programming the much harder game of chess and analyze some of the reasons why there still does not exist a computer program which plays master-level chess.

Since logic is one of a computer's inherent strong points, it should be possible to develop an effective theorem proving program. We first explore the logical systems in which theorem proving researchers work, then examine an early theorem prover for the propositional calculus. In the more powerful system of the predicate calculus a great deal of work has been done with a recently discovered rule of inference called the resolution principle. We will discover that this principle, although not particularly easy for people to work with, offers perhaps the best hope for future theorem proving programs.

Game playing and theorem proving are special kinds of problem solving. In Chapter 14 we examine approaches to generalized problem solving by computer. After looking at suitable problem representations we discuss the well known General Problem Solver in some detail. Three other research efforts are considered more briefly.

The last chapter considers ways of using human language to communicate with machines. After a brief excursion into the domain of linguistic theory we look at the work of Quillian, in which linguistic and environmental knowledge is represented by semantic networks. Winograd's renowned natural language understanding program provides an example of the procedural approach to knowledge representation. We conclude with an examination of Schank's Conceptual Dependency theory of language processing.

As in previous parts of this book the survey of the next few chapters is far from complete. Actually we are treating selected subjects largely from one approach to artificial intelligence, heuristic programming. A heuristic is any strategem for improving the performance of an artificial intelligence program. The heuristic programming approach to artificial intelligence is perhaps the most popular and productive one today. It contrasts with another major approach, exemplified less often in the work we review, which has been called simulation of human thought. In this approach the aim is more to understand and use the features of human intelligence than to apply any technique which works. The dichotomy between these two schools of thought is not a sharp one. Yet a program which played chess much better than any human would be a triumph for heuristic programming but an inaccurate model for those concerned with simulating human thought.

Another sort of dichotomy in artificial intelligence research is between those who feel that systems should learn to behave intelligently and those who feel that intelligence should be programmed into the system in advance. This is somewhat related to the dichotomy in approach mentioned above, since those trying to simulate human thought might be more naturally concerned with the learning that appears to underlie much of human intelligence. Just as heuristic programming is the more popular approach today so are researchers generally not trying to build programs which learn. As they justifiably observe, how can learning be programmed until there is a better understanding of what is to be learned?

Nevertheless, since the focus of this book is adaptive systems—systems which somehow learn from experience—I have chosen to distort the picture of current artificial intelligence research somewhat by frequently selecting as examples systems which exhibit at least a primitive form of learning. Given the current deemphasis on learning, some of these examples are not the most recent work in the field. However, they often stand as landmarks which have yet to be surpassed in any important sense.

11
Pattern recognition

Humans and other animals survive in their complex and changing environments by using sophisticated sensory systems to detect, classify, and interpret patterns of input stimulation. For over two decades workers in artificial intelligence have been trying to approximate mechanically the performance of that ultimate in biological pattern recognizers, human vision. (We will not consider equally important but less numerous efforts toward auditory pattern processing, such as mechanical speech recognition.) Despite this tremendous research investment computers still cannot "see" even a fraction as well as people. In this chapter we look at a few selected pieces of pattern recognition research in order to get an idea of what has been done and how much remains to be accomplished.

It will be useful if we assign pattern recognition efforts to three somewhat arbitrary (and overlapping) stages, as shown in Figure 11.1. In the first stage,

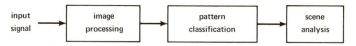

Figure 11.1.   Stages in pattern recognition.

image processing, the input signal is somehow preprocessed to make subsequent tasks easier. This preprocessing may take many forms, from sharpening of edges and elimination of "noise," to normalization of an image through the application of transformations which give it some standard position, orientation, and/or size. We will not have much more to say about image processing in this chapter, since most of the techniques involve solutions to relatively straightforward engineering problems rather than to the kinds of challenges usually considered to require artificial intelligence.

A processed image is suitable material for some sort of *pattern classi-*

fication scheme. A great number and variety of such schemes have been developed, all with the object of identifying or "naming" each input signal by grouping it with others which are somehow equivalent. More precisely, a pattern classification method attempts to formulate an exhaustive set of *equivalence classes* for all possible input stimuli. The classes may be preordained or left to the system to discover. Among the many uses of (visual) pattern classification are recognition of handwritten characters, fingerprints, chromosomes, and tracks in bubble-chamber photographs.

Pattern classification methods can be subdivided along several dimensions. Statistical techniques, which we will not discuss here, use the mathematics of decision theory. Another approach to which we give little attention is called *template matching*. In this method, a pattern to be classified is compared with a set of idealized prototypes (or templates) one for each possible class. The best match determines the classification of the pattern. Template matching is of limited usefulness, but is the basis for many successful optical character readers that work with small ranges of letter sizes and type fonts.

To be contrasted with template matching are the *feature detection* approaches. These methods take a number of "measures" on the input pattern and attempt to combine the resulting values to reach a decision. The features can be as simple as the presence or absence of light at a particular spot, or as complex as the orientations and curvatures of lines. The way in which the values of the features are combined may also be quite complex, although a simple weighted sum of values has been widely used. Feature detection schemes may be subdivided into *sequential* and *parallel* approaches. Sequential methods use information from the evaluation of some features to decide which features to evaluate next. Although sequential methods are more powerful than parallel ones, they are also sufficiently more complex to have been used much less. Discussion of sequential feature detection methods of pattern classification is beyond the scope of this book.

As the term suggests, parallel feature detection methods evaluate the features "all at once." (When this parallel computation is simulated on a serial computer, no feature value is allowed to influence any subsequent evaluations.) Parallel (and, for that matter, sequential) feature detection systems need not employ the same combination of features forever. Some systems can be "trained" through initial presentation of a paradigmatic set of patterns; other systems are programmed to "learn" automatically from experience with correct and incorrect classifications. In either case, the features used and their relative importance ("weights") will change with time.

The first two sections of this chapter will be devoted to parallel feature detection, with an emphasis on approaches capable of learning. In Section 11.1 we will look at some of the earliest ideas and a recent theoretical assessment of the limitations of such systems. In Section 11.2 we will consider one quite successful feature detection program in some detail.

In the last section we turn our attention to the final stage of Figure 11.1, *scene analysis.* Here the goals are much more ambitious, and the problems much more formidable, than in the classification of isolated figures. Effective analysis of complex scenes requires not only identification of the component objects but also a description of how the objects interrelate and combine into larger structures. One recently popular approach to scene analysis tried to apply techniques similar to those used in describing the structure of sentences. These "picture grammars" have proved of limited usefulness outside of specialized applications and will not be considered here. We will consider two interrelated scene analysis sytems which appeared around 1970 and might be said to have ushered in the "modern approach" to this complex task.

To reinforce the arbitrariness of Figure 11.1 we should emphasize that scene analysis can interact with, or even precede, pattern classification. In the analysis of aerial photos, for example, scene analysis techniques may be used to locate relevant objects for subsequent classification.

11.1 Perceptrons

In the late 1950's Frank Rosenblatt of Cornell University coined the term "perceptron" for a class of parallel feature detection systems with learning capabilities. Before considering the perceptron paradigm, however, we should mention a more general abstract model which anticipated many features of perceptrons. This model, called "pandemonium," was developed by Oliver Selfridge at MIT.

Pandemonium consists of a hierarchy of what Selfridge called "demons." At the top of the hierarchy sits a "decision demon," who listens to the "cognitive demons," one for each pattern class, at the next level down. A cognitive demon shouts the name of its class with a degree of loudness proportional to the certainty of the classification. The decision demon awards the decision to whichever cognitive demon is shouting loudest. Cognitive demons get their information (indirectly) from "data demons" at the bottom of the hierarchy. The data demons encode the input and pass it along to one or more layers of "computational demons," which do the real work of detecting and combining features. To improve pandemonium's performance Selfridge suggested several schemes for modifying the computational demons, so that weights of existing features could change and new features could be introduced.

We can illustrate the pandemonium model with a hypothetical system for recognizing (upper-case) letters. If the input were to come from something like a television camera, the data demons might simply digitize the image into a matrix of light intensity levels. The lower level computational demons (feature detectors) would each obtain data from one or more points in this matrix (e.g., the number of "bright" points in the ith column) and pass the values on to the higher level computational demons. These demons would determine weighted sums of subsets of features appropriate to each of the

26 cognitive demons. Then the cognitive demon for, say, the letter G would inspect these inputs for their net "G-ness" and pass on this information to the decision demon. The experimenter would tell the system whether each decision was correct. Performance could hence improve with time, first because the system would be constantly trying small variations in the feature weights and retaining the most successful combination. Also, those features which contributed least to correct decisions would be replaced with new features, which could be built from slight modifications or logical recombinations of existing useful features.

The above example forms a useful introduction to the basic ideas underlying perceptrons. To facilitate further discussion of the class of machines first devised by Rosenblatt, we now introduce some restrictions and some additional terminology. This formal definition of perceptrons will enable us to study the limitations of this feature detection paradigm.

Inputs to a perceptron will be "drawn" on an ordinary, finite two-dimensional plane of discrete points, called R. (R stands for "retina," in recognition of Rosenblatt's view that perceptrons were useful both as pattern classification devices and as models of biological pattern recognition.) A figure or picture on R is an assignment of binary values (0,1) to all the points in R. Alternatively, we may think of the figure as an identified subset of "dark" (value $= 1$) points. In the pandemonium analog, we would require the data demons to report one of just two conditions about each point in the input.

Computational demons in the perceptron model are called *predicates* since they function like the logical entities of the same name in the predicate calculus (to be discussed in Chapter 13). A predicate P applied to a figure X inspects some or all of the points in R to see whether the conditions of the predicate are met. The result is either $P(X) = 1$ (the predicate is "true" on X) or $P(X) = 0$ (the predicate is "false"). Predicates can test for conditions as simple as the presence of a 1 at a particular location in R, or as complicated as the presence of a particular type of figure in R (e.g., a circle). Any predicate which inspects less than the total number of points in R is called a *partial predicate*.

Predicates can be combined to give new predicates either by the normal rules of logic or in an arithmetic fashion. In the latter case we interpret 0 and 1 as numerical rather than logical quantities. A predicate P' is said to be *linear in the set of predicates* P_i, $i = 1, \ldots, n$, if P' is true only when some weighted sum of the P_i exceeds some fixed quantity T, called the *threshold*. That is,

$$P' = \begin{cases} 1 & \text{iff } \sum_{i=1}^{n} a_i P_i > T, \\ 0 & \text{otherwise.} \end{cases} \tag{11.1}$$

Note that the threshold is somewhat like a special purpose pandemonium decision demon. The *weights*, a_i, in Equation (11.1) may have negative as well as positive values.

A *perceptron* may now be defined as any device which can compute all predicates that are linear in some specified set of partial predicates. Thus any change in the set of predicates gives us a new perceptron, while the weights and threshold are adjustable parameters of a particular device. This definition is actually far too general to be of much interest. From the standpoint of practical pattern recognition we would like the basic predicates (feature detectors) to be somehow "easy to compute" and/or "localized." These notions can be formalized by specifying either the maximum *number* of points or the maximum *distance* between points that a predicate may inspect. Thus a perceptron for which none of the partial predicates looks at more than k points will be called a *k-order limited perceptron*. And a perceptron for which the points inspected by any partial predicate must all fall within a circle of specified diameter will be called a *diameter limited perceptron*.

The definitions just developed were actually taken not from Rosenblatt (who frequently worked with more complicated devices) but from an influential work published more than a decade after the invention of perceptrons, by Minsky and Papert of MIT. These investigators were interested in identifying the theoretical limitations on the kinds of geometrical figures which various types of simple perceptrons could classify. While not entirely discrediting the extensive experimental work with perceptrons that occurred during the 1960's, Minsky and Papert do believe that many vastly exaggerated claims about the pattern recognition and learning capabilities of perceptrons have emerged. In the balance of this section we will examine a few of Minsky and Papert's interesting and often surprising results.

We begin with some of the things which can and cannot be done by diameter limited perceptrons. Minsky and Papert have shown that diameter limited perceptrons can function quite well as template matching devices. By partitioning R into regions we can easily arrange to detect an exact match of an input against a particular pattern in a particular position. Yet this is not a particularly impressive or useful ability. On the negative side, it can be shown that no diameter limited perceptron can distinguish the class of figures each consisting of exactly one point anywhere on R.

As a last indication of the limitations of diameter limited perceptrons, let us consider whether they can recognize the class of *connected* figures, those figures which do not have isolated pieces. Minsky and Papert offer an elegant and simple demonstration that diameter limited perceptrons cannot distinguish connectivity. For a given maximum predicate diameter we generate four patterns, each several diameters in length, as shown in Figure 11.2. Note that patterns (b) and (c) are connected while (a) and (d) are not. We can then divide predicates into three types: type 1 predicates can "see" only the left ends of the patterns, type 2 only the right ends, and type 3 only the centers.

If we let P^1 stand for the weighted sum of all type 1 predicates, and so on,

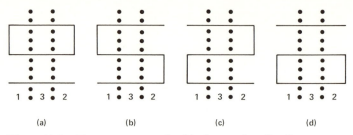

Figure 11.2. Four patterns, each with three regions for diameter limited predicates.

then the combined predicate for connectedness must have

$$P^1 + P^2 + P^3 - T > 0, \tag{11.2}$$

for connected patterns only. [The threshold T has been shifted to the left hand side of Equation (11.2).] Thus on Figure 11.2a the left hand side of Equation (11.2) must be nonpositive. Since only P^1 is affected by a change to Figure 11.2c, its contribution must increase enough to make the left hand side positive. Similarly, P^2 must so increase in going from Figure 11.2a to 11.2b. But *both* of these increases must occur for Figure 11.2d, making the sum even more positive on a pattern which is in fact disconnected. Note that P^3 remains constant across all four patterns. Thus if a diameter limited perceptron could distinguish Figures 11.2b and 11.2c as connected (but not so classify Figure 11.2a), it would necessarily also identify Figure 11.2d as connected. We may therefore conclude that diameter limited perceptrons cannot recognize connectivity.

The discriminative capacities of order limited perceptrons are somewhat more general. Instead of mere template matching, devices of order 6 or less can recognize a given figure anywhere on R, or even rotated 180° about an undetermined point. Convexity is a property which predicates of order 3 can easily be shown to recognize. A figure is convex (by definition) only when the midpoints of all lines connecting any two points in the figure also fall in the figure. If we examine all pairs of distinct points in R and find even one where a point "halfway" between two that are in the figure is not itself in the figure, then the figure fails to be convex. Clearly each predicate need inspect at most three points.

To understand the limitations on order limited perceptrons it is useful to introduce the notion of a *predicate of finite order*. The convexity predicate just discussed is of finite order because the maximum number of points inspected (by each of the primitive predicates of which it is composed) is bounded by a fixed quantity (in this case 3) no matter how large the plane R becomes. In other cases we may need to keep increasing the predicate order needed to distinguish a class of figures as the size of R increases. When the order is thus a function of the number of points in R, so that a nonfinite number of points would have to be inspected in a (hypothetical) infinite plane, we say the order is not finite.

One of Minsky and Papert's more startling results concerns logical combinations of predicates of finite order. The so-called "And/Or" theorem states that there exist predicates of order 1 whose conjunction and disjunction are not of finite order. Thus logical combinations of "easily discriminable" properties may not themselves be so. The parity predicate, which checks whether the number of points occupied by a pattern is odd or even, is another case of nonfinite order. In fact, it is necessary to inspect all the points in R with a single detector in order to determine parity, which clearly violates any notion of locality of operation. Finally, the connectedness property analyzed above for diameter limited perceptrons is not of finite order.

We should not leave the discussion of abstract perceptrons without mentioning learning. Minsky and Papert discuss the *perceptron convergence theorem* in some detail. This theorem states that, for a given set of (partial) predicates and an initially random set of weights, there exists an algorithm which can use information about correct and incorrect classifications to arrive (after a finite number of steps) at a set of weights for correctly performing any discrimination task, provided such a set of weights exists. The algorithm is remarkably simple. Whenever an incorrect classification is made, the weights of those predicates which "contributed" (had values of 1) are adjusted in the direction required to compensate for the error. We will see a rather complex version of this algorithm in the next section.

Although the convergence theorem makes the perceptron seem like an ideal learning machine, we must be cautious about such a conclusion for several reasons. First, convergence is not guaranteed when the classes of patterns are inherently "nonseparable" by the perceptron under consideration. Second, the theorem does not refer to the number of (partial) predicates, and hence weights, that may need adjusting after each error. Recall the "simple" convexity predicate mentioned above, which required inspection of every distinct pair of points in R. For an n by n plane, the number of weights to be adjusted could thus be on the order of n^4. Finally, the convergence theorem says nothing about the number of iterations (error based adjustment steps) required before the optimal set of weights is found. The time of convergence may be intolerably long.

11.2 A feature detection system

In this section we illustrate the use of perceptron like devices in solving practical pattern recognition problems. Rather than attempt any sort of survey of the many extant implementations, we will examine in detail one system, devised about 1960 by Leonard Uhr and Charles Vossler and described as "a pattern-recognition program that generates, evaluates, and adjusts its own operators."

In the operation of the Uhr–Vossler system, an unknown pattern is presented as a 20 by 20 binary matrix. If the pattern does not fill the matrix a rectangular mask is placed around the pattern (touching it on all four sides), so that "blank margin" areas are eliminated from subsequent processing. Next a set of 5 by 5 *operators* (feature detectors, diameter limited predicates) is applied to the pattern. These operators may contain any combination of 0's, 1's, and blanks. Each operator is translated across and down the pattern, one row or column at a time (so that the operator is eventually "centered" over every pattern cell). In each new position it is determined whether the pattern of 0's and 1's in the pattern *matches* the binary entries in the operator. Blanks in the operator signify that the corresponding position in the pattern is irrelevant. Figure 11.3 shows an operator of the sort which might be used to detect upper left corners; also shown are two examples of pattern regions where the operator would match. Note that cells outside the mask match if the operator is zero or blank at the corresponding position.

b	b	b	b	b		1	1	0	0	0					
b	1	1	1	b		1	1	1	1	1		1	1	1	1
b	1	0	b	b		0	1	0	0	0		1	0	0	0
b	1	b	0	b		0	1	0	0	0		1	1	0	1
b	b	b	b	b		1	1	0	0	0		0	0	0	0

(a)   (b)   (c)

Figure 11.3. (a) An Uhr–Vossler operator; (b), (c) two pieces of pattern with which it would match. Blanks in the operator are denoted "b"; the lines in (c) indicate the edge of the pattern.

After all of the matches of a particular operator with the input pattern have been found, four quantities are computed: (1) the total number of matches, (2) the average horizontal position of the matches, (3) the average vertical position of the matches, and (4) the average distance of a match from the center of the mask. Each of these quantities is scaled to a 3-bit value and retained for purposes we consider shortly.

Operators can originate from four sources. First, the experimenter can predetermine any number of operators which he thinks might be useful for the types of patterns being processed. Figure 11.3a is a typical example of a preprogrammed operator. Second, operators can be generated at random, subject perhaps to some constraint like a limitation on the total number of 1's. This method was not used in the experiments discussed here. Third, operators can be "extracted" from the input pattern itself. In this innovative and powerful method, a random 5 by 5 subset of the pattern is selected and (according to rules which need not concern us) blanks inserted for some of the binary entries. This last step generalizes the subpattern and reduces the precision required in matches. Fourth and finally, a new "combinatorial operator" can be produced by logical or arithmetic operations on corresponding measures of two existing operators. These combinatorial operators thus contribute a single value (instead of four) to the total description of the pattern.

In the early stages of an experiment nonpreprogrammed operators are generated with each new input until a preset total is reached. Since Uhr and Vossler typically used around 48 regular operators and an unspecified number of combinatorial operators, each input pattern generated a description consisting of a vector of around 200 3-bit characteristics. Stored in memory for each pattern class is a similar vector of characteristics, built from experience with recent examples of the pattern class. The input pattern is classified by computing a weighted average difference score against each pattern class vector and selecting the class with the lowest score.

Computation of the difference score is rather involved, but must be understood if we are to appreciate the Uhr–Vossler learning scheme. Three types of "amplifiers" or weights are involved. *Pattern amplifiers* consist of 3-bit weights particular to each characteristic of each pattern class. *General amplifiers* are 3-bit weights computed by averaging the pattern amplifiers across pattern classes. Finally there is an *average difference amplifier* for each pattern class. To compute a difference score the (absolute) difference between the pattern class characteristic and the input characteristic is multiplied first by the pattern amplifier and then by the general amplifier for that characteristic. The sum of these doubly weighted differences is then normalized through division by the sum of the products of the corresponding pattern and general amplifiers. Finally, this normalized weighted difference is multiplied by the average difference amplifier for the pattern class to produce the difference score.

It is interesting to note that all these operations could be collapsed into multiplication of the difference vector by a single weight vector for each pattern class, as long as all the amplifier values remained fixed. The reason for the confusing battery of amplifiers is that the different types are modified differently by the learning algorithm, which we now consider.

If the Uhr–Vossler system is to improve its performance its "trainer" must not only give feedback about right and wrong classifications but also identify the correct class when the system errs. Using this information, the program proceeds to modify pattern amplifiers for pattern classes "similar" to the correct one (i.e., where the difference scores were close to, or actually less than, the difference score which *should* have been smallest). Thus the system concentrates on reducing the tendency to confuse similar patterns. For a given similar pattern, each characteristic is compared with the corresponding characteristic in the correct pattern. If a decision based on this characteristic *alone* would have produced a correct classification, the corresponding pattern amplifiers are increased, giving more weight to this "discriminating" feature. If the classification would have been incorrect, the amplifiers are decreased. (Actually the correct pattern amplifiers are not changed unless its overall difference score equalled or exceeded the similar pattern's score. This arrangement changes an already good set of weights hardly at all, but drastically modifies a poor set during the course of processing several similar patterns.)

Once the pattern amplifiers have been adjusted, the stored list of characteristics for the pattern class of the type just processed is updated to reflect this new experience with a pattern of that class. The general amplifiers are then recomputed. Finally the average difference amplifiers are modified by decreasing the one for the correct class in proportion to the number of similar classes, and by increasing the ones for all similar classes.

Since characteristics which have been valuable in discriminating many patterns will have had their various pattern amplifiers augmented frequently, the associated general amplifier averages will be relatively large. This situation forms the basis for computing "success counts" that indicate the relative value of the various operators (averaged over their four characteristics). When its success count drops too low, an operator is replaced by a new one generated according to whatever scheme is currently in use. A new operator enters the stored pattern class vectors with characteristic values based on its application to the most recent example of each pattern type. Initially, all weights for the new operator are small, giving it a success count just sufficient to keep it around until it has a chance to "prove itself."

Having completed this rather sketchy account of the Uhr–Vossler system, we might well ask about the program's performance. We will actually consider the results of a revised program in which some of the flexibility of the system as described above was sacrificed to reduce computation time. In these results it is important to note the difference between "known" and "unknown" patterns. Performance data on known patterns are computed after one or more "training" passes through the set of inputs. Unknown patterns are from the same classes but have not been used in the learning phase.

The program was extensively tested on letters hand printed by different people. For a ten letter set containing four examples of each letter, 100% correct classification was achieved after two training passes, for both known and unknown sets of letters. With a full 26 letter alphabet about five passes through a threefold set of examples were required to achieve 100% performance on known letters and better than 90% on unknown ones.

The program's generality was demonstrated by its performance on line drawings of cartoon faces and simple objects (95% on known and 70% on unknown pictures), on segmented Arabic handwriting (60% and 55%), and on several other tasks. Of particular note was the program's performance on meaningless patterns, where it made considerably fewer errors than did human subjects in an experiment where they had to classify the same patterns. This result suggests that an important component of human pattern classification is the extensive experience we have with the familiar shapes of our environment.

In sum, the Uhr–Vossler feature detection scheme for pattern classification introduced a number of important ideas in the design of perceptron like devices. Its learning algorithm, though perhaps unnecessarily involved, demonstrated the importance of rewarding successful components of systems.

And its performance record still serves as a benchmark for those who would classify isolated and relatively simple patterns. Unfortunately, most "real world" vision tasks do not involve simple, isolated patterns. In the next section we examine two programs which attempt to work with somewhat more natural visual environments.

11.3 Scene analysis

In the late 1960's Adolfo Guzman of MIT devised a program called SEE which analyzes complex groupings of objects. Input to SEE is a coded description of a line drawing representing a collection of convex polyhedral objects (cubes, wedges, pyramids, and so on). SEE uses information from the vertices where lines meet in the drawing to identify the closed regions and the objects to which they belong. A remarkable thing about SEE is that it contains no knowledge of the type of objects it may encounter. The program demonstrates how far it is possible to proceed in scene analysis without a "world model."

SEE is initially presented with a specially coded compact representation of a scene. This information is immediately transformed into the internal representation SEE works with, which contains the following information: (1) an unordered list of (numbered) regions and, for each region, counter-clockwise ordered lists of all neighboring regions, all surrounding vertices, and alternating neighbors and vertices; (2) an unordered list of (lettered) vertices and, for each vertex, its type (see below), position (x and y co-ordinates), and counterclockwise ordered lists of connected vertices, impinging regions, and alternating regions and vertices; and (3) a designation of one or more regions as the background of the scene and not part of any object.

The eight types of vertices with which SEE works are shown in Figure 11.4. The relative angles of the impinging lines can vary considerably in most cases. In order to assign the regions to objects, SEE tries to find evidence which justifies linking regions together. These links may be "strong" or "weak." Some strong links that may often be inferred directly from the vertex type are shown as arcs connecting regions in the vertices of Figure 11.4. Other, more complex, strong links depend on configurations of vertices, such as the case of "matching T" vertices in which the stems are collinear and the tops of the T's face each other. Such a situation is considered strong evidence that an object between the T's is occluding an edge of another object behind it. Weak links arise from far fewer configurations than strong links, and are typically associated with potential "leg" like structures for some kinds of ARROW type vertices.

Guzman calls groups of one or more regions *nuclei*. His merging algorithm attempts to reduce the number of nuclei required to cover all (nonback-ground) regions to one nucleus per object. Merging of nuclei proceeds in three steps: (1) any two nuclei connected by two or more strong links are

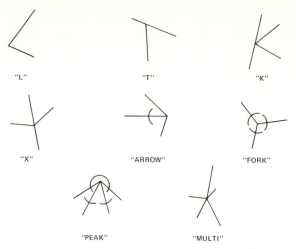

Figure 11.4.   Vertex types used by SEE. "ARROW,"
"FORK," and "PEAK" produce the indicated
strong links.

merged into a single nucleus; (2) when (1) can no longer be applied, any pair of nuclei connected by one strong and one weak link are merged (and (1) is then reapplied if possible); (3) when (1) and (2) can no longer be applied any remaining nucleus consisting of a single region having only one strong link (and no weak ones) is merged with the nucleus to which it is linked. When these surprisingly simple rules have been applied to their fullest extent, SEE usually produces a correct list of objects and their component regions, even for quite complex inputs.

Figure 11.5 illustrates the linking and merging process for a simple example. The scene has 9 regions (number 1 is the background and will not be linked to any others) and 15 vertices. All the strong links shown in Figure 11.5b are of the sorts given in Figure 11.4 except for the matching T situation that links regions 5 and 8 through vertices H and J. There is also a weak ("leg") link between regions 8 and 9, which is based on the fact that lines KM and GD are parallel.

In Figure 11.5c, merge step (1) has been applied to yield four nuclei. Merge step (2) then combines regions 8 and 9 (Figure 11.5d). Finally (Figure 11.5e) merge step (3) is applied to combine region 5 with the 8–9 nucleus. Note that the single remaining strong link satisfies no merge prerequisites. SEE can now report that the scene consists of three objects with regions 2–3–4, 6–7, and 5–8–9.

Although Guzman has shown similar correct analyses of scenes with nearly 50 regions, it should be kept in mind that his approach is limited to well-defined artificial "blocks world" scenes and would fail upon introduction of noise, shadows, textures, and/or curved lines. Guzman and others have since offered some partial solutions to these kinds of difficulties.

Since Guzman's program merely identifies objects without any cog-

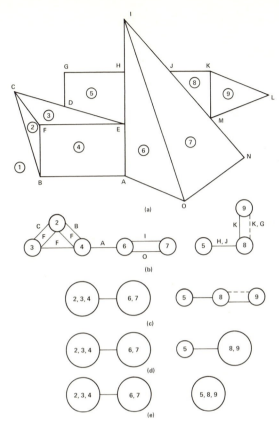

Figure 11.5.   (a) A simple scene; (b) its links; and
(c)–(e) the sequence of region merges done by SEE.

nizance of their identities or functions, it was intended to be used as a "front end" for a more sophisticated scene understanding system. In his 1970 doctoral thesis at MIT, Patrick Winston developed just such a system. As his title, "Learning Structural Descriptions from Examples," suggests, Winston's program can use information gained from experience with (correct and incorrect) instances of structural concepts.

Winston's system accepts as input a Guzman-type output in which the various component objects in the scene have been found. The program is then capable of recognizing the identity of various types of blocks, such as "bricks" and "wedges." Characteristics and relative positions of blocks (and groups of blocks) in a scene are described in terms of relations like "has property of," "one part is," "a kind of," "in front of," "right of," and "supports." Winston's program represents a scene as a network or *description graph* of object nodes and relational connections. This description graph notation has a powerful self-applicability feature, allowing representation not only of simple scenes and sets of scenes but also of relations

141

and comparisons between scenes and even between description graphs themselves.

To illustrate these ideas let us consider Winston's own favorite example, the definition of the general concept or *model* of an "arch." The network describing the "arch" model notes that the scene has three components (*A*, *B*, *C*) of which two (*B* and *C*) are a "kind of" brick and are "standing" with *B* to the "left of" *C*. Further, *B* and *C* "must not abut" each other and must both "support" *A*, which may itself be any "kind of" object. Similar networks can be used to describe other concepts, like "house," "table," and "tent."

As already suggested, the impressive thing about Winston's system is not so much the representational networks themselves as the fact that the system can generate such descriptions from examples. The program learns best from a reasonably skilled trainer who can present a series of examples and counterexamples of the concept to be learned. Winston emphasizes the importance of the "near miss" example. Noninstances of the concept should differ in only small ways from true instances, so the system can easily identify the incorrect features and incorporate appropriate restrictions in the model.

Each alteration of the model is based on a *comparison network* which describes the similarities and differences between the model and the current example. This network is used to modify the model by adding or relaxing restrictions and by removing incorrect or reinforcing correct features. For the fairly simple "blocks world" instances Winston describes, his program learns quite effectively and rapidly.

Bibliography

Guzman, Adolfo. "Decomposition of a visual scene into three-dimensional bodies." *Proceedings of the Fall Joint Computer Conference, 1968* (AFIPS Conference Proceedings, *33*, Part 1), pp. 291–304. Thompson Book Co., 1968.
  A compact and lucid presentation of SEE.

Grasselli, A. (ed.). *Automatic Interpretation and Classification of Images.* Academic Press, 1969.
  An extensive collection of varied and important contributions from the 1960's. Reprints the Guzman paper listed above.

Minsky, Marvin, and Papert, Seymour. *Perceptrons: An Introduction to Computational Geometry.* MIT Press, 1969.
  The basic work on the capabilities of this class of devices.

Nilsson, Nils J. *Learning Machines.* McGraw-Hill, 1965.
  A short and now classic treatment of trainable pattern classifiers, presenting convergence methods and results for a variety of machines.

Hunt, Earl B. *Artificial Intelligence.* Academic Press, 1975.
  A recent comprehensive text with a major section on pattern recognition. See especially Chapters V (Perceptrons), VII (Grammatical Pattern Classification), VIII (Feature Extraction), and XIII (Computer Perception).

Jackson, Philip C. *Introduction to Artificial Intelligence.* Petrocelli Books, 1974.
   Another recent text. Treatment of pattern recognition is limited to scene analysis systems.

Rosenblatt, Frank. *Principles of Neurodynamics.* Spartan Books, 1962.
   The major work by the "inventor" of perceptrons.

Selfridge, Oliver G. "Pandemonium: A paradigm for learning." In *Mechanization of Thought Processes*, HMSO, 1959. Reprinted in the Uhr collection below.
   A concise description of the pandemonium model.

Uhr, Leonard (ed.). *Pattern Recognition.* Wiley, 1966.
   A valuable compendium of early papers on all aspects of the subject: philosophical, experimental, physiological, and computer oriented.

Uhr, Leonard, and Vossler, Charles. "A pattern-recognition program that generates, evaluates, and adjusts its own operators." *Proceedings of the Western Joint Computer Conference*, 1961. Reprinted in the Uhr collection above.
   The original paper on the Uhr–Vossler system.

Winston, Patrick (ed.). *The Psychology of Computer Vision.* McGraw-Hill, 1975.
   A collection of important recent works from MIT on scene analysis and understanding, including Winston's own thesis.

Exercises

11.1. Indicate precisely the restrictions that must be placed on the general pandemonium paradigm to make it equivalent to (a) an order limited and (b) a diameter limited perceptron.

11.2. As presented in Section 11.1, a perceptron can distinguish between just two classes of inputs. How could the model be extended to deal with many classes?

11.3. An *area limited* figure is one which occupies at least (or equivalently, at most) k points on R. It is easy to show that a perceptron of order 1 (or a diameter limited perceptron of diameter 1) can recognize area limited figures for any fixed k. Do so. It is harder to show that a perceptron of order 2 can recognize figures occupying *exactly* k points. [*Hint:* you will need to use all single points and all distinct pairs of points.] Do any results stated in the chapter suggest that diameter limited perceptrons *cannot* recognize figures of exact area?

11.4. For the following Uhr–Vossler operators

1	0	b	b	b		1	0	b	b	b		0	b	1	b	0
0	1	0	b	b		1	0	b	b	b		0	b	1	b	0
b	0	1	0	b		1	1	1	b	b		0	b	b	b	0
b	b	0	1	0		1	0	b	b	b		0	b	b	b	0
b	b	b	0	1		1	0	b	b	b		0	0	0	0	0
	(a)						(b)						(c)			

find all the matches to the input shown below.

```
1 1 1 1 1 1 0 0 0
1 0 0 0 0 0 1 0 0
1 0 0 0 0 0 0 1 0
1 0 0 0 0 0 1 0 0
1 1 1 1 1 1 0 0 0
1 0 0 0 1 0 0 0 0
1 0 0 0 0 1 0 0 0
1 0 0 0 0 0 1 0 0
1 0 0 0 0 0 0 1 0
1 0 0 0 0 0 0 0 1
```

11.5. Use Guzman's merging algorithm to try to identify the objects shown in the scenes of Figure 11.6. (*Note*: the analyses do not require the use of weak link information.)

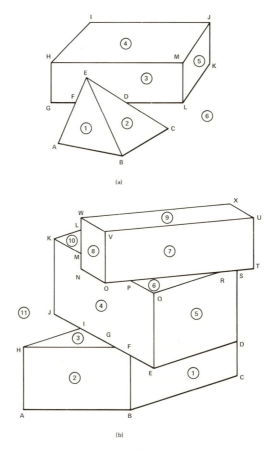

Figure 11.6.   Scenes for Exercise 11.5.

Note: The following exercises assume familiarity with Parts I and II of this book.

11.6. Compare the design of a perceptron with that of (a) a McCulloch–Pitts neuron and (b) a biological neuron.

11.7. Discuss any fundamental similarities and differences between the human visual system and (a) perceptrons in general; (b) the Uhr–Vossler system in particular.

12
Game playing

Game playing programs have long been a popular area of artificial intelligence research, for a variety of reasons. First of all there is usually no argument that the ability to play even a simple game represents a form of intelligent behavior. Second, games are usually fairly easy to implement on a computer because they are already defined in a formal, rule bound manner. Third, games may be arbitrarily complex, ranging from the triviality of tic-tac-toe to the sophistication of master level chess. Fourth, many games can be considered to represent models of real world situations, as shown by the business and war games used in social science research (and for entertainment). Finally, games are a convenient medium in which to study methods of search which are fundamentally important to many areas of artificial intelligence research.

It should be emphasized that not all kinds of games have been of interest in artificial intelligence. Most programs play what game theorists refer to as "two-person zero-sum games." Thus the computer usually interacts with one other player, the opponent (although some work has been done on games of more than two persons, like bridge). The phrase "zero-sum" describes games in which the interests of the players are exactly opposed. One player's loss is always the other player's gain (the two values sum to zero).

The restriction to two-person zero-sum games is not particularly limiting, however, as there are a great variety of such games. Computers have been programmed to play tic-tac-toe (frequently in three dimensions), nim, and blackjack. Especially popular, both because of their challenging complexity and the relative ease of storing positions within the computer, have been board games, like go, checkers, and chess. These last two games will be of primary concern in this chapter. In Section 12.2 we will be examining in some detail a checker playing program famed for its ability to beat excellent human players. In Section 12.3 we will discuss approaches to computerized chess and attempt to identify some of the obstacles which have prevented the development of a program of better than weak tournament-player caliber. Before looking at particular games, however, we first examine some aspects of representation and search common to computer programs for most games.

12.1 Game trees

A *tree* is an abstract structure consisting of *nodes* and *branches*. Each node except the top one, called the *root*, is connected by a branch to exactly one node above it. (Since trees are usually drawn upside down they look more like a root system than a branch system.) If we call the root node level 0, the nodes just below it level 1, and so on, then the *successors* of a node at level n are the level $n + 1$ nodes connected to it by branches. A node without successors, which may occur at any level, is called a *terminal* node.

In the representation of games each node in a tree corresponds to one possible state of affairs or position in the game, while each branch corresponds to a legal move by one of the players. In chess for example the root node is the arrangement of pieces on the board before either player has moved. There are 20 level 1 nodes corresponding to White's possible opening moves, and 400 level 2 nodes since Black has 20 possible replies for each of White's first moves. A particular board configuration or position will be represented at as many different nodes in the tree as there are distinct move sequences leading to it.

Although it is possible to represent some games *explicitly* in terms of their complete trees, such is not the case for most interesting games. In chess for example, it has been estimated that the complete game tree contains on the order of 10^{120} nodes. This figure obviously not only precludes storage of the tree in any foreseeable computer memory but also rules out systematic exploration of the tree in any remotely reasonable amount of time. It is this property of complex games, that we cannot "see to the end" until it is virtually upon us, that makes them interesting to people and a challenge to artificial intelligence.

The alternative to an explicit game tree is an *implicit* one, stored as a set of rules or *generation procedure* allowing the production of all successors of a given node. The game playing program can then make explicit manageable and pertinent portions of the tree in order to decide its next move. When such explicit tree fragments are to be produced we require not only a generation procedure but also one or more *termination criteria* which tell us when we have generated enough nodes. A frequently used termination criterion is the number of levels or *depth* to which the explicit tree is to be generated. Another case when tree expansion must terminate is at the end of the game. (Some very good game playing programs have been written which did not detect all "game over" situations. The threefold-repetition-of-moves draw in chess is particularly easy to overlook.)

Among a variety of potential generation procedures the two almost universally employed are *breadth first* and *depth first* generation. As the names suggest, breadth first generation produces all the successors of nodes at the current level (usually in a fixed order, like left-to-right, for each node) before expanding the tree any deeper. Depth first generation produces a designated (e.g., leftmost) successor of the root, then the designated successor of that successor, and so on. When a termination criterion is satisfied the procedure backs up to the next higher node which has not had all its successors generated, generates the next successor, and again carries through until termination. Figure 12.1 shows a small tree with the breadth first node generation sequence in numerical order and the depth first sequence in alphabetical order.

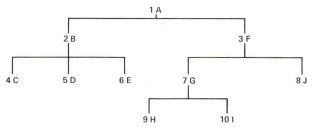

Figure 12.1. Breadth first (numbers) and depth first (letters) generation sequences.

Generation procedures and termination criteria are only the first two components of an effective *search procedure* for game trees. Clearly we also require some way of comparing nodes in order to choose positions which are favorable. Such comparisons are made by an *evaluation function*. These kinds of functions usually compute some *weighted* combination of *features* (the terminological similarity to pattern classification is not coincidental) like piece advantage, potential captures, and mobility. An evaluation function which does not accurately reflect the player's standing in the game will obviously undermine any game playing program, no matter how effectively it searches the tree. In most cases, however, there is no known procedure for producing an optimal evaluation function, a situation which has always plagued game playing efforts.

Given a suboptimal function, evaluation is usually improved somewhat if the function is applied to positions as far in the future as possible. The current move can then be made with some confidence in its consequences several moves down the tree. Most game playing programs therefore use some sort of *backing up* procedure which computes the value of the current position on the basis of values of nodes further down the tree. The most common such method is the *minimax* backing up procedure. Viewed from the standpoint of the player called MAX (for whom high values are advantageous), this procedure assumes that MIN (the opponent, who seeks low values) will select alternatives which minimize MAX's possible gains.

Correspondingly, MAX will choose moves which maximize his own possible gains.

Figure 12.2 shows a hypothetical explicit game tree fragment which has been generated to a depth of three levels (node letters show the depth first sequence). The bottom level nodes have all been assigned values (shown in parentheses after node letters) by some evaluation function. Values for the intervening nodes (shown in parentheses next to node letters) have been filled in by the minimax backing up procedure. Thus in going from level 3 back to level 2 (and from level 1 back to level 0), it is assumed that MAX will always choose the alternative giving the largest value. But in backing up from level 2 to level 1 MIN is moving and will attempt to minimize MAX's gain. The result of the backing up indicates that MAX should now move to the node S, assuring him a value of at least 10 three levels later. When com-

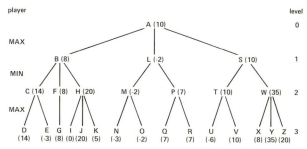

Figure 12.2. Fragment of a game tree showing minimax backing up.

bined with a depth first generation procedure, the minimax method yields a search procedure known as the *depth first minimax procedure*.

We have now seen all the essential components of a search procedure: generation procedure, termination criteria, evaluation function, and backing up procedure. But there are a number of refinements to game tree search which can often considerably reduce the effort involved. The most important refinement is the *alpha-beta* procedure. To introduce this procedure, consider what happens on evaluation of node J in Figure 12.2. We know MIN will choose the smallest value from C, F, and H if he has to move from B. And we know F has value 8. When we find a value of 20 for J we know H will have at least this value backed up, since we back up maxima for MAX's move. Therefore we need not look at node K. If its value is smaller than 20 it will not affect H; if it is larger, H will be an even more unlikely choice for MIN. So we can effectively rule H out of consideration (and not even bother to back up a value to it) once we find the value of J to be greater than 8. The quantity 8 is the value of *beta*.

In general, when backing up maximal values, beta is the smallest such maximum yet encountered among the descendents of a given node at the next higher level. When a lower level node (like J) allows us to rule out further consideration of a higher level node (like H), we say that a *beta cutoff* has been encountered. Another beta cutoff occurs in Figure 12.2 at node *Y*, when the value of 35 exceeds the beta value of 10.

Alpha is defined, in a manner analogous to beta, as the largest minimum yet encountered in a subtree when backing up minima for MIN's move. Clearly MAX will not move so as to achieve a smaller backed up value. One *alpha cutoff* occurs in Figure 12.2. When alpha is 8 (based on *B*) the *M* value of -2 indicates that it is pointless to evaluate further successors of *L*, since it will be at least that small and thus never chosen by MAX. Although the savings from the use of the alpha-beta procedure may seem trivial in this example, they can be considerable in the typical case where each node may have dozens of successors.

The number of alpha and beta cutoffs found in searching a tree can be increased by exploring the best moves first. This observation has led to a refinement of the alpha-beta technique called *plausibility ordering*. In this method the first level nodes are effectively rearranged so that the depth first search examines the most promising positions first. In order to rank the first order nodes in rough order of plausibility, some information is needed. This information may be obtained by simply applying the evaluation function at that level, without any backing up of values. In general, a *shallow search* may be carried out, with values backed up from some fraction of the depth used for the actual minimax values.

The methods so far described introduce no additional risk to the basic method of depth first minimax search. If the evaluation function is sufficiently accurate, and if the opponent always chooses his best move (both of which assumptions underlie the basic method), shallow search based plausibility ordered alpha-beta searches will produce the same move selections as the unrefined method. Additional refinements (heuristics) have been proposed which "prune" the tree by failing to explore nodes which are *unlikely* to contain the optimal alternatives, thus running some risk of missing the best move.

The forward pruning techniques we consider are based on the results of a shallow search at successive levels of the tree. In *n-best forward pruning* only the *n* most likely successors are explored at each level. In *tapered forward pruning* the value of *n* is decreased as the depth of search increases, leading to the greatest elimination of nodes where they are most numerous. Finally, there is *convergence forward pruning* which keeps running track of the current alpha and beta values in a subtree. When the difference between these values becomes small (the largest minimum is close to the smallest maximum), exploration may be terminated on the assumption that there is little further information to be gained from the subtree.

12.2 The Samuel checker player

In this section we examine rather carefully a checker playing program which A. L. Samuel first described in 1959 and substantially revised in 1967.

Samuel has emphasized that he was using the game of checkers to explore general problems of effective machine learning. Yet his work remains not only an outstanding example of a learning system but also probably the most successful game playing program yet devised. We will begin with a complete description of the 1959 version, then consider the major changes and improvements reported in 1967.

Samuel originally employed a standard depth first minimax search procedure. His termination criteria were fairly involved. First, the entire tree is explored to a depth of three levels. Further subtrees are then generated if the next move is a jump, the last move was a jump, or an exchange is possible. Further and more restrictive conditions permit expansion to a maximum depth of 20 levels. This principle of terminating expansion of subtrees when no "interesting" activity arises, at so-called "dead" positions, is an important feature of many game playing programs. Another consideration in expansion of checker trees is the fact that jumps are mandatory and hence considerably narrow the number of possible successors along such paths.

Samuel's evaluation function was a linear combination of weighted numerical scoring parameters. Some 40 such parameters were available, having been intuitively determined by Samuel, partly on the basis of discussions with checker experts. Typical parameters measured features like piece advantage, center control, exposure, threat of fork, back-row control, and mobility. Samuel was not entirely satisfied with the set of parameters. He would have preferred to define a "complete" set on some formal grounds, or even to let the program generate its own parameters, but could find no satisfactory implementation of either of these alternatives.

At any given time the program would be using from 10 to 20 of the available parameters. Both the identity of the currently active parameters and the relative importance (weights) attached to them were subject to alteration by learning schemes we will consider shortly. But there was one parameter too important to leave to the whim of the learning mechanisms, so it did not appear in the polynomial at all. Whenever the board position was characterized by an inability of either side to move (the technical condition for "game over" in checkers), the fact that the game would be won or lost in that position took precedence over the normal evaluation function.

The first of Samuel's three types of learning schemes is called *book learning*. In this method the program works through recorded "book games" representing expert play, evaluating all possible moves from each position. During this process, information is separately tabulated for each weighted parameter, indicating the number of moves which it rated higher (H) or lower (L) than the expert's actual move. Thus large values of L and small values of H tend to reflect agreement with the expert's decision, and vice versa. Samuel used the data so collected to compute a sort of "correlation function," $C = (L - H)/(L + H)$, ranging from -1 (when the parameter never predicted the book move) to $+1$ (when the parameter always predicted the book move). The value of C for a given parameter can be used to adjust the weight of that parameter in a direction which will cause it to make a better contribution to the evaluation function.

Another use of C can occur after book learning during which all the weights are equal. The resulting correlations can be scaled if necessary and used as initial estimates for weights in an evaluation function which is to be subjected to other forms of learning. Thus a parameter which makes "random" predictions ($L = H$) will have an "initial weight" of zero and would not be used at all in the evaluation function. Note that parameters for which C is close to -1 are quite useful, as long as their weights are negative.

Samuel called his second learning scheme *rote learning*. In this method the program stores frequently encountered board positions together with their backed up evaluations. When such values are retrieved during play they can either speed up search, since the minimaxing need not be repeated, or effectively extend the depth of search. To make this scheme reasonably economical and effective, Samuel had to devise three procedures. The first was a means of storing board positions for fast retrieval. To this end Samuel ordered positions according to their relative frequency of occurrence and grouped them by total number of pieces, presence or absence of kings, and other easily detected features. The second procedure involved elimination of redundancies in stored positions through symmetry considerations. Finally it was necessary to find a means for eliminating less useful positions when new ones were to be added to storage. To implement such a replacement scheme Samuel associated with each position a parameter which measured its frequency of use during recent play. The parameter was periodically incremented but also halved whenever the position was used. Positions with the largest values for this parameter were candidates for replacement.

Neither of the two learning methods so far discussed allows the program to improve its performance (evaluation function) dynamically, on the basis of its actual experience during competitive play. Samuel's last, and most important, contribution was a method of *generalization learning*. Although this type of learning can be carried out during a game against a human opponent, Samuel has devised a method of "bootstrapping" the program's performance through play against itself. In this form of play, Black uses the best evaluation function yet developed and holds it constant through the game. White starts with the same function and attempts to improve it during play. If White wins, Black is given the improved function and the cycle begins again. If White loses too often (say, three times running), it is considered to be on the wrong track and is given a drastically and arbitrarily modified evaluation function.

Generalization learning attempts to capitalize on the superiority of backed up evaluations by comparing the static value, s, of a position at the bottom of a tree fragment with the backed up value, b, which can be computed when that point in play is actually reached. If s exceeds b the program fared worse than its own prediction. Thus the accuracy of the evaluation function can be improved by giving more weight to negative terms and less to positive terms. The weights are adjusted by a fraction of their magnitude, so that the terms contributing most to the error will change the most. Similarly, when b exceeds s weights need to be adjusted in the opposite direction to prevent the program from undervaluing good positions. This account has somewhat simplified Samuel's involved procedure for modifying the evaluation function.

Generalization learning also involves a mechanism for replacing terms which are making little contribution to evaluation because their weights are close to zero. A rejected term is placed at the bottom of a "reserve list" and replaced by the term at the top of the list. The scheme is arranged so that a term is replaced every eight moves on the average, and may expect another "chance" 176 moves later.

Except for some minor additional refinements and expedients, we have now fully described the 1959 version of Samuel's checker player. Let us consider its performance. Using rote learning the program learned to imitate master play during the opening moves and played a reasonable end game, but performed quite poorly during the middle game. The overall learning rate was quite slow, but continuous. With generalization learning, by contrast, the program was somewhat weak in the opening and end game but learned to play a very good middle game. Generalization learning thus appeared to be much more adaptable and less rigidly structured than rote learning. Samuel suggested but did not implement a scheme combining the advantages of the two forms of learning. Perhaps the crowning achievement of the program was its defeat in 1962 of the former Connecticut checkers champion.

But Samuel was not content with his program's performance. After several years of additional experience (including several losses to checker masters), he summarized the major defects in the first version of the checker player as follows: (1) inadequate methods for pruning the tree and terminating search; (2) the assumption of parameter independence, as reflected in the linear combination of terms; (3) slowness of learning; (4) the lack of an ongoing strategy of play; and (5) the inability of the program to generate useful new parameters. In his 1967 paper Samuel reported solutions to defects (1) and (2) and some progress on (3) and (4). Defect (5) remains unsolved.

The main changes in the second version of the checker player were in the areas of search procedure and evaluation function. To replace simple depth first minimax search Samuel introduced the alpha-beta technique combined with plausibility ordering based on shallow search. He also added forward pruning (both tapered and convergent) and modified his termination criteria so that less plausible paths terminated earlier. The many details of these refinements as implemented by Samuel will not be discussed here.

With respect to the evaluation function, Samuel had long been aware

153

that it was unrealistic to assume that parameters do not interact. To replace a simple linear combination of weighted values he used the technique of multilevel *signature tables*. To understand the idea of a signature table we begin with a simple example. Suppose we have just three binary parameters, which can sum to a net evaluation of 0, 1, 2, or 3. If the parameters are not independent then the three possible ways in which a sum of 2 may be obtained could reflect very different situations. We can take such interactions into account by constructing a table of all possible values of the function for each binary combination from 000 through 111. We can thus assign different evaluations to 110, 101, and 011, despite the fact that they all sum to 2. But as we increase the number of parameters it quickly becomes impractical to take all interactions into account. With just 8 10-valued parameters our table requires 100 million entries.

Samuel's compromise was to *group* the parameters into subsets (or "signature types") which hopefully contained parameters most likely to interact significantly with each other. If we divide the 8 parameters mentioned above into two groups of 4, each table has only 10,000 entries. Since Samuel wanted to combine some 24 parameters he first reduced the number of possible values they could assume to 3 or in some cases 5. This mapping to a smaller range did not appear to restrict the flexibility of the evaluation significantly. Next Samuel sought a workable allocation of parameters into small groups. Since there is really no basis for deciding which parameters in the checkers evaluation function will have the most important interactions, Samuel divided them somewhat arbitrarily into six groups of four parameters each (one 5-valued and three 3-valued).

As shown in Figure 12.3, outputs from these six 135-entry tables were grouped into two sets of three 5-valued variables and evaluated by two tables with 125 values each. The two 15-valued outputs were finally fed into a 225-entry table to produce a single value for the board position. Samuel thus reduced the number of table entries from nearly a trillion to 1,285, at the cost of ignoring the vast majority of higher order interactions.

To test the signature table evaluation method Samuel tried it on a book learning task similar to the one he had used for the linear combination approach. In this case the result of counting H and L predictions for each combination of values in each signature group could serve as a basis for an initial estimate of that table entry and as a means for modifying it with experience. The signature table based book learning turned out to be superior to the linear combination approach, despite the essentially random allocation of variables to tables. As another measure of the worth of signature tables, Samuel found that the evaluation function rated book moves first or second some 64% of the time (and first, second, third, or fourth some 90% of the time), after having been trained on a set of 170,000 book moves. Samuel has apparently not discussed combining signature table evaluation with generalization learning.

A final potential value of signature tables might be in the introduction of

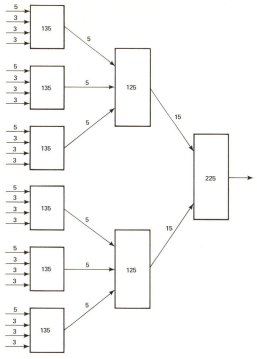

Figure 12.3. Samuel's 3-stage signature table
scheme. Values on lines indicate numbers of
permissible variable values. Values in boxes
indicate table sizes.

"strategic thinking" into the checker player. To counteract the tendency of
the present program to view each move as a brand new problem, parameters
might be grouped into signature types in a manner related to long range
goals in the game. Strategies could then be introduced and modified through
adjustment of the higher level table entries. Samuel has discussed but not
implemented such a feature.

12.3 Chess playing

The mechanization of chess has been a popular idea ever since the late
18th century, when Baron von Kempelen exhibited his chess automaton.
The quality of this machine's game became understandable when the human
inside was revealed. In this section we consider some highlights in the history
of computer chess playing, with more emphasis on ideas than on specific
programs. We will also consider the basic features of the more successful
present day approaches. Finally we will look at some possible reasons why
no program has yet played chess anywhere near as well as Samuel's program
plays checkers.

The modern history of automated chess begins with a 1950 paper by

Claude Shannon, of communication theory fame. In this conceptual study Shannon laid the groundwork for most subsequent programs and was the first to suggest many of the general principles of game playing we discussed in Section 12.1. Among Shannon's ideas were evaluation by linear combination of weighted features, learning by modification of the weights, the minimax backing-up procedure, and tapered forward pruning. He also suggested that evaluations be made only of "quiescent positions," those for which the available moves would not significantly change the evaluation. Thus an exchange of material, for example, should be followed to completion before evaluation, a concept which Samuel employed in checkers by following jump sequences to their conclusions.

Noting the important differences in playing style among the various phases of a chess game, Shannon proposed that different algorithms be employed for the opening, middle, and end games. Recall that Samuel found different learning methods effective in different phases, although he did not actually combine the methods. Finally, we note Shannon's suggestion that a chess program should be designed to play in much the same way as people do. While this condition is certainly not a prerequisite to artificial intelligence, it may well be that the sort of strategic thinking envisioned for checkers by Samuel will prove indispensable for a superior chess playing program.

Although a couple of programs capable of weak amateur play were implemented in the interim, the next advance in ideas about chess playing came in the late 1950's from Newell, Shaw, and Simon (about whom we shall hear much more in subsequent chapters). These investigators proposed a scheme tied closely to their interests in the simulation of human thought processes. The program thus has a strong strategic or goal-oriented flavor. Move generation is based on an ordered list of goals produced at the outset of each move by a preliminary analysis routine. Comparative evaluation is carried out not on individual positions in the tree but with respect to how such positions satisfy various goals in the goal list. While some of the Newell–Shaw–Simon goals, like "material balance" and "center control," correspond to the features evaluated in other programs, others like "development" clearly have a more global nature.

One problem with the Newell–Shaw–Simon program was that it failed to capture the continuity of human strategic thinking because it generated a new list of goals at each move, regardless of those which had previously been in effect. Because of this and other problems the program's (postopening) play was quite poor and hence not extensively tested. Despite these difficulties the goal-directed approach to game playing was an important contribution and one which may be revived in connection with chess playing in particular.

The last several years have witnessed a proliferation of chess programs. These are regularly pitted against each other in national and international computer chess tournaments. The similarities among most current programs are more apparent than their differences. Evaluation functions tend to be linear combinations of weighted features. Tree search is by minimax backing up with alpha-beta and a number of other pruning refinements. Few programs attempt any sort of automatic learning, although their designers are continually "patching in" various improvements. And no currently successful program embodies a significant strategic or goal-directed component.

One dimension along which present programs vary is the relative amount of effort devoted to extensive exploration of the tree, as opposed to time spent carefully evaluating a selection of nodes. Thus one of the better playing programs ("Mac Hack" written by Greenblatt and others) applies a sophisticated evaluation function to a small subset of possible moves, while another ("TECH" by Gillogly) uses an extremely crude scoring function, based solely on material difference, but attempts to explore as many nodes as possible. Since these programs play with approximately equal skill it would seem there is a trade off in computer chess, between "brute force" exploration and sensitive, selective evaluation.

Yet neither of the two programs just mentioned, nor any of their competitors, plays particularly well by human standards. Chess players are ranked internationally by a numerical scheme which assigns the value 2,200 as the lower limit for "master" players. The poorest tournament players typically have a ranking of at least 1,200. The best chess programs have been estimated at around 1,400 to 1,500, although such figures are unreliable because of the limited number of games on which they are based. In any case, a chess program has never even come close to beating a master player in a serious game. Why should this be the case after nearly two decades of computer chess research?

First, it must be acknowledged that chess is an extremely complicated game. We should not expect simple application of the techniques that allowed Samuel to produce a master checker player to do the same for chess. Given the improvement in Samuel's program resulting from the introduction of signature tables, however, chess programmers might be well advised to consider nonlinear evaluation functions. On the other hand, some investigators suspect that numerical combination of features is a dead end for chess and should be abandoned in favor of other approaches.

Inbuilt learning procedures might also improve chess programs. After all, people seem to learn to play better chess mainly from experience, although study of chess theory and master games is also useful. On the other hand, it is perhaps too much to expect that learning techniques will be of significant use before more effective static methodologies and representations have been discovered.

A final problem with most current programs hearkens back to the work of Newell, Shaw, and Simon, and to Samuel's latest ideas for his checker player. What we need is some means of instilling and maintaining long range strategic goals in our chess playing algorithms. Such goals certainly govern most of the moves made and local tactics used by successful human players.

Since suggestions along these lines have recently been made, a revival of goal-directed computer play (in chess and other games) may be just around the corner.

Bibliography

The book by Jackson in the Chapter 11 Bibliography has a good chapter on game playing, covering search procedures, the Samuel checker player, and programs for chess, go, poker, and bridge.

Feigenbaum, Edward A., and Feldman, Julian (eds.). *Computers and Thought*. McGraw-Hill, 1963.
An excellent collection of papers from the "first decade" of artificial intelligence research. Section 2 on game playing contains Samuel's first paper and the article on chess playing by Newell *et al.*.

Newborn, Monroe. *Computer Chess*. Academic Press, 1975.
A thorough historical study with details of many important games.

Newell, A., Shaw, J. C., and Simon, H. A. "Chess playing programs and the problem of complexity." *IBM Journal of Research and Development*, *2*, 1958, pp. 320–355. Reprinted in the Feigenbaum and Feldman collection above.
A good study of the inherent problems in programming a chess player, with descriptions of several early programs.

Newell, A. and Simon, H. A. *Human Problem Solving*, Prentice-Hall, 1972.
A massive research compendium with a good chapter on their own and other approaches to chess playing. Considerable overlap with the above article.

Samuel, A. L. "Some studies in machine learning using the game of checkers." *IBM Journal of Research and Development*, *3*, 1959, pp. 211–299. Reprinted in the Feigenbaum and Feldman collection above. And "II—Recent progress," *9*, 1967, pp. 601–617.
The two papers on the famous checker player.

Shannon, Claude E. "Programming a digital computer for playing chess." *Philosophical Magazine*, *41*, 1950, pp. 356–375.
The classic first study of the challenge of computer chess playing.

Slagle, James R. *Artificial Intelligence: The Heuristic Programming Approach*. McGraw-Hill, 1971.
A good introduction to selected artificial intelligence topics. Game playing is treated in chapters 1, 2, and 3.

Exercises

12.1. Using symmetry considerations to reduce the number of distinct positions, create a partial game tree for tic-tac-toe (3 by 3 Xs and Os) by expanding at least one of the nodes at each level, until all paths have terminated.

12.2. For the game tree fragments in Figure 12.4 show the order in which the nodes would be visited by a depth first and by a breadth first search.

12.3. For the game tree fragments in Figure 12.4 and the evaluations given in the

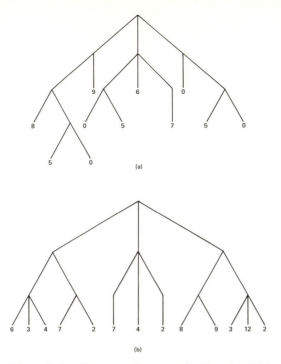

Figure 12.4.   Game tree fragments for Exercises 12.2 and 12.3.

terminal nodes, (1) show the minimax backed up values through to the root node, and (2) identify all alpha and beta cutoffs which could normally occur in a depth first search of the tree. (Maximizing player moves first.)

12.4. Give a comparative analysis of the learning methods employed by the Uhr–Vossler pattern classification program (Section 11.2) and the Samuel checker player.

12.5. For some simple game with which you are quite familiar (e.g., nim, blackjack, 3-dimensional tic-tac-toe) draw up a set of specifications for a computer program to play the game. Include a method for representing the game positions and all the components of a search procedure.

13
Theorem proving

Human intelligence reaches one of its rarified heights in the ability of mathematicians to prove difficult theorems. Since computers are designed for mathematical manipulation it is not surprising that a good deal of effort has gone into attempts to automate theorem proving. Perhaps surprisingly, artificial intelligence has yet to make significant contributions to mathematics. It would seem that we do not sufficiently understand, or cannot adequately implement, the principles people use to discover proofs. In fact, the most recent and impressive progress in mechanical theorem proving has been made by application of principles which human theorem provers find difficult to use· This situation provides some evidence that artificial intelligence may be attainable with little or no consideration of its human counterpart.

In this chapter we first examine the logical systems within which most theorem proving work has been carried out. Then, in Section 13.2, we consider an early and rather successful program for proving theorems in the propositional calculus. Section 13.3 contains an introductory discussion of resolution principle theorem proving in the predicate calculus, the area of greatest current activity.

It should be emphasized that there is no clear dividing line between the subject of this chapter and the problem solving research discussed in Chapter 14. Newell, Shaw, and Simon incorporated many of the principles of their Logic Theorist (Section 13.2) in their General Problem Solver (Section 14.2). In addition, resolution theorem proving methods have been used in a variety of problem solving programs.

13.1 Logic systems

The simpler of the two systems which have served as a framework for most mechanical theorem proving is called the *propositional calculus*. Extensively developed by Whitehead and Russell in their early 20th century classic *Principia Mathematica*, this system is also known as propositional logic, sentential calculus, and (informally) as "symbolic logic."

The basic entities, or primitives, in the propositional calculus are *propositions* (sentences) which are symbolized $p, q, r, s, \ldots$. A proposition symbol stands for an assertion ("The sky is blue," "It is raining," "$x = y$") which may be *true* (T) or *false* (F). Propositions may be combined into more complex assertions by the use of operators, analogous to the familiar arithmetic operators of addition, multiplication, and so on. These *logical connectives*, however, combine propositions into logical expressions whose truth or falsity is a function of the truth value (T or F) of each component proposition. In general, logical connectives map combinations of n propositions onto the set (T, F). When $n = 1$, the only mapping of interest reverses the truth variable of a proposition. We symbolize this *negation* operator with a minus sign and read $-p$ as "not p."

When $n = 2$ (which is as high as we need go) there are 16 possible binary logical connectives (comprising all the distinct ways truth values can be assigned to the four possible pairs of proposition values). Figure 13.1 shows the mappings for the *conjunction* ($p \& q$, "p and q"), *disjunction* ($p \vee q$, "p or q"), and *implication* ($p \to q$, "p implies q") operators.

p	q	p & q	p v q	p → q
T	T	T	T	T
T	F	F	T	F
F	T	F	T	T
F	F	F	F	T

Figure 13.1   Three binary logical connectives.

It is not difficult to show that the set of connectives in Figure 13.1 (together with negation) is *complete* in the sense that all other binary mappings can be expressed in terms of conjunction, disjunction, implication, and negation. In fact we can dispense with implication since

$$p \to q = -p \vee q \tag{13.1}$$

and even with either conjunction or disjunction since

$$p \& q = -(-p \vee -q), \qquad p \vee q = -(-p \& -q). \tag{13.2}$$

There are even some other binary connectives which are complete in themselves. For ease of understanding, however, we usually work with all of the connectives in Figure 13.1.

Although the simple expressions in Equations (13.1) and (13.2) clearly "make sense," we require a formal means of determining whether more complex expressions are constructed properly. We thus introduce the following recursive definition of *well-formed formulas* ("wffs"):

1. A proposition is a wff.
2. If A and B are wffs, then so are $(-A)$, $(A \& B)$, $(A \lor B)$, and $(A \rightarrow B)$.
3. There are no other wffs.

To avoid introducing parentheses around all subexpressions, as required by this definition, we can adopt a convention which specifies a *precedence hierarchy* for logical operators. Thus, unless parentheses dictate otherwise [as in the right hand sides of both equations in (13.2)], all negations will be evaluated first, followed by all conjunctions, then by all disjunctions, and finally by all implications. The various instances of a given operator can be processed in left-to-right order.

A propositional calculus formula is not especially meaningful until a truth value has been assigned to each of its component propositions. Such an assignment is called an *interpretation* of the formula. For any given interpretation we can use the formula evaluation rules to determine if the formula as a whole has the value true or false under that interpretation. A formula which is true under all possible interpretations is a *valid* formula or a *tautology*. A formula which is true under no interpretation is an *inconsistent* formula or a *contradiction*. A *consistent* (*satisfiable*) formula is true under at least one interpretation.

Two formulas (A, B) are *equivalent* $(A = B)$ if they have identical truth values under all possible interpretations. Thus Equations (13.1) and (13.2) show examples of equivalent formulas. It is often useful to convert a propositional formula into an equivalent but standardized form. One common such form is called the *conjunctive normal form* (CNF). A CNF formula consists of conjunctions of subformulas, where each subformula is a disjunction of single propositions or their negations. Any formula can be converted to an equivalent CNF expression by application of relations like those in Equations (13.1) and (13.2), together with the commutative, associative, and distributive relations that hold for logical operators.

To illustrate conversion of a formula to conjunctive normal form we begin with

$$(p \& (q \rightarrow r)) \rightarrow s.$$

Replacing both implications by their equivalents [Equation (13.1)] gives

$$-(p \& (-q \lor r)) \lor s.$$

Applying Equation (13.2), we may write first

$$(-p \lor -(-q \lor r)) \lor s,$$

and then

$$(-p \lor (q \& -r)) \lor s,$$

having also used the fact that $-(-q) = q$.

Distributing the disjunction with $-p$ through the conjunction,

$$((-p \vee q) \& (-p \vee -r)) \vee s.$$

Distributing the disjunction with s through the result gives

$$(-p \vee q \vee s) \& (-p \vee -r \vee s),$$

where associativity of disjunction allows removal of internal parentheses. The last expression is in conjunctive normal form, consisting of a conjunction of two disjunctions of propositions and their negations.

To prove a theorem in the propositional calculus we typically try to show that one formula follows logically from a set of other formulas. Such demonstrations are carried out within a formal deductive apparatus containing *axioms* and *rules of inference*. Axioms are usually rather "obvious" formulas which are assumed valid without proof and used as a basis for proving other results. In any deductive system with given rules of inference a good set of axioms should be *complete* (sufficient to prove all valid formulas in the system), *consistent* (not leading to proofs of contradictory results), and *minimal* (not containing any "extra" axioms which could be proved using the others). It should be noted that for systems more complex than the propositional calculus these properties are not always attainable.

In *Principia Mathematica* Whitehead and Russell were able to prove a vast number of theorems using the following five axioms (not actually a minimal set, since the fourth was later shown to be redundant).

$$1: \quad (p \vee p) \rightarrow p$$

$$2: \quad p \rightarrow (q \vee p)$$

$$3: \quad (p \vee q) \rightarrow (q \vee p)$$

$$4: \quad (p \vee (q \vee r)) \rightarrow (q \vee (p \vee r))$$

$$5: \quad (p \rightarrow q) \rightarrow ((r \vee p) \rightarrow (r \vee q))$$

The other component of a deductive system is the rule of inference. One or more such procedures are needed to generate new valid formulas from existing ones. Three rules of inference were used in *Principia Mathematica*: (1) *substitution*, which allows replacement of all occurrences of a proposition in a formula by any given wff; (2) *replacement*, which allows any logical connective to be replaced by its definition in terms of other connectives [definitional equivalence, as in Equation (13.1), can be established by testing all interpretations]; and (3) modus ponens or *detachment* which allows inference of B from both A and $A \rightarrow B$.

We may now define a *theorem* more formally. A given (well-formed) formula A is a theorem if and only if there exists a finite sequence of (well-formed) formulas A^1, A^2, A^3, ... such that the last member of the sequence is A and each other member is an axiom, a previously proved theorem, or a derivation from the previous members by some rule of inference. The sequence of formulas is called a *proof* of A. We conclude this introduction to the propositional calculus with a short proof of a simple theorem, $(p \rightarrow -p) \rightarrow -p$.

1. $(p \vee p) \rightarrow p$, by axiom 1 (above)
2. $(-p \vee -p) \rightarrow -p$, by substitution of $-p$ for p
3. $(p \rightarrow -p) \rightarrow -p$, by replacement of $(-A \vee B)$ with $(A \rightarrow B)$

We now develop the basic ideas of the (first-order) *predicate calculus*, the logic system in which most current theorem proving research is carried out. We have already done quite a bit of the groundwork, since the predicate calculus is an extension of the propositional calculus which allows us to deal with individuals, relations between individuals, and properties of individuals and sets of individuals. We continue to denote propositions by $p, q, r, \ldots$ and to use the same set of unary and binary logical connectives.

To those structures we add *individual constants*, denoted $a, b, c, \ldots$, which symbolically identify particular items in the *domain of discourse*, D (e.g., people, numbers, days of the week). We use the last letters of the alphabet $(z, y, x, \ldots)$ to denote *individual variables* which may range over all of the individuals in D. *Functions* of one or more variables and/or constants will be denoted $f, g, h, \ldots$ and will map objects or groups of objects in D into other objects in D. Thus in the domain of numbers we might represent negation by $g(x)$, addition by $f(x, y)$, and 3-way multiplication by $h(x, y, z)$, so that $h(g(2), 6, f(3, 1))$ would denote -48. Any expression of this sort, which evaluates to an object or set of objects in D, is known as a *term*. Defined recursively, a term is (1) a constant, (2) a variable, or (3) a function of terms.

The predicate calculus gets its name from the entities used to describe or relate terms. These *predicates* are denoted $P, Q, R, \ldots$ and map terms onto the truth values T and F. Thus if D is people, $P(a)$ might assert that individual a has red hair, while $R(c, b)$ might claim that b is a sibling of c. Any predicate of terms (or simple proposition) in the predicate calculus is known as an *atomic formula*.

The last group of predicate calculus entities consists of the *quantifiers*, of which there are just two. The *universal* quantifier, denoted (x) and read "for all x," when applied to a formula asserts that the formula is true for all possible substitution instances of the variable x (the entire domain D). The *existential* quantifier, denoted (Ex) and read "there exists an x," asserts that the formula is true for at least one of the possible values of x. In general a quantifier does not apply to all occurrences of its variable in a formula but only to those which fall within its range or *scope* (delimited if necessary by appropriate parentheses). Such variables are said to be *bound* by the quantifier while other occurrences of the same variable symbol may be *free* of quantification.

We can now define recursively the well-formed formulas (wffs) of the predicate calculus, as follows:

1. Any atomic formula is a wff.
2. If A and B are wffs then so are $(-A)$, $(A \& B)$, $(A \lor B)$, and $(A \to B)$.
3. If A is a wff and x is a (free) variable in A, then $((x)A)$ and $((Ex)A)$ are wffs.
4. There are no other wffs.

As for the propositional calculus, a precedence hierarchy allows omission of many parentheses. To the rules given previously we need add only that quantifiers are to be evaluated first, along with negations. Thus the scope of (x) in $(x) - P(x) \lor Q(x)$ is just $-P(x)$; the x in $Q(x)$ is a free variable.

Interpretation of predicate calculus formulas requires specification of the domain, D, an assignment of elements of D to individual constants, and assignments of "meanings" (mappings) with respect to D to all functions and predicates. For example, if D is the positive integers, F denotes equality, f is the addition function, and the constants a and b are 3 and 5 respectively, then the formula $(Ex)F(f(x, a), b)$ asserts that there is an x such that $x + 3 = 5$. The formula happens to be true under the given interpretation. But just as for the propositional calculus, predicate calculus formulas are classed as valid (true for all interpretations), satisfiable (true for at least one interpretation) and inconsistent (true for no interpretations). Also as before, two predicate calculus formulas are equivalent if and only if they have identical truth values under all interpretations.

A useful type of formula equivalent to any given predicate calculus formula is its *prenex normal form*. In this form all quantifiers have been "swept" to the front of the formula, so that each of them has all the rest of the formula (called the *matrix*) as its scope. The most awkward aspect of converting formulas to prenex normal form can be "moving negation through quantifiers" where the following (sensible) equivalences apply:

$$-(x)A = (Ex) - A, \qquad -(Ex)A = (x) - A. \tag{13.3}$$

Since conversion to prenex normal form is an implicit step in preparing formulas for resolution theorem proving, we will be illustrating the method in Section 13.3.

The notions of axiom, rule of inference, proof, and theorem carry over directly from the propositional calculus to the predicate calculus. In Section 13.3 we will be examining a particular predicate calculus proof method which uses a rule of inference known as the resolution principle and which is the basis for most current work in mechanical theorem proving.

13.2 The Logic Theorist

In this section we briefly discuss an early theorem proving program which contrasts sharply with the resolution based approach. For one thing, this program proves theorems in the (simpler and less powerful) propositional calculus. More significantly, Newell, Shaw, and Simon's Logic Theorist (LT) was intended as much as a simulation of human reasoning as a contribution to theorem proving. In any case, LT gave a tremendous boost to artificial intelligence research of the times (mid-1950's), both because it was one of the first reasonably successful mechanizations of intelligent behavior and because its development was accompanied by the appearance of the first of the list processing programming languages, which have since become a mainstay of artificial intelligence programs in all areas.

LT used the axioms, definitions, and rules of inference set out in *Principia Mathematica*, and tried to prove theorems from that work. Theorems were attempted in the same order as presented by Whitehead and Russell, so that the same use could be made of previously proved theorems in proving new ones.

LT's basic approach involves the generation of *disjunctive subgoals*, a specific form of the problem reduction representation we will be discussing in the next chapter. Beginning with the main goal of establishing the truth of the theorem, LT tries to reduce the problem to a set of more easily attainable goals, any one of which, if satisfied, will allow immediate attainment of the main goal. Subgoals can be broken down into subsubgoals, and so on. LT explores a promising problem reduction path until it can go no further, then backs up and tries a new subproblem. We will set out LT's search algorithm more precisely after examining the methods used to reduce a goal to subgoals.

There are three such methods. *Substitution* attempts to find an axiom or prior theorem that can be transformed into the expression to be proved by substitutions for variables and replacement of connectives. Thus the substitution method of subgoal generation employs principles from two rules of inference (substitution, replacement). *Detachment* uses the same principle as the rule of inference with the same name; that is, if B is to be proved, detachment looks for an axiom or theorem of the form $A \rightarrow B$, then attempts to prove A as a subproblem. *Chaining* can attack the problem of proving $A \rightarrow C$ from either of two directions. Forward chaining seeks a prior result $A \rightarrow B$ and sets up $B \rightarrow C$ as a subproblem, while backward chaining seeks $B \rightarrow C$ and sets up $A \rightarrow B$. Chaining was not an inference rule used by Whitehead and Russell, but can be shown to be equivalent to two successive detachments.

LT's "executive routine" or search algorithm can be described as five steps:

1. Using all the axioms and theorems it has been told to assume, LT attempts substitution in the original problem.
2. If (1) fails, detachments are attempted and substitution tried on each new subproblem; if detachment cannot be used, the subproblem is added to a subproblem list.

3. If (2) fails, the same approach is tried with forward. then with backward, chaining.
4. If (3) fails, then subproblems are taken from the subproblem list and attacked again using combinations of methods.
5. The procedure terminates if a proof is found (any subproblem is solved), if time or memory limitations are exceeded, or if there are no untried subproblems on the list.

Newell, Shaw, and Simon employed several heuristic techniques to reduce the search effort. Substitution and other subproblem generation methods were applied only to pairs of expressions which could be successfully "matched" by transformation of logical connectives. The matching procedure itself was in turn employed only for sufficiently similar expressions. Similarity was determined by a comparison of criteria like total number of variables, number of distinct variables, and so on. The combination of similarity tests and matching procedures served to screen out subproblem generation attempts that had little hope of success, and to speed up the generation process when the methods were applicable.

LT's performance was impressive, for its time. It successfully proved 38 of the first 52 theorems in *Principia Mathematica*. Solution times (on the rather slow computer then available) ranged from a few seconds to many minutes, perhaps somewhat faster than logic students could generate the same proofs. (On a modern computer the times would be reduced to the order of half a minute or less.) The example below consumed the greatest amount of time (45 minutes) of any successful proof. LT had the five axioms and 20 previously proved theorems to work with. The expression to be proved was the familiar relation $(-q \rightarrow -p) \rightarrow (p \rightarrow q)$.

(1)	$A \rightarrow --A$	previous theorem
(2)	$p \rightarrow --p$	substitution of p for A
(3)	$(A \rightarrow B) \rightarrow ((B \rightarrow C) \rightarrow (A \rightarrow C))$	previous theorem
(4)	$(p \rightarrow --p) \rightarrow ((--p \rightarrow q) \rightarrow (p \rightarrow q))$	substitution of p for A, $--p$ for B, and q for C
(5)	$(--p \rightarrow q) \rightarrow (p \rightarrow q)$	detachment, using (2) and (4)
(6)	$(-A \rightarrow B) \rightarrow (-B \rightarrow A)$	previous theorem
(7)	$(-q \rightarrow -p) \rightarrow (--p \rightarrow q)$	substitution of q for A, and $-p$ for B
(8)	$(-q \rightarrow -p) \rightarrow (p \rightarrow q)$	chaining of (5) and (7)

Q.E.D.

To conclude this discussion of propositional calculus theorem proving we should mention the work of Wang (also known for his formulation of Turing machines). Several years after the Logic Theorist, Wang programmed a computer to prove theorems from *Principia Mathematica* and was able to prove more (and more difficult) theorems orders of magnitude faster than Newell, Shaw, and Simon's program. At the time, Wang and others argued that his results vitiated the Logic Theorist methodology. From the present perspective, however, the Logic Theorist remains a milestone in artificial intelligence research, first because it spearheaded the simulation of human thought approach, and second because it advanced the case for heuristics in a way Wang's purely mechanical procedures could never do.

13.3 Resolution theorem proving

In 1965 the logician J. A. Robinson reported the development of a new inference rule for the predicate calculus. He also proved that his *resolution principle* was "sound" (producing only valid wffs) and "complete" (producing all valid wffs). While not especially convenient or intuitive for people, the resolution principle is ideally suited to computer implementation and forms the basis for almost all current research in mechanical theorem proving.

Without going into the complex logical basis for resolution based inference, we can understand the central idea underlying the method in the following terms. A proof that some formula W logically follows from a set of formulas S is equivalent to the claim that every interpretation satisfying S also satisfies W. If such is the case then no interpretation can satisfy the union of S and $-W$. Resolution theorem proving tries to show that that union is unsatisfiable by deriving a special formula called the "null" clause or resolvent from it. The method is thus a special form of "proof by contradiction."

Before resolution theorem proving techniques can be applied to a theorem, certain preliminary steps must be executed. First, if the premises and conclusion to be proved are stated in English, they must be expressed in predicate calculus notation. We will illustrate this process later. Second, the conclusion to be proved must be negated. Third, all the formulas including the negated conclusion must be converted to what is known as *clause form*. A clause is a formula in prenex normal form with no quantifiers shown because existential quantifiers have been eliminated and all variables are assumed to be universally quantified. The matrix of a clause consists solely of disjunctions of atomic formulas and their negations, known collectively as *literals*. While conversion to clause form (from more general formulas or even directly from English statements) is usually quite easy, the general algorithm has no fewer than eight steps.

We now consider these steps, illustrating the operations with the unusually complex formula

$$(x)[P(x) \to [(y)Q(x, y) \& -(y)(P(y) \to R(f(x, y)))]].$$

Step 1. Use Equation (13.1) to remove implication signs:

$$(x)[-P(x) \lor [(y)Q(x, y) \& -(y)(-P(y) \lor R(f(x, y)))]].$$

Step 2. Use Equations (13.2) and (13.3) to reduce the scopes of negation signs to single predicates:

$$(x)[-P(x) \lor [(y)Q(x, y) \& (Ey)(P(y) \& -R(f(x, y)))]].$$

Step 3. Rename quantified variables, if necessary, so that each quantifier has a unique variable:

$$(x)[-P(x) \lor [(y)Q(x, y)L \& (Ez)(P(z) \& -R(f(x, z)))]].$$

Step 4. Eliminate existential quantifiers. For all such quantifiers which do not fall within the scope of universal quantifiers we may simply replace $(Ew)P(w)$ with $P(a)$ where a is the constant whose "existence" the quantifier asserts. In a case like $(v)(Ew)Q(w)$, however, there is some (possibly distinct) w for *every* v, so we must write $(v)Q(h(v))$ where h is a function that selects the w which exists for each v. Constants and functions introduced in this step must be new to the formula. Our example becomes:

$$(x)[-P(x) \lor [(y)Q(x, y) \& (P(g(x)) \& -R(f(x, g(x))))]].$$

Step 5. Convert to prenex form by moving all (universal) quantifiers to the front of the formula:

$$(x)(y)[-P(x) \lor [Q(x, y) \& P(g(x)) \& -R(f(x, g(x)))]].$$

Step 6. Put the matrix of the prenex form into conjunctive normal form:

$$(x)(y)[(-P(x) \lor Q(x, y)) \& (-P(x) \lor P(g(x))) \& (-P(x) \lor -R(f(x, g(x))))]$$

Step 7. Drop the universal quantifiers. From this point we assume that all variables are universally quantified.

Step 8. Eliminate the conjunctions by separating the formula into distinct clauses, each of which will be a disjunction of literals:

$$-P(x) \lor Q(x, y)$$

$$-P(x) \lor P(g(x))$$

$$-P(x) \lor -R(f(x, g(x))).$$

Given a set of clauses derived from the premises and negated conclusion of a theorem the resolution principle generates new clauses by *resolving* pairs of clauses in the set. These new clauses are added to the set and may be used in the generation of further *resolvents*. It can be shown, although we will not do so, that if the original set of clauses is unsatisfiable (the theorem is provable) resolution will eventually produce a clause containing no literals, the so-called *null resolvent*.

To produce a resolvent of two available clauses we require that at least one atomic formula appear with opposite signs in the two "parent" clauses.

The resolvent then consists of a disjunction of all other literals in both parent clauses, after removal of the literal(s) differing only in sign. Thus from the clauses $-P(x) \vee R(x)$ and $-R(x) \vee Q(x)$ we may infer the resolvent $-P(x) \vee Q(x)$ by combining the literals left after removing $R(x)$ and $-R(x)$. This simple example actually provides a rare demonstration of the intuitive plausibility of the resolution principle For if we write the clauses in implication form, we are inferring $P(x) \rightarrow Q(x)$ from $P(x) \rightarrow R(x)$ and $R(x) \rightarrow Q(x)$. With more literals in each clause (and the possibility of more than one pair dropping out), it is usually much less apparent why resolvents are reasonable inferences.

Another artificially simple feature of the above example was the "nice" coincidental appearance of $R(x)$ and $-R(x)$ in just those forms in the parent clauses. Usually it is necessary to perform one or more *substitutions* in the parent clauses as a first stage in the resolution process. The process of finding suitable substitutions is properly termed *unification*. If a set of clauses can be unified (i.e., can produce resolvents), a procedure called the *unification algorithm* can be used to find the simplest substitution (or "most general unifier") that does the job. Although the details of this algorithm need not concern us, we should note that it is effective in the sense that it will report that a set of clauses *cannot* be unified when such is the case.

We now consider the legal substitutions that may be made in a pair of clauses without altering their truth values. In order to avoid confusion (and possible error) from coincidentally identical variable names, substitution should be applied to clauses which have no variable names in common. If this is not already the case we simply *rename* some or all of the variables in one of the clauses. Now since all variables are understood to be universally quantified, each specifies any object in the domain. We can therefore substitute any new or existing variable name for *all* the occurrences of any given name in order to bring literals in the clauses into closer correspondence.

We can also substitute any constant or function for all the instances of any variable in the two clauses, since such substitutions simply limit the range to one or more of the objects for which the variable stood. We *cannot* however make any substitutions which would change or increase the identified set of objects, since such substitutions could alter the truth value of the clause. Thus we may not substitute variables for functions or constants, nor may we replace any constant or function with any other constant or function.

To illustrate how substitution can be used in producing resolvents, we consider the two clauses

(1) $\qquad\qquad\qquad -P(a) \vee Q(f(x), y, c) \vee R(y)$

(2) $\qquad\qquad\qquad S(x, y) \vee P(x) \vee -Q(y, b, c).$

Renaming variables, by application of "primes" to variables in (2) which also happen to appear in (1), gives us

(2a) $S(x', y') \vee P(x') \vee -Q(y', b, c).$

Now we can substitute a for x' in (2a) producing

(2b) $S(a, y') \vee P(a) \vee -Q(y', b, c).$

which can be resolved with (1) to give

(3) $Q(f(x), y, c) \vee R(y) \vee S(a, y') \vee -Q(y', b, c).$

Alternatively we might substitute b for y in (1) *and* $f(x)$ for y in (2a), giving the different resolvent

(4) $-P(a) \vee R(b) \vee S(x', f(x)) \vee P(x').$

Thus different substitutions can give different resolvents. It should also be noted that (3) and (4) can be further resolved against the original formulas, with appropriate further substitutions.

The number of possible resolvents arising from even a small set of original clauses can obviously grow very rapidly. It would therefore be quite in-efficient to try to prove a theorem by generating resolvents at random and waiting for the null clause to appear. For this reason, researchers have proposed and experimented with a large number of heuristic *strategies* for resolution theorem proving, in order to reduce the number of resolvents generated and direct the theorem proving program along promising lines. We mention just a couple of the simpler schemes. The *unit preference* strategy attempts to resolve clauses with as few literals as possible (ideally one of the parent clauses should be a single-literal or *unit* clause). The *set-of-support* strategy tries to identify a set of "relevant" clauses and always include at least one member of this set as a parent in every resolution. For the purposes of this introductory discussion the examples we work with are sufficiently elementary that no further consideration of strategies is required.

In addition to the potential explosion of resolvents, another difficulty with resolution theorem proving arises when the putative theorem is in fact invalid. In such a case the resolution method may never terminate. We can thus never be sure whether a program has not terminated because the proof is difficult to find or because no proof exists. One partial solution to this problem is to interrupt the theorem proving attempt after a fixed amount of time and spend some time attempting to prove the negation of the theorem. If this fails, the original proof attempt can be taken up where it was left off, and the alternation continued. The alternation will lead to a proof or dis-proof if the putative theorem is valid or unsatisfiable but not if it is invalid and satisfiable. (Incidentally, this problem of not always being able to disprove invalid formulas is not limited to the resolution methods. The predicate calculus itself is termed *undecidable* because there does not exist an effective procedure for showing that any particular formula does *not* logically follow from a given set of formulas.)

To conclude our discussion of resolution theorem proving we work through two examples, starting with an initial English statement of the theorem and ending with the null clause. First, consider the following theorem: "If there are no compassionate professors, and if all competent professors are compassionate, then no competent professor exists." If we let $S(x)$ indicate that x is compassionate, and $P(x)$ that x is competent, then the predicate calculus formulas for the premise are

(1) $-(Ex)S(x)$ and   (2) $(y)(P(y) \rightarrow S(y))$,

while the denial of the conclusion is $--(Ez)(P(z))$ or just

(3) $(Ez)(P(z))$.

(Note that we have avoided duplication of variable names to reduce the necessity for renaming prior to substitution.) In clause form,

(1') $-S(x)$ (2') $-P(y) \vee S(y)$ (3') $P(a)$.

With substitution of x for y in (2'), resolution of (1') and (2') yields just $-P(x)$. Substituting a for x in this resolvent and using (3') as the other parent yields the null resolvent, proving the theorem.

As a second example we prove the somewhat more complicated theorem: "A police officer questioned everyone who knew the victim and did not have an alibi. Some of the criminals knew the victim and were questioned only by criminals. No criminal had an alibi. Therefore some of the police officers were criminals." Let $P(x)$ mean that x is a police officer, $Q(x, y)$ that x questioned y, $K(x)$ that x knew the victim, $A(x)$ that x had an alibi, and $C(x)$ that x is a criminal. The first premise yields the following formula

$$(x)((K(x) \,\&\, -A(x)) \rightarrow (Ey)(P(y) \,\&\, Q(y, x))),$$

which can be readily shown to produce the two clauses:

(1) $-K(x) \vee A(x) \vee P(f(x))$ (2) $-K(x) \vee A(x) \vee Q(f(x), x)$.

The second premise produces

$$(Ez)(C(z) \,\&\, K(z) \,\&\, (w)(Q(w, z) \rightarrow C(w))),$$

which yields the clauses

(3) $C(a)$ (4) $K(a)$ (5) $-Q(w, a) \vee C(w)$.

The last premise is $(v)(C(v) \rightarrow -A(v))$ producing clause

(6) $-C(v) \vee -A(v)$.

Finally the denial of the conclusion is $-(Ex)(P(x) \,\&\, C(x))$ or, in clause form,

(7) $-P(x) \vee -C(x)$.

The proof requires eight resolution steps, in which the substitutions should be apparent from the resulting resolvents.

$$(8) \quad -A(a) \qquad \text{from (3) and (6)}$$
$$(9) \quad A(a) \vee P(f(a)) \qquad \text{from (1) and (4)}$$
$$(10) \quad P(f(a)) \qquad \text{from (8) and (9)}$$
$$(11) \quad A(a) \vee Q(f(a), a) \qquad \text{from (2) and (4)}$$
$$(12) \quad Q(f(a), a) \qquad \text{from (8) and (11)}$$
$$(13) \quad C(f(a)) \qquad \text{from (5) and (12)}$$
$$(14) \quad -P(f(a)) \qquad \text{from (7) and (13)}$$

Finally we resolve (10) and (14) to obtain the null clause.

Bibliography

Both the Hunt and Jackson books in the Chapter 11 Bibliography treat resolution theorem proving. Hunt gives an especially thorough treatment of strategies. The Feigenbaum and Feldman collection listed in Chapter 12 contains the Logic Theorist paper below and two articles on proving geometry theorems. The fourth chapter of the Newell and Simon book (also listed in Chapter 12) includes a backward look at LT from a more modern perspective.

Chang, C-L., and Lee, R. C-T. *Symbolic Logic and Mechanical Theorem Proving.* Academic Press, 1973.
A good introduction to propositional and predicate calculus in Chapters 2 and 3, followed by a thorough treatment of many varieties of resolution.

Newell, A., Shaw, J. C., and Simon, H. "Empirical explorations with the Logic Theory Machine." *Proceedings of the Western Joint Computer Conference*, 1957, pp. 218–239.
A thorough discussion of the structure of LT, together with a careful analysis of early experience in proving actual theorems.

Nilsson, Nils J. *Problem-Solving Methods in Artificial Intelligence.* McGraw-Hill, 1971.
The last three chapters contain one of the best concise treatments of resolution theorem proving and its uses.

Robinson, J. A. "A machine oriented logic based on the resolution principle." *Journal of the Association for Computing Machinery, 12*, 1965, pp. 23–41.
The (technical) article which first reported the new rule of inference.

Wang, H. "Towards mechanical mathematics." *IBM Journal of Research and Development, 4*, 1960, pp. 2–22.
The work which was considered by some to have superseded the Logic Theorist.

Exercises

13.1. Using (if you wish) the previously established theorems $A \rightarrow (A \vee B)$ and $(A \rightarrow B) \rightarrow (-B \rightarrow -A)$, prove the following theorem from *Principia Mathematica*, $-(p \vee q) \rightarrow -p$. Compare your time with LT's 12 minutes (realizing that LT had no instruction about useful prior theorems).

13.2. Convert the following predicate calculus formulas to clause form.
  (a) $[(Ez) - Q(z)] \rightarrow [-(z)Q(z)]$
  (b) $[-(Ex)P(x)] \rightarrow [(x)(y)(Q(x, y) \rightarrow -R(y))]$
  (c) $(v)(Eu)[(P(u, v) \rightarrow Q(v, w)) \& (Q(v, w) \rightarrow R(u, v))] \rightarrow [(Eu)(v)(P(u, v) \rightarrow R(u, v))]$

13.3. Find all the possible resolvents (if any) of the following clause pairs.
  (a) $Q(u, v, a)$ and $Q(u, f(v), a) \vee -Q(c, f(u), u)$
  (b) $-P(a, g(a))$ and $P(x, x) \vee -Q(x)$
  (c) $R(x, f(y, y), x)$ and $R(x, z, x) \vee -R(w, z, w)$

13.4. Translate the following theorems into predicate calculus formulas, convert to clause form, and prove using resolution.
  (a) If the king is served by all subjects who serve someone, and if no subject serves nobody, then every subject serves the king.
  (b) If all logicians are rational, and if anyone who understands a rational person is rational, and if there exists a psychotic who understands a logician, then some rational person is a psychotic.
  (c) If every person has a mother, and if x is the mother of y and y is the mother of z imply that x is the grandmother of z, then everyone has a grandmother.

13.5. Since the predicate calculus is a generalization of the propositional calculus, there is a resolution principle for the latter system too. (a) Describe the necessary mechanics in formulating and resolving formulas in propositional calculus. (b) Prove the theorem at the end of Section 13.2 using propositional calculus resolution methods.

14
Problem solving

To prove a theorem is to solve a problem. Finding the best move in a game solves a problem. And even analyzing the components in a visual scene may contribute to the solution of a problem (say, for a robot which has the task of finding and manipulating a particular object). In its broadest sense, then, mechanical problem solving encompasses virtually all of artificial intelligence research. The focus of this chapter, however, is on those contributions which have aspirations to *generality*, those which concentrate more on the problem solving *process* than on solutions to particular problems.

We begin with some theoretical considerations. We examine the two predominant general methods of representing problems for processing by computer. And we consider how spaces defined by such representations can be efficiently and effectively searched for problem solutions. In the second section we discuss in some detail the well known General Problem Solver. During the nearly two decades of this program's history, it has been applied with some success to more than a dozen distinct types of problems, a claim to generality that has not been seriously contested by any other extant program. Finally, in Section 14.3, we sample some of the many other problem solving programs and procedures that have arisen in recent times.

14.1 Problem representations

Ideally a problem should be represented in a fashion that is both easy to implement on a computer and readily amenable to the manipulation and search procedures of problem solving routines. Much of the burden imposed by the first of these criteria has been lifted by the development of special purpose programming languages designed to handle data structures like lists and character strings. Although we will not be discussing such languages it should be noted that, through them, artificial intelligence has been indirectly responsible for a good deal of the computer's relatively recent ascension from the status of a glorified desk calculator to its true role as a general purpose symbol manipulator.

Among the many problem representations that have been tried at one time or another, two have predominated. These are the *state space* and *problem reduction* representations. Associated with each is a variety of *search procedures* suited to exploring the space induced by the representation, in order to find a solution to the problem. Nils Nilsson of the Stanford Research Institute has devoted a majority of his book *Problem Solving Methods in Artificial Intelligence* to an excellent discussion of state space and problem reduction representations and search procedures. The following presentation incorporates many of his ideas and examples.

First we need a new mathematical structure. While trees of the sort we used to represent games are frequently sufficient for either type of problem representation, the more generalized structures known as graphs are usually more suitable. A (directed) *graph* consists of a set of *nodes*, pairs of which may be connected by (directed) lines called *arcs*. If there is an arc from node *i* to node *j*, then *j* is called a *successor* of *i*. A sequence of nodes in which each is the successor of the preceding node defines a *path* from the first to the last node in the sequence. The *length* of a path is the number of arcs it contains. A path which closes on itself by returning to the initial node is called a *cycle*. The *depth* of a node (relative to a particular initial node) is the length of the shortest path to the node.

Trees can now be seen as special cases of graphs in which the following restrictions apply: (1) there is exactly one node (the root) which is the successor of no other node; (2) all other nodes are successors of exactly one node; and, hence, (3) there can be no cycles. Just as for trees, graphs may be defined explicitly or implicitly. In the latter case we require a function or rule which generates all the successors of any given node. As for trees, we search implicit graphs by making some portion of the graph explicit.

In a state space representation the nodes of a problem graph correspond to descriptions of the possible "states of the world" as relevant to the problem at hand. In the special case of a board game we already know that the states can be described in terms of the arrangements of pieces on the board. The arcs in a state space problem graph correspond to operators which change a given state into its successor(s). We often label arcs with the operators they represent. For game trees we have seen how moves function as operators.

Although a problem space is fully described by all its nodes and arcs, we still do not know what corresponds to the operation of "solving the problem." This notion can be realized if we denote one or more nodes as *starting nodes* and one or more nodes as *goal nodes*. Then a solution to (one particular version of) the problem consists of finding a path from a (designated) starting node to any goal node. Notice that it is especially important for a solution finding algorithm to be able to recognize a goal node when it encounters one. Goal nodes will usually have (legal) successors, which make it easy for the search to go right past the goal.

Frequently the object of a problem solving method is to find not just any solution but one which optimizes some measure. Thus we often seek the *shortest* path from starting node to goal node. Or, if some operators take more time or resources to apply, we may associate a cost with each arc and try to find the *minimum cost* solution. If all arcs have unit cost, the two criteria are equivalent.

Independently of the criterion of solution optimality, we may also wish to minimize the search effort (number of nodes examined) of a problem solving method. Nilsson calls a search algorithm *admissible* if it always finds a best (minimal cost) solution (providing any solution path exists). Of course any algorithm which simply examines all possible paths is admissible, even if wholly impractical. An admissible algorithm is also *optimal* if it expands (generates the successors of) no nodes other than those expanded by any other algorithm which has access to "less information" (a phrase we will clarify later).

Before looking more carefully at state space search methods let us consider an example of a state space representation. The problem we deal with is the well known "Tower of Hanoi" puzzle in which a stack of variable diameter disks must be transferred from the leftmost to the rightmost of three pegs by moving one disk at a time and never placing a larger disk on top of a smaller one. Although the solution can be generalized to any number, three disks make for a simple but interesting problem.

Following Nilsson, let us denote a *state* of the problem by a triple of numbers specifying the peg positions of the large, intermediate, and small disks (in that order), assuming the pegs are numbered from left to right. Since only legal states will be included we may assume that whenever two or three disks are on the same peg, larger disks are always below smaller ones. The starting state in this representation is thus 111, while the goal is 333. A graph of the 27 possible states is shown in Figure 14.1. Note that each state is a successor of all its successors, since any operation can be immediately reversed. The operations themselves, sufficiently simple that they need not be shown on the graph, consist of moving the top disk on peg i to a distinct peg j, for all six i–j combinations. Since the graph is small enough to be shown explicitly, the shortest solution path can be seen to consist of the eight nodes running down the right hand side of the outside triangle.

The notions of breadth first and depth first search (see Section 12.1) carry over fairly directly from game trees to problem graphs, with two important additional considerations. First, because a graph may contain cycles we must keep track of which nodes have been visited in order to avoid "going around in circles." Second, because the solution to the problem is contained in the path traversed (rather than in the achievement of some

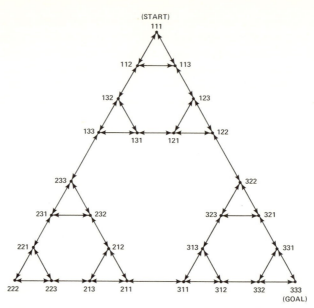

Figure 14.1. State space representation for 3-disk Tower of Hanoi puzzle.

"winning" state), we must remember the *sequences* of nodes traversed by using some sort of "reverse pointer" system. After reaching a goal node, we can then recreate the solution by tracing backwards to the start node.

Simple, undirected depth or breadth first search is usually as inefficient for problem graphs as it is for game trees. In the latter case we have seen how alpha-beta cutoffs and various pruning methods can considerably reduce the search effort. These techniques required an evaluation function which measured the goodness of various game positions. An analogous notion can be introduced into problem graphs if we realize that the game evaluation functions were in sense measuring "closeness to a win." Thus we require some way of comparing nodes in a problem graph with respect to which is most likely to be on a shortest path to a goal node. Good problem graph evaluation functions are typically as difficult to find as good game tree ones. Usually we work with some (heuristic) estimate of the true function. The efficacy of the search depends on the quality of the estimate.

Although any more detailed consideration of state space search is beyond the scope of our discussion, we should not leave this form of problem representation without mentioning a method developed by Nilsson and his colleagues, called the A* algorithm. In this algorithm $g(n)$ represents the minimum distance (or cost) from the start node to node n, $h(n)$ the minimum from node n to a goal node, and $f(n) = g(n) + h(n)$ the minimum length of a solution path via node n. The algorithm uses $h'(n)$, an estimate of $h(n)$, so that the evaluation function estimating $f(n)$ is $f'(n) = g(n) + h'(n)$. (This form is actually for trees. For graphs we must also estimate $g(n)$ by $g'(n)$ since the shortest path to node n may not have been followed. But using the actual path as an estimate of $g(n)$ turns out not to affect the algorithm's behavior if h' is *consistent* in that $h'(m) - h'(n)$ is the true cost of a minimal path from m to n.) In operation, the A^* algorithm always next expands the (breadth first) node with smallest value of $f'(n)$.

Nilsson has shown that A^* is admissible, providing that $h'(n)$ is a lower bound on $h(n)$. Algorithm A is called *more informed* than algorithm B if A computes a lower bound on $h(n)$ that is everywhere strictly greater than that computed by B. Nilsson has shown that A^* is optimal in the following sense: if A and A^* are admissible algorithms such that A^* is more informed than A, then for any graph, if a node is expanded by A^* it is also expanded by A (provided the above mentioned consistency holds for h' of A).

As an illustration of h' (i.e., a consistent lower bound on h), consider the following estimate of the remaining number of operations required at any node in the Tower of Hanoi graph (Figure 14.1): $h' = $ number of disks not in their final positions on the rightmost peg, plus the number of obstructing disks, where an obstructing disk is either on top of another disk on the left or middle peg, or in the wrong position on the right peg.

We turn now to the second major representation used in problem solving research, that of problem reduction. In this approach graph structures are again employed, but with some important differences from their use in state space representations. First, problem reduction graphs are frequently smaller, mostly because more implicit problem analysis is accomplished by the complex reduction operators than by the simple state transformation operators. Second, it is often possible to carry out problem reduction with tree structures instead of the more complex graph structures. There is less likelihood of solving the same subproblem more than once, compared to state spaces where a given state may typically be reached through many paths and will thus be a successor of many nodes.

The third and most important distinctive feature of problem reduction graphs is the special types of nodes employed. When a problem node has been reduced to subproblems, from one to all of the successor nodes may need to be "solved" in order to consider the original node solved. If any one of the successors suffices we have a disjunctive situation, called an *OR node*. If all the successors must be solved we have an *AND node*. We distinguish AND nodes by tying the arcs together with a horizontal line, as will be illustrated in Figure 14.2. When solving a node depends on a complex combination of AND and OR conditions among its successors, the situation can be simplified by introducing "dummy" nodes so that all nodes are of the simple AND and OR types. Such a tree (graph) is called an *AND/OR tree* (graph). In the remainder of this section, we consider representations and search procedures for subproblem AND/OR trees.

As already suggested, the nodes in a problem reduction tree correspond to *problem descriptions*. The root node describes the problem to be solved. Level one nodes describe the subproblems, the solution to one (if the root

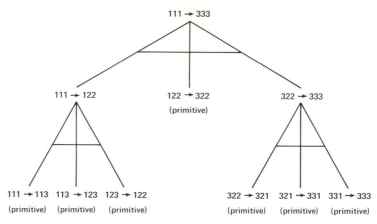

Figure 14.2.   Subproblem tree for Tower of Hanoi puzzle.

node is an OR node) or all (if an AND node) of which amounts to solving the main problem. Subproblems may be reduced to subsubproblems, and so on, until the tree terminates in a group of nodes describing problems whose solutions are trivial. These *primitive* problems can be solved immediately either because their solutions are already known to the system or because the solution transformations are elementary operations in the problem's state space. The ability to detect primitive problems is just as crucial to the problem reduction approach as is the ability to recognize goal states in the state space approach.

The arcs in a problem reduction tree represent the application of *problem reduction operators*. Several such operators may be applicable to a given node, giving a number of alternative solution paths. The nature of problem reduction operators, as well as of problem descriptions and primitive problems, is highly problem dependent and can best be illustrated by example.

We return to the Tower of Hanoi problem and describe it and its associated subproblems in terms of transforming one state into another. As shown in Figure 14.2 the root node of the problem reduction tree is thus 111 → 333. Now in order to get all of the disks on the right hand peg, we must clearly put the biggest one there. That task becomes primitive (requiring a single move) if the right hand peg is empty and the big disk is alone on the left hand peg; the associated subproblem is 122 → 322. To isolate the big disk we must *also* (this is an AND node) find a way to put the other two disks on the center peg (subproblem 111 → 122). If we can solve both of these subproblems *and* figure out how to get the two smaller disks from the center peg to their correct positions on top of the big disk on the right hand peg (subproblem 322 → 333), then the main problem is solved. But neither of the two outside level one nodes in Figure 14.2 is a primitive problem (since movement of two disks is required). So each of these nodes is further reduced to three ANDed primitive problems by the sort of reasoning just employed.

180

A solution to all seven primitive problems can now be "backed up" to a solution of the main problem at the root node.

This example illustrates the frequent, and sometimes deceptive, similarity between the problem reduction and state space problem solving methods. As Nilsson observes, state space search employs a trivial kind of problem reduction, since each step along a solution path produces a slightly simpler equivalent problem. The problem reduction approach is actually more general in that it provides a way to search separately for subpaths and to connect such subpaths into full solutions. The more general method is not used in every case because of the often immense difficulties in finding appropriate subproblem descriptions and problem reduction operators.

Searching AND/OR trees, in either breadth first or depth first order, is much like searching game trees, except for some important pruning and termination considerations. We may recursively define the *solved* nodes of a tree as the terminal nodes (primitive problem descriptions), any OR nodes with at least one solved successor, and any AND nodes with all successors solved. Similarly the *unsolvable* nodes are nonterminal nodes with no successors, OR nodes with no solvable successors, and AND nodes with one or more unsolvable successors. In searching an AND/OR tree for a subtree that represents a solution to the problem, we clearly need not examine any (additional) successors of solved nodes, since *any* solution suffices. Similarly, it is pointless to expand any successors of unsolvable nodes. Finally, every time we place a new node in the solved or unsolvable category we must check back through the search tree to see if it is now possible to consider the original problem solved or unsolvable. The possibility of showing rather early in the search that a problem is unsolvable (with the available operators) often gives the problem reduction approach an advantage over the state space formulation.

Nilsson has developed an ordered search algorithm for AND/OR trees which has points of similarity to the A^* algorithm for state graphs. The cost of a solution tree may be defined as either the total number of arcs in the tree or the length of the longest path in the tree. In both cases Nilsson provides a recursively defined estimator $h'(n)$ of the cost of a solution tree rooted at n. This estimator can then be used to order for expansion nodes generated in a breadth first search, in a fashion similar to the use of h' in A^*. Nilsson has demonstrated the admissibility but not the optimality of this ordered search algorithm.

14.2 The General Problem Solver

In the late 1950's Newell, Shaw, and Simon were led by their work on the Logic Theorist (see Chapter 13) to initiate research on the General Problem Solver (GPS). Partly because of its origins, GPS was first applied to problems expressed in the propositional calculus. The system has subsequently developed through half a dozen major modifications and been used to solve a great variety of problems. Our discussion will focus on the latest version of GPS. In addition, we will emphasize the operation and performance of the GPS problem solving algorithms, to the point of neglecting its contribution to the simulation of human behavior. It should never be forgotten that a model of the way people reason in solving problems was a major concern in the work of Newell and his colleagues.

GPS searches a type of problem reduction tree in which the root node represents the main goal (problem to be solved) and successors represent various types of subgoals. Search of the implicit tree is guided by a general technique called *means-end analysis*. Subgoals are generated in this method by finding and attempting to reduce *differences* between the initial state and the goal state expressed in the main goal. In GPS terminology, such states are called *objects*. For any given problem, GPS is supplied with a *task environment* containing the differences that might be encountered and a *difference-ordering* which places the differences in estimated order of difficulty of reduction. Differences are reduced by the application of *operators*, which are supplied as part of the task environment, along with a *table of connections* indicating which operators are applicable to reducing which differences.

The GPS "problem solving executive" can attempt to achieve four types of goals: (1) *transform* object A into object B, possibly by going through a series of intermediate objects; (2) *reduce difference D* on object A, by modifications of relevant features of A; (3) *apply operator Q* to object A, thus generating a new object; and (4) *select* the elements of a set S which best fulfill criterion C, where C is stated with respect to some object (e.g., "select element of S most similar to object A"). To achieve any goal the executive invokes one of a set of applicable *methods*. If all such methods fail, other goals are attempted, and so on, until GPS either solves the problem or gives up.

Since there are more than a dozen methods and submethods, we cannot consider them individually or in detail. To illustrate the hierarchical nature of method interactions we consider a typical sequence which might be invoked in an attempt to satisfy a *transform* type goal. The global TRANS-FORM-METHOD calls upon the MATCH-DIFF-METHOD which detects all differences between the two objects and uses SELECT-DIFFER-ENCE to determine the most difficult. If a goal can then be constructed to reduce this difference, control passes to the REDUCE-METHOD which selects a suitable operator and attempts to create a goal of applying this operator to the initial object. Depending on the type of operator to be applied, one of several OPERATOR-METHODS is used. This kind of intricate methodological tour is fortunately not necessary to understand the operation of GPS at the level and for the examples of interest to us. We will analyze problems in terms of the goal trees GPS creates for them.

To illustrate the way in which GPS solves a problem, let us consider its behavior on the relatively simple, and now classic, "Monkey Task." This problem is set in a rectangular roofed cage with an integral "place numbering" system to specify locations on the floor. At (or over) three distinct such locations are a monkey, a box, and (suspended from the ceiling) a bunch of bananas. The monkey can walk around, move the box around, climb the box, and grasp the bananas if they are within reach. To reach the height of the bananas the monkey must be standing on the box. The problem is to find the sequence of steps required for the monkey to get the bananas. Phrased carefully, the solution goes as follows: (1) the monkey walks from his initial place to the place of the box; (2) the monkey pushes the box from its initial place to the place under the bananas (and therefore moves himself to the same location); (3) the monkey climbs the box; (4) the monkey grasps the bananas. Let us see how GPS goes about finding this solution.

As its TOP-GOAL GPS wants to transform the INITIAL-OBJECT into the DESIRED-OBJECT. The INITIAL-OBJECT has the monkey in place 1, the box in place 2, and the monkey's hand empty. The DESIRED-OBJECT has the bananas in the monkey's hand. Four operators are defined, each with one or more associated *pretests* to see if the current object is suitable for the application of that operator. The operators are: (1) CLIMB (pretest: monkey's place equals box's place) which causes the monkey's place to become on-box; (2) WALK-TO-X (pretest: X is in the set of places) which changes the monkey's place to place X; (3) MOVE-BOX-TO-X (pretests: X is in the set of places, monkey's place is in the set of places and equals box's place) which changes the box's and monkey's places to X; and (4) GET-BANANAS (pretests: box's place equals under-bananas, monkey's place equals on-box) which causes the monkey's hand to contain the bananas. Three differences are specified. In order of increasing difficulty, $D1 =$ (a difference in the) monkey's place, $D2 =$ box's place, and $D3 =$ contents of monkey's hand. For this problem the table of connections is nonselective; all operators may be useful in reducing all differences.

Figure 14.3a shows a tree of the 13 goals GPS generated in solving the Monkey task; the goals are numbered in the order in which they were generated. The INITIAL-OBJECT, DESIRED-OBJECT, and differences were specified above. Intermediate objects generated by GPS are shown in Figure 14.3b. Note that GPS first attempts to reduce the most difficult difference ($D3$) which results in an attempt to apply GET-BANANAS. It then becomes apparent that $D2$ must be reduced, generating an application of MOVE-BOX, which in turn requires the use of WALK to reduce $D1$. With Goal 4 satisfied, attention is turned to the other successor of Goal 3. It is but a few more steps until the problem is successfully solved. Goal 13 simply discards the place information from OBJECT-4 to make it identical to the DESIRED-OBJECT.

GPS solved the Monkey task relatively quickly; processing of 13 goals required the equivalent of less than two minutes on a contemporary computer. More representative performance figures were demonstrated on tasks involving symbolic integration (22 goals), letter series completion (27 goals),

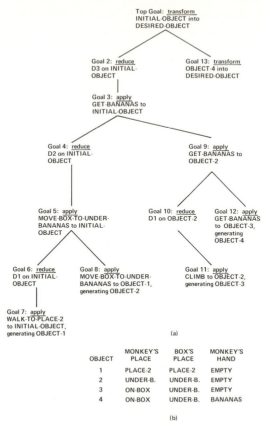

Figure 14.3. (a) Goal tree and (b) intermediate objects for GPS solution of Monkey Task.

a 4-disk Tower of Hanoi puzzle (46 goals), and resolution principle proof of a predicate calculus theorem (56 goals). GPS was also successfully applied to another half-dozen widely varying puzzles and tasks.

It must be noted that a good deal of the impressive flexibility and generality of GPS depends on the experimenter's ability to specify functional task environments, useful operators, and effective difference orderings and connection tables. Nevertheless, GPS was certainly the first truly multipurpose problem solving program, and remains one of the outstanding demonstrations of generality in artificial intelligence. In the next section we take a brief look at some of the more recent efforts in general problem solving, many of which have been strongly influenced by aspects of GPS.

14.3 Other problem solving programs

The following thumbnail sketches of three general purpose problem solving systems indicate the nature of recent research in the area. Three important concepts not explicitly discussed previously in this chapter emerge from these examples. First we will discover the strong interconnections between problem solving and mechanical theorem proving. Second we will see how important the notion of *planning* the solution to a problem has become. Finally we will encounter some attempts to include a learning component in problem solvers, so that experience with previous problems of a given type can facilitate future performance.

Our first example is the MULTIPLE (MULTIpurpose Program that LEarns) system developed in the mid to late 1960's by James Slagle and his colleagues at the National Institutes of Health. MULTIPLE searches an implicit AND/OR goal tree and tries to develop a constructive proof that the top goal is achievable in terms of a set of lower level goals. The system consists of two independent parts. The Proving Program (PP) uses an experimenter supplied subgoal generation mechanism to expand goal nodes in order of their "promise" for finding an early solution. A node's promise is calculated by a combination of two evaluation functions to be described shortly. The other component of MULTIPLE is the Learning Program (LP), which attempts to improve the evaluation functions used by PP, on the basis of experience with problems of a general type.

PP evaluates a node according to its *probability* and *merit*. A goal's probability is the likelihood that it can be achieved. The closer this value can be forced to 1 (or 0), the closer the program is to proving (or disproving) the node. An AND node's probability can be backed up as the product of the probabilities of its subnodes. The backing-up formula is only slightly more involved for an OR node. A (sub)node has merit to the extent that expanding it is expected to change the probability of the top node and to be relatively cheap in terms of effort. Merit values can be calculated from a measure called the *self-merit* of individual nodes, computed as the ratio of the expected change in the goal's own probability to the expected cost of expansion.

Given functions for probability and self-merit, PP searches a tree by trying to expand the most meritorious unexpanded goals, while backing up probability and merit values from new unexpanded goals to the top goal. PP was originally tested with evaluation functions supplied by the experimenter and with the learning component of MULTIPLE inoperative. The performance of the system, in proving that wins could be forced by a particular side in a game called kalah, proved superior to an adaptation of the alpha-beta tree search algorithm to the same problem.

In subsequent experiments with resolution based proofs of predicate calculus theorems, the LP component was incorporated. Initial evaluation functions supplied to PP contained features like number of literals in goal clause and number of resolutions possible from goal clause. After preselection of 13 such features, LP used the results of PP's experience to produce optimal weights for linear combinations of the features. The results of several experiments showed that LP significantly improved MULTIPLE's performance on problems within a particular domain (e.g., plane geometry, group theory). While experience in one such domain did not transfer well to another domain, a system learning from experience in many domains showed good flexibility when extended to new problem types.

Our second example of a recent problem solving system is the STanford Research Institute Problem Solver (STRIPS) developed by Fikes, Nilsson, and others. STRIPS employs a combination of resolution theorem proving and GPS-like means-end analysis to achieve goals for a robot which navigates in a "world" consisting of several rooms with interconnecting doors. The STRIPS problem space is defined by three entities: (1) a *world model* which maintains a current description of the "floor plan" of the environment and the contents of the rooms, in terms of predicate calculus formulas (e.g.,

> PUSHABLE (BOX2),
> INROOM (BOX2, ROOM3),
> INROOM (ROBOT, ROOM1),
> CONNECTS (DOOR2, ROOM2, ROOM5),
> STATUS (LIGHTSWITCH, OFF));

(2) a set of *operators* (actually operator schemata) which govern the robot's actions and which have associated *preconditions* for their application, and well defined *effects* on the world model (e.g., $goto(x)$, $pushto(x)$, $turnonlight(x)$, $climbonbox(x)$, $gothrudoor(d, x, y)$); (3) a goal condition expressed as a predicate calculus formula.

To generate a search tree of subgoals, STRIPS first applies its theorem prover to see if the main goal is a logical consequence of the initial world model. If not, the incomplete proof is used to generate a "difference" between the model and the goal. Operators relevant to "reducing" the difference are applied to generate subgoals. This methodology, reduction of differences by selection of relevant operators which meet appropriate preconditions, is derived rather directly from GPS. Like MULTIPLE, STRIPS employs an evaluation function to order subgoals for expansion.

The STRIPS system as just described was able to perform tasks like turning on a lightswitch (by climbing on a box) and pushing three boxes together, developing search trees of around a dozen goals to do so. The next major addition to STRIPS was a capacity for generalizing solutions to particular problems into *plans* which could be applied to future tasks. Such generalization requires careful substitution of variables for individual constants throughout the sequence of operators used to solve the original problem. The result is a sort of operator-sequence schema, called a *macrop*. To deal with the complex problem of macrop applicability, the STRIPS designers developed an ingenious structure (called a *triangle table*) for determining whether a given plan or any subplan pieces of it could be used to operate on the current world model. Planning using triangle tables has provided as much as a threefold speedup in STRIPS solutions of robot movement problems. This improvement in performance is naturally counter-acted somewhat by the amount of time required to find applicable plans, especially when the number of available plans becomes large.

Our third and final example of a problem solving system carries the notion of planning even further. In fact PLANNER, developed by Carl Hewitt and his colleagues at MIT, is not so much a problem solving system as a general purpose artificial intelligence language, which can be used to program the achievement of goals by plan formulation in a wide variety of applications. In the next chapter, for example, we will see that a subset of PLANNER called MICRO-PLANNER has been used as an important component of a natural language understanding system. Since its inception in the late 1960's several versions of PLANNER have been described, but not fully implemented. Since the language is still evolving, our discussion will be limited to brief descriptions of some of the major features of PLANNER.

PLANNER stores its "knowledge of the world" in a *data base* which consists of two kinds of structures. The first kind we have seen before. *Factual knowledge* is stored in the form of assertions expressed as predicate calculus formulas, similar to those used in STRIPS model of the world. The second component of the data base represents *procedural knowledge* in the form of (predicate calculus) theorems and programs. PLANNER was one of the first systems to incorporate the important notion that much of the knowledge people use in solving problems is of the "how to" form. Thus PLANNER *consequent* theorems express ways to reason, to reduce prob-lems to subproblems, and to act so as to accomplish desired goals. Other types of theorems allow the system to deduce the logical implications of adding or deleting assertions in the data base. An important feature of the way PLANNER expresses goals is the option for incorporation of experi-menter supplied *recommendations* of useful approaches to achieving the goal.

An important aspect of the control structure with which PLANNER operates on the data base is *automatic failure-driven backtracking*. When a search fails to produce a desired object (or, more generally, to evaluate a given expression), the language provides for return to the most recent choice point and reinitiation of search along a new path. The idea of backtracking in this fashion was of course used in GPS and other early problem solving systems. What PLANNER innovates is a language feature which frees the programmer from coding the backtrack mechanism. The PLANNER con-trol structure also incorporates *multiprocessing*, in which (simulated) parallel search from several "control loci" can be carried out.

One of PLANNER'S most significant contributions is *pattern directed* search of the data base. Assertions can be retrieved on the basis of their format. Procedures can be sought which "promise to accomplish" particular kinds of objectives. Thus when new items are added to the data base, their presence need not be accommodated by adjustment of existing routines. An item will automatically be accessed when it fulfills the requirements of the current pattern. Like automatic backtracking, pattern directed search has antecedents in earlier problem solving systems (e.g., the GPS connection-table matching of differences and operators); but PLANNER implements the idea in a much more general and convenient form.

There are of course some problems with PLANNER. Some of the difficulties have been remedied in later versions of the system. Other issues have led to the development of alternative general purpose artificial intelligence languages. In any case, it cannot be disputed that recent work on such languages has given artificial intelligence research a tremendous boost.

Bibliography

Many works relevant to problem solving have been listed in the Bibliographies of the previous few chapters. Both the Hunt and Jackson books (Chapter 11) treat representations, search, and several specific systems including GPS, STRIPS, and PLANNER. Hunt's coverage is more extensive and formal. Feigenbaum and Feldman reprint an early GPS paper, while Newell and Simon give a somewhat updated account from the viewpoint of modelling human reasoning. Slagle develops the Monkey task for GPS, as described in Section 14.2, and provides a good introduction to his MULTIPLE system. (See Chapter 12 for all three books just mentioned.) Nilsson's *Problem Solving Methods in Artificial Intelligence* (listed in Chapter 13) is probably the best systematic treatment of representation and search, as discussed in the first section of this chapter. The book below offers the most comprehensive treatment of GPS, including a full description of how all tasks were solved by the latest version.

Ernst, George W., and Newell, Allen. *GPS: A Case Study in Generality and Problem Solving*. Academic Press, 1969.

Exercises

14.1. Formulate a state space representation and show the complete problem graph for the Missionaries and Cannibals Problem, described as follows. Three missionaries, three cannibals, and a rowboat are on the left bank of a river. The boat can hold at most two people. Everyone can row. Figure out how to get all six people over to the right bank subject to the constraint that the number of cannibals on a bank may never exceed the number of missionaries there (unless there are no missionaries at all on that bank), so that no missionaries will be ganged up on and eaten.

14.2. Using the h' function suggested in Section 14.1, carry out an A^* search of the Tower of Hanoi graph in Figure 14.1. Indicate all nodes actually visited in the search.

14.3. An AND/OR tree in which all odd-level nodes are OR nodes and all even-level nodes are AND nodes corresponds closely to a two-person game tree. (a) Describe the correspondence precisely. (b) Discuss the use of game tree search methods for such problem trees.

14.4. Formulate a GPS representation and solution for the Three Coins Problem, described as follows. Three coins are placed on a table such that the middle one shows heads and the other two tails. Give a sequence of *exactly* three moves which will cause all the coins to show the same face, where a *move* corresponds to turning over exactly two of the three coins. [*Hint:* the desired object must include the value of "3" for a counter which keeps track of the number of operator applications.]

14.5. Formulate a GPS representation and solution for the (3-disk) Tower of Hanoi problem. [*Hint:* for a proper difference ordering GPS will make no mistakes in proceeding to the solution of this problem.]

15
Natural language processing

Despite the apparent lack of effect, people frequently talk to their machines. To replace such fruitless monologs with productive dialogs is probably the most important and most ambitious goal of artificial intelligence. Since nearly all of man's intellectual activities involve language, a full mechanical language processing capability would seem to imply competence in most aspects of human intelligence.

The above observation was made as early as 1950 by Alan M. Turing (of Turing machine fame) when he proposed his well known "test" for machine intelligence. Turing suggested that an interrogator sit in a room with two teletypes, one with a human at the other end of the line, and one with a computer. The interrogator questions the two (unidentified) conversants and attempts to determine which is which. Ideally, the experiment should be repeated many times, with the same program but different people. If the machine is correctly identified no more than half the time it can be said to manifest human-like intelligence in the sense that it has "passed" Turing's test.

The Turing criterion has been subject to considerable criticism, some of which was anticipated by Turing in his early discussions. It would, for example, be rather pointless to require that a computer slow down its arithmetic operations to human rates. Nevertheless Turing's test has yet to be passed, and does serve to emphasize the fundamental role of natural language processing in artificial intelligence.

It should be noted that Turing did not require the computer to understand or produce speech. Automatic speech recognition and production is an important area of contemporary AI research. But our discussion will be concerned exclusively with efforts to communicate with machines via written language. Presumably an effective speech processor could be added as a "front end" to a language processing program, at some future date.

In this chapter we first introduce a few important concepts about natural language contributed by the science of linguistics (Section 15.1) and then describe in some detail three recent research efforts which illustrate the variety of current approaches to the language processing problem. Before beginning these investigations however, we take a quick look at some highlights in the history of language processing by computer.

The earliest work on natural language automation involved attempts to have computers translate from one language to another. Such Mechanical Translation (MT) projects assumed that only a *dictionary*, listing the equivalent words in each language, and *grammar*, describing how to order and inflect (put "endings" on) the output, would suffice. Eventually it became clear that natural language was too complex for such simple analyses. Translation without *understanding* the meaning of sentences was found to be a dead end. Such understanding is now considered to require knowledge of both the *context* of utterances (what has been said before) and the *environment* ("world," domain of discussion) in which they are uttered. After more than a decade of intensive research, MT projects were largely abandoned in the early 1960's. Enough more has since been learned about natural language structure and automation so that MT again appears to be a reasonable research prospect.

With the demise of MT research, investigators turned to problems of understanding restricted kinds of utterances in a single language. Most of these early artificial intelligence programs (and many recent ones as well) can be described under the general heading of Question Answering systems. Using a fairly small data base, frequently represented as some sort of list structure, such programs attempt to derive the questioner's meaning, search the data base for an answer, and express the answer in more or less natural English. Of the many such "first generation" language processing systems, we mention only two.

An early system which came surprisingly close to passing the Turing test, at least for short periods of discourse, was Joseph Weizenbaum's ELIZA. ELIZA plays the role of a psychiatrist discussing the conversant's problems, a situation in which unconnected remarks and sudden shifts of topic are not too surprising. The program actually does very little processing. Input sentences are matched against form classes, key content words extracted, and responses produced from groups of standard utterances, sometimes with the conversant's keywords inserted. The following, partly hypothetical dialog indicates both ELIZA's deceptive conversational abilities and its true weaknesses.

Human: My boyfriend made me come here.
ELIZA: Your boyfriend made you come here?
Human: He says I'm depressed.
ELIZA: I am sorry to hear you are depressed.
Human: It may be because of my father.

ELIZA: Tell me more about your family.
Human: Asdfghjkl.
ELIZA: Why do you say that?
Human: Qwertyuiop.
ELIZA: Are you certain of that?

A contemporary of ELIZA was Bertram Raphael's SIR (Semantic Information Retrieval) system. Although SIR really did not understand language much better than ELIZA, it could manipulate a small set of relations among the items of discussion and thus carry out a primitive form of reasoning in attempting to answer questions. SIR accepted information and questions in a quite limited format. Here is a portion of an actual dialog with SIR.

Human: Every boy is a person.
SIR: I understand.
Human: A finger is part of a hand.
SIR: I understand.
Human: Each person has two hands.
SIR: The sentence is ambiguous; please rephrase.
Human: There are two hands on each person.
SIR: I understand.
Human: How many fingers does John have?
SIR: I don't know whether finger is part of John.
Human: John is a boy.
SIR: I understand.
Human: How many fingers does John have?
SIR: How many finger per hand?
Human: Every hand has five fingers.
SIR: I understand.
Human: How many fingers does John have?
SIR: The answer is ten.

The "ambiguity" in the Human's third sentence arises because SIR does not know whether to use the relation "has-as-parts" or "has" in the sense of ownership. Note that SIR is capable of identifying the information it requires to answer a question.

15.1 Linguistics

It is difficult to appreciate current research in natural language processing without some knowledge of basic terminology and concepts in the field of linguistics. In this section we consider relevant highlights of *descriptive* (English) linguistics, that branch of the science concerned with providing a systematic account of the structure of present day utterances.

Linguists describe language phenomena at several hierarchically organized levels. The lowest level description of spoken language is in terms of its elementary sounds, the study of which is known as *phonology*. Roughly, a group of similar speech sounds which function in the same way, and which may be substituted for each other without changing the meaning of an utterance, is called a *phoneme*. Depending on the language and on the precise definition of a phoneme, linguists may find from 30 to 80 phonemes in a human language. English is usually described in terms of about 40 phonemes of which perhaps 10 will be "vowel" sounds and the rest "consonants." We will not really be concerned with phonology in this chapter, since the systems we study all use written input and output. The basic unit of written language is called the *grapheme*. Although more careful definitions are possible, it will suffice in our discussion to consider the set of English graphemes as consisting of the alphabetic characters, punctuation marks, and the blank. Since these symbols may be assigned direct computer representations, graphemic analysis is usually a trivial aspect of (written) language automation.

The second level of linguistic analysis is *morphology*. A *morpheme* is the minimal meaningful unit of a spoken language and consists of a sequence of one or more phonemes. In English many simple words are morphemes, but so are various inflectional sounds which convey meaning, like the plural endings. When two or more phoneme sequences function in the same way to convey the same meaning (such as the different plural sounds in "cars," "trucks," and "buses") they are considered to be *allomorphs* of the same morpheme. Natural language processing systems frequently have to deal with the morphemic components of written words. Thus it is useful to be able to segment a word like "unknowables," to find its root form ("know"), and to determine the meaning change effected by each of the additional morphemes ("un-," "-able," "-s").

The way in which meaningful components are put together to form an utterance (or sentence) is the subject of *syntax*. The notion that a sentence is made up of a hierarchy of constituents has been central to most of the many theories of syntax. Such a constituent structure can be represented in terms of a tree, like that shown for a simple sentence in Figure 15.1a. A set of

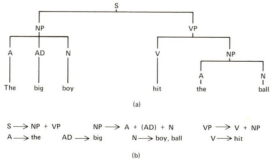

Figure 15.1. (a) Parse tree and (b) phrase-structure rules for a simple English sentence.

Abbreviations: S—sentence; NP—noun phrase; VP—verb phrase; A—article; AD—adjective; N—noun; V—verb.

Parentheses indicate optional component in product of rule; two rewriting choices are separated by commas.

rewriting or *phrase-structure rules* which can generate the sentence with the constituent relations of Figure 15.1a is shown in Figure 15.1b. (Phrase-structure rules are of the context free type, as described in Section 4.4.) Such rules may be used not only to generate sentences but also to analyze, or *parse*, them into constituent structures. Trees like that shown are sometimes called *parse trees*.

Modern theories of syntax are so complex that we can only sketch their general features. The present day approach to syntax is the product of a revolution in linguistics largely attributable to the writings of one man, Noam Chomsky of MIT (whose work on formal grammars was discussed in Section 4.4). In his 1957 book *Syntactic Structures* Chomsky demonstrated the inadequacies of simple phrase-structure grammars as accounts of natural language phenomena. He argued for the addition of *transformations* which could restructure the so-called "kernel sentences" in a variety of obligatory and optional ways. Thus given two simple active declarative sentences, one might be made passive, the other negated, and the two conjoined by successive application of three transformations. These ideas were the beginning of the *generative-transformational* view of syntax, a view which in a considerably evolved and altered form remains the most popular approach today.

In 1965 Chomsky introduced a number of major revisions to generative-transformational theory, in a book called *Aspects of the Theory of Syntax*. The syntactic portion of the new theory included a *base* component to generate *deep structures* and a *transformational* component to produce *surface structures* from deep structures. The base was further divided into a *categorial component* (the phrase-structure rules) and a *lexicon* or dictionary of words. Each word in the lexicon was described in terms of its "part of speech" and a number of *selection restrictions* governing the contexts in which it could be used. Thus certain verbs, like "eat," might be required to have an animate subject, while others, like "talk," a human one.

The transformational component of the 1965 model differed in many ways from the earlier theory. For one thing, transformations which changed the meaning of an utterance (like negation) were no longer permitted, so that all content of an utterance had to come from the base component. A second major change was that many base level components typically contributed to the surface structure of even a simple sentence. Although deep structures are not usually expressed in English, we might imagine the sentence of Figure 15.1 as a result of combining deep structures corresponding to the two elementary propositions "The boy is big" and "The boy hit the ball."

The Chomskian view of language tended to separate the syntactic or structural aspects and treat them as logically prior to the *semantic* (meaning) content of utterances. The 1965 model did incorporate semantic considerations into the selectional restrictions of the lexicon; but the theory as a whole still tended to view semantics as something of an afterthought, to be worked out separately from a sentence's structure. Many linguists, including several of Chomsky's students, took exception to this "back seat" role for semantics and formulated new theories in which semantics figured more prominently and at an earlier stage in utterance production.

One such theory was the *case grammar* developed by Fillmore and others. Case grammar analysis of a sentence regards the verb as a central focus, to which most other components relate according to a half-dozen functional roles or cases. Thus in the sentence "Bill opened the door in the hall with the key," "Bill" is in the *agentive* case, "hall" is *locative*, and "key" is *instrumental*. In Section 15.4 we will be discussing a language processing system which incorporates similar notions of case in its semantic analyses.

Lest the above discussion convey the impression that all important syntactic theories are Chomskian in their origins, we should emphasize that alternatives have always existed. In Section 15.3 we will examine a very successful language processing system which employs the Systemic Grammar approach developed in Britain by Halliday.

15.2 The work of Quillian

In the mid-1960's M. Ross Quillian developed two related models of natural language information representation and storage. Of the three currently popular formats for representing meaning and storing knowledge, Quillian's systems typify the *semantic network* approach. In such systems conceptual entities are represented by the nodes of a graph-like structure. Links between the nodes may be labelled to indicate various types of relationships among concepts. In the next section we will be looking at an outstanding example of a second format, *procedural* representation. We will not illustrate the third approach, that of *logic based* representation, in this chapter. An idea of how such systems employ predicate calculus to organize and store knowledge can be derived from our discussion of the STRIPS problem solving system in the last chapter (although STRIPS was not, of course, specialized for processing natural language).

In this section we first take a brief look at the model proposed by Quillian in his 1966 Carnegie–Mellon University doctoral thesis, then consider the more refined "Teachable Language Comprehender" (TLC) he described in 1969. It should be emphasized that Quillian's work was very much in the "Carnegie–Mellon tradition" of Newell and others, in that he regarded his systems as simulation models of human language processing.

The semantic network of Quillian's thesis model contained nodes representing individual occurrences of words (or concepts). For each concept there was a unique *type node*, linked to configurations of other nodes which embodied definitions of various meanings of the concept, and an unlimited number of *token nodes*, one for each occurrence of the concept in the definitions of other type nodes.

Figure 15.2a shows the six major kinds of links which could occur between

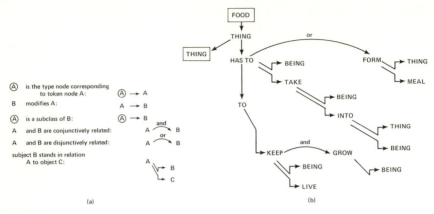

Figure 15.2. (a) Types of links and (b) definition of FOOD in Quillian's semantic network.

pairs of nodes. Figure 15.2b is an example of an encoding of the two definitions of the concept "food," based on the following simplified dictionary entry: "That which living being has to take in to keep it living and for growth. Things forming meals." Type nodes are circled in the figure; but only one of the token to type pointers is shown, although a similar pointer would exist for each token node.

Quillian's program consisted of three routines for constructing and operating on the semantic network. The first routine accepted hand-coded versions of dictionary definitions and incorporated them into a fully interconnected net. Computer memory size limited a network to about 20 major concepts. The second routine demonstrated the system's understanding of interrelated concepts by comparing pairs of words. The routine started at the type nodes for the given words and simulated a parallel search along all paths until one or more intersections were found. Such intersections were used by a third routine to express relations between concepts in rough English output.

Thus when asked to process the pair of concepts CRY and COMFORT, the search routine found an intersection in the concept SAD of paths from the second sense of CRY and the third sense of COMFORT. The output was: "CRY2 IS AMONG OTHER THINGS TO MAKE A SAD SOUND. TO COMFORT3 CAN BE TO MAKE SOMETHING LESS SAD." When more than one intersection was found for the same or for different senses of the concept pair, all relations were reported.

Although Quillian's thesis model did not communicate with the user in particularly fluent English, such was not its objective. What the system did demonstrate was the power of semantic networks in the representation and processing of natural language concepts. Many present day semantic network based systems owe a good deal to Quillian's early work.

Quillian's TLC model employs a semantic memory network developed from his thesis research, but uses quite different processing routines to "understand" natural language input and add its meaning to the memory structure. That structure consists of *dictionary*, a set of *units*, and a set of *properties*. The dictionary is simply a list of all distinct English words known to the system. There is a pointer from each word to at least one unit.

A unit represents a concept, usually one meaning of a dictionary word, although the system can work with concepts for which it has no names. Each unit typically has one pointer to a *superset* unit and pointers to zero or more properties. Thus TLC defines concepts in a manner analogous to the classical approach of putting an object in its class (superset) and distinguishing it from other members of its class (by its distinctive properties). Quillian also provides for storing logical operations and quantifier-like modifiers in a unit, although it is not clear that use was ever made of these features in the (limited) implementation of TLC.

A property is a generalized attribute-value pair. Typical examples would be pairs like "color-green," and "speed-fast"; but also included are proposition object relations ("under-water") and verb object relations ("hit-ball"). A property thus has at least two pointers, one to the unit representing its attribute and one to the unit representing its value. Properties can have an unrestricted number of further pointers to subproperties (which can themselves have subsubproperties, and so on). Finally, a property may have pointers to one or more *form tests* which are used to carry out a crude type of syntactic analysis. Figure 15.3 shows how the TLC representation of two Volkswagens, one red and one green, might involve five dictionary entries, six units, and two properties.

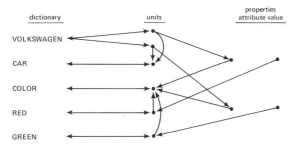

Figure 15.3.   A possible TLC memory fragment.

TLC tries to comprehend English input by translating it into an appropriate coding in the same format as the memory structure. The new information can then be added to the memory network. TLC is thus considered to have understood an input utterance if the system can integrate the utterance into its existing memory structure. TLC begins to process an input by seeking one or more *candidate units* (potential meanings) for each word in the utterance. In the memory structure of Figure 15.3, two candidates would be associated with the word Volkswagen if it appeared in an input phrase.

TLC next carries out a (simulated) parallel search for intersecting paths along superset chains originating in the various candidate units for different words. This search, which is not essentially different from the intersection method used in Quillian's earlier model, will hopefully identify the most reasonable combination of candidate units that can be associated with the utterance. New units can then be constructed, with information from both the search and the input being used to build appropriate superset and property pointers. New properties are created for new information about existing concepts. Before actually modifying memory, TLC applies the above mentioned form tests, to check that its interpretation of the input does not violate simple syntactic constraints.

Like its predecessor, TLC is not intended to be a conversation machine. Thus the system's output is quite primitive. TLC indicates its understanding of an input expression by rephrasing it in terms of existing components of its memory structure. Of more use to the informed user is TLC's non-linguistic output. By displaying its encoding of the input into memory format, TLC presents unambiguous evidence of how it has understood the utterance.

TLC represented one of the earliest attempts to use almost exclusively semantic (as opposed to syntactic) information in processing natural language. The system also placed a good deal of emphasis on understanding language in context. Quillian's ultimate objective was to "educate" TLC with long stretches of connected discourse, perhaps of the type found in children's books and stories. Several contemporary systems have similar goals. On the negative side, TLC might be criticized for not using *enough* syntax, for allowing its memory structures to expand unnecessarily, and for its primitive output. These problems have all been solved to some degree by Gordon McCalla in his successor to TLC, called MUSE (a Model to Understand Simple English).

15.3 The work of Winograd

For his 1971 Ph.D. thesis at MIT Terry Winograd developed a natural language understanding system which remains one of the most impressive pieces of work in the field to date. Winograd's system simulates a robot called SHRDLU (apparently named after the sequence of seventh to twelfth most frequent letters in written English), which lives in a tabletop "blocks world" environment containing a box and several colored pyramids and cubes of assorted sizes. SHRDLU keeps track of the positions of the blocks and can pick them up and rearrange them. The system accepts natural English input and responds by executing commands, answering questions, and otherwise conversing with the experimenter.

Figure 15.4 shows a block diagram of most major components of SHRDLU, with arrows indicating interactions among the various syntactic, semantic, reasoning, and environmental manipulation components. The

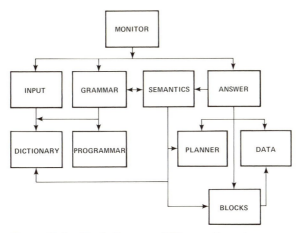

Figure 15.4.   Block diagram of Winograd's system.

MONITOR is a small program which invokes other routines to initiate and terminate processing of an input utterance. INPUT works with information in the DICTIONARY to carry out morphemic analysis on input sentences, and provides GRAMMAR with strings of words together with their definitions found in another part of the DICTIONARY. GRAMMAR coordinates the understanding process through its analysis of the basic units of English structure. The syntactic theory underlying Winograd's system is Halliday's Systemic Grammar, which we briefly describe later. In the SEMANTICS block are routines which assist GRAMMAR in interpreting the input.

PROGRAMMAR is a special language Winograd devised to do parsing by interpreting grammars written as programs. PROGRAMMAR builds and maintains a parse tree for an input sentence. ANSWER converts the system's responses to fluent English and keeps track of discourse in order to take context information into account. PLANNER (actually MICRO-PLANNER) is a subset of the deductive language developed by Hewitt (see Section 14.3) which is used throughout analysis. Among many other things, PLANNER deduces facts about the environment. BLOCKS is a group of PLANNER theorems which embody the system's knowledge about its physical environment and how goals may be achieved in that environment. Finally, DATA contains PLANNER assertions which describe the objects in the current scene.

Before looking more closely at some features of Winograd's system, we consider its remarkable performance, as illustrated by fragments of the sample dialog reported by Winograd. In this dialog, lower case letters indicate inputs, while SHRDLU's responses are in upper case. The response "OK" means that a requested action has been carried out in the environment.

pick up the big red block.
OK.
grasp the pyramid.

199

I DON'T UNDERSTAND WHICH PYRAMID YOU MEAN.
find a block which is taller than the one you are holding and put it into the box.
BY "IT" I ASSUME YOU MEAN THE BLOCK WHICH IS TALLER
    THAN THE ONE I AM HOLDING.
OK.

. . . .
how many blocks are not in the box?
FOUR OF THEM.
is at least one of them narrower than the one which I told you to pick up?
YES, THE RED CUBE.
is it supported?
YES, BY THE TABLE.
can the table pick up blocks?
NO.
can a pyramid be supported by a block?
YES.
can a pyramid support a pyramid?
I DON'T KNOW.
stack up two pyramids.
I CAN'T.

. . . .
will you please stack up both of the red blocks and either a green cube or a
    pyramid?
OK.

. . . .
had you touched any pyramid before you put the green one on the little cube.
YES, THE GREEN ONE.
when did you pick it up?
WHILE I WAS STACKING UP THE RED CUBE, A LARGE RED BLOCK,
    AND A LARGE GREEN CUBE.
why?
TO GET RID OF IT.
why did you do that?
TO CLEAN OFF THE RED CUBE.
why did you clear off that cube?
TO PUT IT ON A LARGE GREEN CUBE.
why did you do that?
TO STACK UP THE RED CUBE, A LARGE RED BLOCK AND A LARGE
    GREEN CUBE.
why did you do that?
BECAUSE YOU ASKED ME TO.
how did you do it?
BY PUTTING A LARGE RED BLOCK ON THE TABLE; THEN LETTING
    GO OF IT; THEN PUTTING A LARGE GREEN CUBE ON IT; THEN
    LETTING GO OF THAT CUBE; THEN PUTTING THE RED CUBE
    ON THAT CUBE; THEN LETTING GO OF THAT CUBE.
how many objects did you touch while you were doing it?
FOUR OF THEM.
what did the red cube support before you started to clean it off?
THE GREEN PYRAMID.
there were five blocks to the left of the box then.
NO, ONLY FOUR OF THEM: THE RED CUBE, TWO LARGE GREEN
CUBES, AND A RED BLOCK.

. . . .

200

does a steeple
SORRY, I DON'T KNOW THE WORD "STEEPLE."
a "steeple" is a stack which contains two green cubes and a pyramid.
I UNDERSTAND.
are there any steeples now?
NO.
build one.
OK.

We can obviously not go into much detail about a system as complex and massive as Winograd's. The remainder of our discussion describes highlights of SHRDLU's syntax, semantics, and knowledge representation. We begin with a brief consideration of Systemic Grammar. Halliday's theory of syntax deals with three levels of syntactic units. The highest level of organization is the *clause*. There are three kinds of major clause (imperative, declarative, and question) and an assortment of secondary clauses. Clauses consist of combinations of four types of *groups* (noun, verb, preposition, and adjective). A group is described by its component *words*, of which there are some 18 types ("determiners," "classifiers," "nouns," and so on), and by a variety of *features* denoting things like tense, number, and the role of the group in the sentence. This organization leads to systemic grammar parse trees which are typically smaller, shallower, more highly branched, and composed of more complex nodes than parse trees produced by generative-transformational grammars.

Parsing is carried out by specialized routines which look for expected constituents of clauses or groups, guided by the syntactic features which have been discovered. Thus a fragment of a simplified noun-group program might seek a determiner, then an adjective, then a noun. The procedure could report failure at any point in the search, allowing backtracking to alternative parsing routines. Note that SHRDLU's syntactic knowledge is thus largely of a *procedural* sort, represented in the form of programs written in the special purpose PROGRAMMAR language.

Winograd also makes extensive use of procedural representations for SHRDLU's knowledge base. The meaning of an input utterance is represented as a PLANNER program. Knowledge of what can be done in the environment is coded in the PLANNER theorem base, while descriptions of actual or hypothetical block configurations are kept in the PLANNER data base (the only nonprocedural part of SHRDLU'S knowledge).

As illustrated in the sample dialog, SHRDLU has a well developed ability to interpret fragmentary utterances (such as "why?" or "is it supported?") correctly, in terms of what has previously transpired in both the discourse and the world. In fact, Winograd's system was one of the first to deal at all effectively with the issue of *context*. SHRDLU handles this and other problems associated with interpretation of the semantic structure of utterances through the use of another procedural device, the "semantic specialist" routines.

These programs, of which there are about a dozen, are "experts" in analyzing particular syntactic structures and the meanings of the words they contain, in order to construct PLANNER expressions for use in reasoning and question answering. The semantic routines interact with the syntactic analysis. Thus the noun group specialist might be invoked as soon as a noun group has been successfully parsed (or even during parsing). Systemic grammar is particularly suited to introduction of semantic considerations quite early in syntactic processing. Constant checking to see if what has been parsed so far makes sense can eliminate a good deal of wasted syntactic analysis in a language understanding system.

15.4 The work of Schank

Since the late 1960's Roger Schank and his students at Stanford have been developing a theory of human language understanding. In both its use of network-like representations and its emphasis on modelling man's mind, Schank's work is very much in the tradition of Quillian's research. Although he is not greatly concerned with producing programs that perform like Winograd's, major aspects of Schank's theory have been implemented on the computer and appear to offer valuable insight and direction for research on natural language processing by machine.

Schank's basic premise is that people understand language by mapping utterances into a *conceptual base*. Since a great variety of utterances may have essentially the same meaning, the mapping is many to one. Further, the relations between the components of conceptual representations and the English words in the corresponding sentences may be indirect and not at all obvious. Finally, conceptual representations frequently contain a lot less information than the typical listener infers from an utterance. As these ideas imply, Schank is much more concerned with semantics than with syntax. He actually regards syntactic categories as temporary devices which are sometimes convenient to use while analyzing the meaning of an utterance.

The primitive units of conceptual analysis are *concepts*, which occur in three major types. A *nominal*, like "man" or "book," is a concept which can be thought of by itself, and which often invokes a "picture" in the mind. Nominals are abbreviated by PP, for "Picture Producer." The second type of concept is an *action* (abbreviated ACT), like "move" or "grasp," which can be executed by (some) nominals. Although actions sometimes correspond to words identified syntactically as verbs, "grow" for example is not an action but its result. We will shortly see that Schank has classified all common ACTS into a small number of primitive categories. The third and final basic concept type is the *modifier*, which occurs in two forms that are similar to the syntactic categories of adjective and adverb. A "Picture Aider" (PA), like "little" or "alive," specifies an attribute of a nominal. An "Action Aider" (AA), like "quickly" or "strongly," specifies an attribute of an action.

Two or more concepts may be connected by a dependency relation.

Schank specifies a set of about 15 such relations in the form of *conceptual rules*. These rules are used to tie together all the concepts in some complete idea into a *conceptual dependency diagram*. Figures 15.5 and 15.6 respectively show some of the more important conceptual rules and some very simple examples of conceptual dependency diagrams corresponding to sentences.

In Figure 15.6, action concepts are not usually represented as any of the English words in the sentences. Schank prefers to fit all ACTs into roughly a dozen categories. These "primitive actions" might be considered to characterize human thought at its most basic levels. We cannot consider all the varied ramifications of each primitive action. Some of the physical actions, like PROPEL, MOVE, GRASP, SPEAK, INGEST, and EXPEL, are fairly self-explanatory. The three "transfer" type actions appear quite frequently. PTRANS means to change the location of a physical object, ATRANS to transfer an abstract quality like control or ownership, and MTRANS to move conceptual information around among mental "loci" like memory and consciousness (thus serving to encode verbs like "learn" and "forget"). CONC roughly means to "think about," while MBUILD refers to combining thoughts in a "reasoning fashion."

One advantage of representing natural language utterances in terms of primitive actions is that it simplifies and generalizes various reasoning

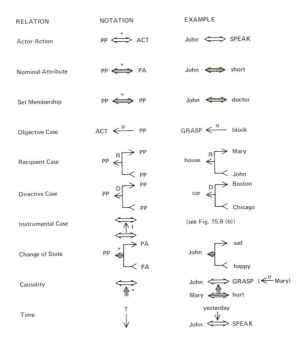

* may be marked for past tense (p), future tense (f), conditionality (c), and other features.

Figure 15.5.   Some of Schank's Conceptual Rules.

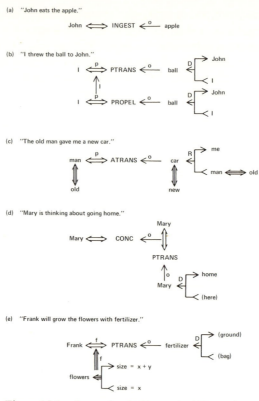

Figure 15.6. Some simple Conceptual Dependency diagrams.

processes that a computer program might carry out. For each of the primitive ACTs, Schank has proposed a number of probable inferences that could immediately be generated from even isolated utterances represented in his format. Thus we might assume that if an actor PROPELs an object and the object is not fixed, then the object is PTRANSed. Similarly, if an actor INGESTs an object and the object is edible, then the actor becomes more nourished.

Some of the more recent work of Schank's group has been directed toward computer implementation of aspects of the theory. A system called MARGIE (for Memory, Analysis, Response Generation, and Inference on English) consists of three components (each of which constituted a separate Ph.D. thesis!): a natural language analyzer, a conceptual memory system, and a program for generating English responses from conceptual representations. We conclude our discussion of Schank's work with a few words about each of these components.

MARGIE's analyzer attempts to discover the meaning of an input sentence and represent it in conceptual dependency notation. The program processes the input word-by-word and uses the new information associated with each successive word to build and refine expectations about what is to follow. The emphasis is thus on what the component words can predict about the meaning structure of the input, not on how they are organized into syntactic structures. As in all his work, Schank here uses syntax as a "last resort." This approach resembles Quillian's and contrasts with Winograd's strategy of inserting semantic considerations to guide a basically syntactic analysis.

The memory system converts the output of the analyzer into a format more convenient for computer storage and attempts to integrate the new information into the existing semantic data base. Thus if the system already knows about a "John" and a "Mary" it will identify further information about these characters with the existing concepts, providing nothing in the input suggests that other people with the same names might be involved.

The memory system also extracts "subpropositions" or self-contained assertions which may be contained in the main propositions of input sentences. Then all main and subpropositions are supplied to the inference generating routines. These inferences can be much more sophisticated than the simple ones mentioned above as derivable from primitive ACTs. Thus from the input "John gave Mary an aspirin," the system can infer the following as probable:

> "John believes that Mary wants an aspirin."
> "Mary is sick."
> "Mary wants to feel better."
> "Mary will ingest the aspirin."

In the course of generating inferences, the memory system also attempts to "clean up" the data base by filling in gaps and connecting related information together.

The third component of MARGIE is required to produce the English output for the inferences. The first step in this generation procedure is the conversion of conceptual representations to complex structures called "syntactic case networks." Transforming such networks to English is done by means previously developed by workers outside of Schank's group.

The case network representation gives MARGIE another capability in addition to inference generation. Because paths through this network can terminate with either first or subsequent choices of semantically equivalent English expressions, MARGIE can operate in a "paraphrase mode" and produce literally hundreds of quite varied versions of the original input. Here, for example, are two paraphrases produced for the sentence "John prevented Bill from giving a banana to Mary by selling a banana to Rita."

> "Bill was unable to give a banana to Mary because Rita traded John some money for a banana."
> "Rita bought a banana from John caused Mary not could get a banana from Bill."

As the last sentence shows, MARGIE does not always speak especially good English, certainly not as good as SHRDLU's. On the other hand (and without denigrating Winograd's impressive accomplishments), generation of syntactically pleasing output has been possible since ELIZA. Much more progress remains to be made on genuine understanding of natural language before we might expect a machine to pass Turing's test.

Bibliography

The Jackson and Hunt books listed in the Chapter 11 Bibliography both contain good introductory discussions of natural language processing.

McCalla, Gordon I., and Sampson, Jeffrey R. "MUSE: A Model to Understand Simple English." *Communications of the ACM, 15,* 1972, pp. 29–40.
An improved version of Quillian's TLC system.

Minsky, Marvin (ed.). *Semantic Information Processing.* MIT Press, 1968.
A collection of early papers, mostly abridged versions of MIT Ph.D. theses. Many important early systems are described, including Raphael's SIR and Quillian's thesis model.

Quillian, M. Ross. "The Teachable Language Comprehender: A simulation program and theory of language." *Communications of the ACM, 12,* 1969, pp. 459–476.
The basic description of TLC.

Schank, Roger C. "Conceptual Dependency: A theory of natural language understanding." *Cognitive Psychology, 3,* 1972, pp. 552–631.
A thorough discussion of Schank's theory at an intermediate stage of its development.

Schank, Roger C. *The Fourteen Primitive Actions and their Inferences.* Stanford Artificial Intelligence Memo AIM-183, March, 1973.
A full discussion of the role of ACTs in Conceptual Dependency Theory.

Schank, Roger C., and Colby, Kenneth M. (eds.), *Computer Models of Thought and Language.* Freeman, 1973.
A recent collection of papers, including major contributions by Schank, Winograd, and other workers in the field.

Turing, A. M., "Computing machinery and intelligence" *Mind, 59,* 1950, pp. 433–460.
Reprinted in the Feigenbaum and Feldman collection (see the Chapter 12 Bibliography).
The Turing test, proposed and defended.

Weizenbaum, Joseph. "ELIZA—A computer program for the study of natural language communication between man and machine." *Communications of the ACM, 9,* 1966, pp. 36–45.
The original description of ELIZA.

Winograd, Terry. "Understanding natural language." *Cognitive Psychology, 3,* 1972, pp. 1–191.
The entire issue devoted to a condensation of Winograd's thesis. The same material has been published as a book (*Understanding Natural Language,* 1972) by Academic Press.

Winograd, Terry. *Five Lectures on Artificial Intelligence.* Stanford Artificial Intelligence Memo AIM-246, September, 1974.

An introduction to current research problems in natural language understanding. Lecture 1 considers previous systems; Lecture 2 describes SHRDLU.

Bibliographical note for Part III: Listed below are three major continuing series of artificial intelligence publications which have not been mentioned in the individual chapter Bibliographies. These volumes regularly contain a broad spectrum of recent contributions by leading investigators.

Machine Intelligence
> Beginning with Volume 1 in 1967, at least seven volumes of this Edinburgh University series have appeared under various editorships (usually including Donald Michie and/or Bernard Meltzer). North American publication by American Elsevier.

Proceedings of the International Joint Conference of Artificial Intelligence
> Preprints of the "IJCAI" conference papers have appeared under various publication arrangements for the conferences in 1969 (Washington, D.C.), 1971 (London), 1973 (Stanford), and 1975 (Tblisi, USSR).

SIGART Newsletter
> A bimonthly publication of the Special Interest Group on Artificial Intelligence of the Association for Computing Machinery (ACM). Contains letters, discussions, abstracts, reviews, announcements, and other informal contributions.

Exercises

15.1. Compare the relative strengths and weaknesses of network and procedural representations of knowledge for natural language understanding systems. Discuss how the two representations might be combined.

15.2. A language processing system might be said to "learn" in various ways and at various levels. For Quillian's, Winograd's, and Schank's systems, discuss and compare the feasibility of learning in the following senses: (a) addition of new words or concepts by extension of existing data structures; (b) addition of new kinds of knowledge encoded in new types of data structures; (c) addition of control structures for parsing and/or producing new syntactic patterns; and (d) addition of new control structures for processing semantic information. In each case, indicate whether the systems as they stand (i) can learn automatically from experience, (ii) need to be "told" what is learned (perhaps in a specially coded format), or (iii) must be reprogrammed to incorporate the "learning" changes.

Index